Reframing difference

Beur and *banlieue* filmmaking in France

CARRIE TARR

Manchester University Press

Manchester and New York

distributed exclusively in the USA by Palgrave

Published by Manchester University Press
Oxford Road, Manchester M13 9NR, UK
and Room 400, 175 Fifth Avenue, New York, NY 10010, USA
www.manchesteruniversitypress.co.uk

Distributed exclusively in the USA by
Palgrave, 175 Fifth Avenue, New York,
NY 10010, USA

Distributed exclusively in Canada by
UBC Press, University of British Columbia, 2029 West Mall,
Vancouver, BC, Canada V6T 1Z2

British Library Cataloguing-in-Publication Data
A catalogue record for this book is available from the British Library

Library of Congress Cataloging-in-Publication Data applied for

ISBN   0 7190 6876 2 *hardback*
EAN   978 0 7190 6876 8
ISBN   0 7190 6877 0 *paperback*
EAN   978 0 7190 6877 5

First published 2005

14 13 12 11 10 09 08 07 06 05   10 9 8 7 6 5 4 3 2 1

Typeset
by Northern Phototypesetting Co. Ltd, Bolton
Printed in Great Britain
by Bell & Bain Ltd, Glasgow

Reframing difference

Beur and *banlieue* filmmaking in France

Manchester University Press

Contents

List of illustrations

Every effort has been made to obtain permission to reproduce the figures
illustrated in this book. If any proper acknowledgement has not been made,
copyright-holders are invited to contact the publisher.

Acknowledgements

This book consists of a collection of essays on *beur* and *banlieue* filmmaking in France, written over a period of some ten years. Together they chart the development of the phenomena which came to be known as *cinéma beur* and *cinéma de banlieue* from the 1980s through to the early 2000s. I am indebted to the staff at Manchester University Press for the opportunity of revising them for publication, and to *L'Esprit createur, Etudes Transnationales, Francophones et Comparées/Transnational, Francophone and Comparative Studies, Iris, Modern & Contemporary France*, Oxford University Press, *Portsmouth Working Papers* and Wallflower Press for permission to reprint a modified version of articles which were first published with them. I would also like to thank the British Academy for funding a study visit to Paris which enabled me to research the final two chapters.

Thanks are also due to Ginette Vincendeau for inviting me to write my first article on *beur* cinema, to Dominique Blüher, Diane and Michel Dincuff, Danielle Robinson, Alec Hargreaves and Will Higbee for assistance in procuring videos, to Andy Belsham for his technical assistance, to Lieve Spaas, Stephen Barber and other colleagues at Kingston University for their encouragement and, above all, to Frank McMahon for his unfailing intellectual, moral and practical support during the book's gestation.

Introduction

There is a moment in Eric Rochant's comedy *Vive la République!* (1997) when a group of (mostly) unemployed young people, who have decided to set up a new political party to challenge what they perceive as the exclusionary politics of the French Republic, agree that the one *beur* present (a young man of Maghrebi origin) should represent both *blacks* and *beurs* (figure 1). The film mocks their token and ineffectual mobilisation of 'politically correct' Anglo-Saxon discourses on democracy and multiculturalism. But its simultaneous awareness of difference and refusal to take it seriously draw attention to the fault lines in the universalist discourses of French Republicanism. Since the French Revolution, France has prided itself on being the land of equality, founded on an abstract concept of universal citizenship which renders ethnic, gendered, religious or class difference irrelevant (Hargreaves 1995: 160; Rosello 2003: 136). The acknowledgement of difference, which underpins the multi-culturalist policies and practices of countries such as Britain and the USA, has therefore been rejected as leading to undesirable forms of 'communitarianism'. Yet the heterogeneous, multicultural nature of contemporary postcolonial France – and the inequalities in the way its diverse cultures are valued – would appear to be self-evident.[1]

At the turn of the millennium, a number of concessions were made in relation to universalist principles, such as the enactment of the law on parity, which requires a quota of women candidates to be selected for parliamentary elections, and the establishment of the PACS (the Pacte Civil de Solidarité), which legalises the relationships of same-sex couples. However, the question of religious and ethnic difference continues to provoke divisive public debates. Since 1989 a series of '*foulard* affairs', instances of Muslim girls refusing to remove the Islamic head-scarf in school, have fomented controversy about the place of religious symbols within the secular institutions of the Republic. The wearing of the *hijab* is seen as so threatening to the Republican principles of universalism and laicity, as well as to the freedom of women, that in February 2004 the national assembly voted

1 The founder members of a new political party in *Vive la République!* (1997).

to ban such symbols in school rather than encourage tolerance for signs of difference. At the same time, initiatives taken by the Institut d'Etudes Politiques in Paris to privilege student intakes from schools in disadvantaged areas have been criticised for compromising the Republican concept of equality. Debates about (and resistances to) France's changing identity as a plural, multi-ethnic society are thus at the forefront of public preoccupations. The aim of this book is to assess the ways in which filmmaking in France might contribute to such debates by foregrounding the voices and subjectivities of ethnic others and thereby reframing the way in which difference is conceptualised.

The core focus of the book is the appearance and after-effects of two related phenomena in the history of French cinema, *cinéma beur* and *cinéma de banlieue*. The term *cinéma beur* was first coined in a special issue of *Cinématographe* in July 1985 to describe a set of independently released films by and about the *beurs*, that is, second-generation immigrants of Maghrebi descent, one of the most prominent being Mehdi Charef's *Le Thé au harem d'Archimède* (1985). *Cinéma de banlieue* emerged within French film criticism in the mid-1990s as a way of categorising a series of independently released films set in the rundown multi-ethnic working-class estates (the *cités*) on the periphery of France's major cities (the *banlieues*), the most significant of which was Mathieu Kassovitz's *La Haine* (1995). In both cases, the labels have proved controversial and potentially reductive (see Hargreaves 1999; Higbee 2001a). My use of the slightly different terms, *beur* and *banlieue* filmmaking, aims not to reify particular categories of films but to emphasise filmmaking as a set of (changing) practices, whether it be *beur* filmmaking (the work of directors of Maghrebi descent, though the term could also cover other forms of *beur* authorship) or *banlieue* filmmaking (the work of directors aiming to represent life in the *banlieue*). What the majority of these two permeable and overlapping sets of films have in common, however, is a concern with the place and identity of the marginal and excluded in France. This study foregrounds representations of the *beurs* in these (and other) films, first because of the existence of a significant but generally little-known and little-discussed corpus of films made by *beur* filmmakers themselves (included in the filmography), and second because, as the descendants of immigrants from France's former colonies in the Maghreb, the *beurs* have been the most visible, the most stigmatised and the most dynamic ethnic minority in postcolonial France. As I have argued elsewhere, dominant French cinema has, until relatively recently, tended to suppress or marginalise the voices and narratives of the nation's troubling postcolonial others and (re)produce ethnic hierarchies founded on the assumed supremacy of white metropolitan culture and identity (Tarr 1997). Arguably, then, films by and about the *beurs* offer a touchstone for measuring the extent to which universalist Republican assumptions about Frenchness can be challenged and particular forms of multiculturalism envisaged and valued.

The chapters which follow braid together the double focus on *beur* and *banlieue* filmmaking. On the one hand they trace the history of *beur* filmmaking practices from the margins to the mainstream, from low-budget autobiographically inspired features to commercial filmmaking, and assess their effectiveness in addressing questions of identity and difference. On the other, they attempt to gauge the significance of place in the construction of identity through an analysis of films set in the multi-ethnic *banlieue*.[2] In each case, the representation of ethnicity is linked to questions of gender and authorship through the comparison of male and female, white and *beur*-authored films. In a final chapter, *beur* filmmaking is compared with that of displaced filmmakers from Algeria, who also address questions of place and identity in metropolitan France.

Before elaborating further on the context of *beur* filmmaking in France and the aesthetic and ideological issues raised by *beur* and *banlieue* filmmaking, the word *beur* itself (and its later variant *rebeu*) needs some further explanation. A neologism derived from Parisian backslang (*verlan*) by young second-generation immigrants of Maghrebi descent in the early 1980s (see chapter 1), its playful inversion and truncation of the syllables of the word for 'Arab' originally denoted both an awareness of the negative meanings of 'Arab' in the French imaginary, and a refusal to be trapped in those meanings. However, since its incorporation into majority French discourses, many of those it refers to have rejected the term, fearing that it has become simply another way of trapping them in a ghetto.³ In the 1990s, second- and third-generation Maghrebis have tended to designate themselves according to their origins (as in 'd'origine algérienne / marocaine / tunisienne') or more generally as 'd'orig-ine maghrébine' ('of Maghrebi origin'). The latter is an apparently neutral expression which recognises the possibility of a bicultural identity. Yet it is also problematic, first because the term Maghrebi obscures the historical, geo-graphical and cultural specificity of the origins of those it designates,⁴ and sec-ondly because the emphasis on origins risks endorsing an essentialist notion of identity as pre-given, rather than acknowledging that identities, including those of the majority white French population, are constantly in process. The difficulty of naming the *beurs* is clearly indicative of their problematic status within French culture.⁵ What is important, however, is that, until and unless the unmarked term 'French' is automatically (and visibly) understood to include all France's citizens, whatever their origins, it should be qualified not just for those who are 'of Maghrebi origin', but also for the 'white' or 'majority' French (many of whom are themselves the descendants of immigrants⁶). This book alternates the term *beur*, maintained because of its historical significance and as a convenient short form, with the term 'of Maghrebi descent', which has the virtue of not reifying origins, while acknowledging the shortcomings of both terms.

Beurs, banlieues and the French Republic

If France has prided itself on being the country of the 'rights of man' (*sic*) and a 'terre d'accueil', a land hospitable to foreigners, that reputation has been seri-ously eroded by its treatment of immigrants from the Maghreb and their descendants (Ben Jalloun 1997; Rosello 2001). An understanding of the social and historical context in which *beur* and *banlieue* filmmaking has developed is needed in order to appreciate the significance of their interventions in French culture.

   While it is generally assumed that the descendants of immigrants in France eventually become assimilated into French society, there has been resistance to the integration of the *beurs*, due in large measure to the legacy of French colo-nialism in the Maghreb (Silverman 1992; Stora 1992; Hargreaves 1995). Although the *beurs* themselves were either children at the time of the Algerian War of Independence (1954–1962), or born thereafter, their lives have been deeply affected by hostility in France towards 'Arabs'⁷ and Islam, generated by the bitter conflicts of the war, the enforced 'return' of the *pied noirs* (the French settler population) and the visible presence of Arab and Berber immigrants on French soil. The racist policies of Jean-Marie Le Pen's extreme rightwing Front National gained national prominence during the 1980s,⁸ and anti-Arab racism and Islamophobia have been reinforced by worsening relationships between the West and the Arab world (the oil crises, the Gulf War, the Palestinian conflict and, following 9/11, the 'war on terrorism' in Afghanistan and Iraq) and by events in Algeria (the rise of Islamic fundamentalism, the failure of democracy, and the horror of a decade of terrorism and internal civil war). While various movements in France have attempted to combat racism and Islamophobia – including SOS Racisme and France Plus, created in the 1980s – attempts to promote the participation of the *beurs* (and others) in the democratic life of the nation have been largely ineffectual, and continuing discrimination against the descendants of non-European immigrants, exacerbated by the influence of the Front National, maintains a climate in which the settlement and integration of the *beurs* remains precarious.

It is worth noting that many *beurs* have been brought up in ignorance of their family and community histories. First-generation Algerian immigrants, recruited as cheap, temporary labour to fuel French industry during the 'trentes glorieuses' (the thirty 'glorious' years of postwar economic growth), tended not to transmit their histories to their offspring. Often illiterate men from rural areas, suffering from the trauma of exile, they had expected to return to the newly independent Algeria, and did not envisage putting down roots in France, even when, in the 1970s, immigration for work was suspended and family immigration became the norm. They remained silent, in part through a sense of loss and guilt at not taking part in the rebuilding of Algeria, in part through shame at the invidious treatment they received in France, documented in Yamina Benguigui's *Mémoires d'immigrés* (1997–98).[9] Official histories have been similarly silent both about the contribution of immigrants to the development of French society and, specifically, about France's harsh treatment of the Algerians.[10] Until relatively recently, for example, there has been a collective amnesia about events which took place on or around 17 October 1961, when between 100 and 200 peaceful demonstrators against the curfew imposed on Algerian immigrant workers by the chief of Police, Maurice Papon, were drowned, shot, or beaten to death, and thousands more were arrested, detained or deported (Stora 1992: 306–10). There is no doubt, given the need for memory in the construction of a collective identity, that such silences have been disempowering for the second (and later the third) generation. They have also prevented the majority French from assuming their responsibilities for the development of a democratic, egalitarian postcolonial society.[11]

Economic and urban planning factors have also affected the ability of the descendants of Maghrebi immigrants to integrate into French society. Their coming of age coincided with the period when the economy came under pressure as a result of the oil crises of the 1970s. De-industrialisation and mass unemployment meant that, unlike their fathers, a high proportion of the second generation suffered (and continues to suffer) from exclusion from the job market. Furthermore, thanks to lower levels of educational achievement and discriminatory practices on the part of employers and employment agencies, they have been affected by unemployment far more seriously than their white peers.[12] Their location in the *banlieue* has been another factor in their exclusion. First-generation immigrants were housed in hostels or lived in the shanty-towns (*bidonvilles*) which grew up on the outskirts of major cities in the late 1950s and early 1960s. In the mid-1960s, during de Gaulle's presidency, the shanty-towns were replaced by *grands ensembles*, enormous low-rent high-rise housing estates in the areas now known as the *banlieues*, specifically designed to re-house the families of immigrant workers and displaced workers from the countryside. The spatial and social segregation of their inhabitants, which continues to the present day, effectively recreated the colonial geographic model of a city composed of adjacent but mutually exclusive parts.

The coming to power of François Mitterrand and the Parti Socialiste in 1981 entailed hopes for a more progressive approach to immigration than had been demonstrated by the rightwing administration of the 1970s. The second generation, conventionally represented as a generation which had lost its bearings, with no roots, no hope, no future (Wihtol de Wenden 1999: 233), seized the opportunity to make its presence felt (see chapter 1). The 1983 March for Equality and against Exclusion was renamed the March of the *Beurs* by the media (Bouamama 1994) and, together with other public manifestations, propelled the *beurs* into the public arena as active participants in debates about integration, nationality and citizenship.

However, if the *beur* movement drew attention to the anger and frustration experienced by young people living in the *banlieue* estates, intensified by high levels of unemployment and '*bavures*' ('blunders') occasioned by the abuses of police power, the media were more interested in manifestations of violence in the *banlieue*, ranging from *rodeos* (the theft and burning of cars) and drug-dealing to full-scale riots.[13] By the early 1980s, dominant media discourses had begun to consolidate the notion of the *banlieue* as a 'problem', and *banlieue* youths as, for the most part, ethnic minority youths linked to crime and violence. The 1995 bombings orchestrated by Khaled Kelkal (an isolated fundamentalist terrorist from a *banlieue* in Lyons), reinforced the idea that the *banlieue*, home to a large proportion of the Muslim population of France, was also a recruitment ground for terrorists. The association of the *banlieues* with a lack of law and order not only fed the agenda of the Front National and legitimated rightwing policies for heavy-handed policing methods, it also influenced debates on the rights to French nationality for those of immigrant origin, and on policies towards immigration control and the status of immigrants.

Studies of life in the *banlieues* in the 1990s and early 2000s suggest that the social and material conditions necessary for integration have got worse rather than better, with another generation of young people knowing nothing but unemployment, a phenomenon which is not typical of earlier patterns of immigration (Amara 2003). In addition to problems of degraded housing, poverty, failure at school and the disintegration of the family, the *beurs* have also suffered from increasingly hostile attitudes towards non-European (that is, non-white) immigrants in France and the implementation of tough immigration policies. The return of the Right to power in 1993, followed by Jacques Chirac's election as president in 1995, saw the introduction of a series of laws restricting the rights of immigrants in France, notably the Méhaignerie and Pasqua laws of 1993 and the Debré law of 1997, which were not overturned when Lionel Jospin and the Left came to power in 1998. The restriction of access to French nationality for the French-born children of foreign parents meant that young people of Maghrebi descent whose parents had not claimed French nationality themselves were obliged to apply for it once they reached the age of sixteen (Freedman 2000: 17). One of the results has been 'the destabilisation of young people born or brought up in France but deprived of the assurance that they will be able to live there permanently' (Lochak 1997: 44).[14] Thanks to measures enabling the police to stop and detain individuals suspected of being illegal residents, they also suffer from the invidious *délit du faciès*, the crime of simply looking different, which makes them vulnerable to police harassment. In these circumstances, it is not surprising that young males may express their alienation through undesirable, antisocial and hypermacho behaviour. The shift of patriarchal authority from the fathers to *les grands frères* ('the older brothers') has also led to a notable regression in the situation of women in the *banlieue*.

Beur women (or *beurettes*) came to the attention of the media in particular through their resistance to arranged marriages, mediated through accounts of their *fugues* – running away from home – or of their families tricking them into marriages back in Algeria. Their attempt to negotiate new roles for themselves, often through performing better at school than their male peers, has been deemed to make them potentially more assimilable into Western culture. Indeed, for a number of *beur* women activists, the *beur* movement of the early 1980s also generated a contestation of women's oppression within the patriarchal Arabo-Berber-Islamic sex/gender system. However, though *beur* women may aspire to the freedoms and individualism enjoyed by their white peers, they generally also desire to maintain affective links with their family and culture of origin (Flanquart 2003). This may be one of the factors at play in the '*foulard* affairs', which have revealed how Judeo-Christian ethnocentrism and hostility towards Islam are embedded in the supposedly secular French education system, as well as in elite discourses on laicity across the political spectrum (Nordmann 2004). Although the wearing of the veil can be interpreted in a variety of ways, not least as an effect of fundamentalist oppression, it can also be understood as a way for young women to express their identity in opposition to dominant norms (Dayan-Herzbrun 2000).[15]

A new phase of activism on the part of *beur* women was initiated in the early 2000s, following the burning to death of a young woman, Sohane, in Vitry-sur-Seine in October 2002, and the publication by Samira Bellil of her first-person account of gang rapes in the *banlieue* (*les tournantes*), which exposed the way young *banlieue* women may be punished by the *grands frères* if their behaviour does not conform to expected norms (Bellil 2002). Using the slogan 'Ni Putes Ni Soumises' (which translates roughly as 'Neither Slags Nor Slaves'), a group of *banlieue* women organised a 'March of Women from the Estates for Equality and against the Ghetto', which ended with a demonstration of 30,000 people in Paris on International Women's Day, 2003. The new movement is at pains to point out that their protest is directed not just against 'the macho behaviour of the men in our estates who deny us our most elementary rights in the name of a "tradition"', but also against 'a society which shuts us away in ghettos dominated by poverty and exclusion' (Amara 2003: 146).[16]

If by the early 2000s first-generation Algerian immigrants have largely abandoned their dreams of a return to Algeria, the relationship of the *beurs* to the French state is still problematic. Celebrations of the French victory at the World Cup in July 1998, with a multi-ethnic football team including star *beur* player Zinedine Zidane, momentarily gave strength to the belief that France had successfully achieved the transition to a multicultural *black-blanc-beur* society. Yet the booing of the Marseillaise and the pitch invasion by youths from the Parisian *banlieues* at the historic, supposedly friendly, match between France and Algeria in 2001 seemed to suggest that, on the contrary, the *beurs* identified more strongly with their Algerian roots. Zaïr Kédadouche (2002: 23) suggests that young people have become so alienated by France and its symbols that Algeria, which is seen as having won against France, politically and morally as well as militarily, now enjoys a mythic status. For Azouz Begag, however, their behaviour can be interpreted rather as a plea for recognition (Begag 2003: 86). The precariousness of their position was underlined by Le Pen's surprise relegation of Jospin into third place during the first round of the presidential elections of 2002. Even though voters anxious to consolidate a plural, multicultural France ensured that Le Pen was subsequently defeated by Chirac, the electoral successes of the Front National are symptomatic of a country still unsure of its identity and riven by racism. Figures published by the Commission Nationale des Droits de l'Homme in 2000 suggest that 63 per cent of the 'French' think there are too many 'Arabs' in France (Kédadouche 2002: 65).

At the same time, there is no doubt that the socio-cultural integration of the overwhelming majority of French citizens of Maghrebi descent is proceeding apace (Wihtol de Wenden 1999: 236). Many of those referred to as the *beur-*

geoisie (as opposed to the *rebeus* of the *banlieue*) have achieved success as writ-ers, musicians, designers, sportspersons, filmmakers and actors, as well as teachers, researchers, social workers, business persons and even MEPs.[17] The *beurs* have been particularly influential in the growth of *banlieue* youth culture in France, successfully appropriating and developing the practices of black American hip-hop culture (Bazin 1995). France also boasts a high rate of mixed marriages (Begag 2003: 33) and, despite the *foulard* affairs, there is evi-dence to suggest that the practice of Islam in France is not an obstacle to inte-gration (Cesari 1999; Flanquart 2003). Nevertheless, citizens of Maghrebi descent are significantly under-represented in the boardroom, in the conven-tional political parties and in the national assembly.[18]

As writer–researcher Begag argues, representations play a key role in the struggle for the meaning of Frenchness and the promotion of equality.[19] For Begag, Zidane's image as a French football champion (Zizou) and the warm reception accorded in 2001 to Aziz, a young *beur*, after he had been expelled from *Loft Story*[20] are heartening demonstrations of the principles of Republi-can integration at work (Begag 2003: 90). At the same time, the subjects of Yamina Benguigui's 2003 TV documentary, *Aïcha, Mohamed, Chaïb ... Engagés par la France*, recruits of Maghrebi descent in the French army, repeat-edly identify themselves not as French, but as Arabs and/or Algerians in France. Arguably, their attitude suggests not that French society has broken down into 'communitarianism', but rather that, by the early 2000s, France has become sufficiently recognisable as a plural society that its citizens of Maghrebi descent no longer feel it necessary to deny their difference. It remains to be seen whether *beur* and *banlieue* filmmaking endorses such a view.

Beur filmmaking

According to Benedict Anderson's formulation (1983), the nation is an 'imag-ined community', constructed through the repeated performance of particular narratives and discourses. Mainstream French cinema has been notoriously reluctant to perform a critique of France's role as an exploitative colonial or neo-colonial power but instead has narrated the nation in ways which shore up a monolithic sense of white France's cohesiveness and cultural superiority. Its treatment of decolonisation and immigration has tended to contribute to the stigmatisation and othering of first-generation immigrants from the Maghreb and their descendants. In the 1980s, ethnic minority others feature primarily as marginalised and/or stereotyped characters, contributing to the dominant media construction of immigrants/*beurs* as deviants and/or outsiders (Minces 1989). They appear in *policiers* (crime dramas) such as *Police* (Maurice Pialat, 1985) or *L627* (Bertrand Tavernier, 1992) as criminals or prostitutes (figure 2); or in more concerned, liberal films, such as *Tchao Pantin* (Claude Berri, 1983)

2 A policeman (Gérard Depardieu) gets embroiled with a young woman of Maghrebi origin (Sophie Marceau) in *Police* (1985).

or *Train d'enfer* (Roger Hanin, 1985), as victims and subsidiary to the central white characters. In each case they are the objects of, and contained within, a white eurocentric gaze and discourse which, as Shohat and Stam argue, 'takes for granted and "normalizes" the hierarchical power relations generated by colonialism and imperialism, without necessarily even thematizing those issues directly' (Shohat and Stam 1994: 2). In the 1980s, there was a perceived need for alternative narratives of nation which would challenge hegemonic representations of Frenchness and allow the so-called 'second generation' (the sons and daughters of immigrants from the Maghreb) to emerge as citizens, subjects and agents in their own right.

In the early 1980s, a considerable body of video films and documentaries by filmmakers of Maghrebi descent was produced in artisanal conditions outside normal production and distribution circuits (see *CinémAction/Tumulte*, 1981, *CinémAction* 24, 1983, and *CinémAction/Hommes et Migrations* 56, 1990). Super 8 films by the Mohamed Collective (such as *Le Garage, Zone immigrée* and *La Mort de Kader*) played an important role in making the second generation visible as cultural entrepreneurs (Mohamed 1981; Bosséno 1983).[21] Short fiction films by Farida Belghoul (*C'est Madame la France que tu préfères?*, 1981, and *Le Départ du père*, 1983) and Aïssa Djabri (*La Vago*, 1983) were critically acclaimed and gave expression to the identity crisis and, in the case of *La Vago*, the socio-economic disadvantages facing the 'second generation'. The breakthrough into full-length feature filmmaking aimed at a mainstream audience came in 1985 with Costa-Gavras' sponsoring of Mehdi Charef's *Le Thé au harem d'Archimède*, winner of the Jean Vigo Prize, the same year as Rachid Bouchareb made *Baton Rouge*.[22] From 1994 to 1999, eleven other filmmakers of Maghrebi descent wrote and directed their first films (including three women) and nine more made (or co-directed) their first films between 2000 and 2003 (including one woman).[23] By 2003, eight of these had also gone on to make a second film.[24]

In most cases it has not been easy for them to get funding for their films. Several made their first feature films completely outside the conventional film industry circuits, and they took many years to complete, notably *Hexagone* (1994) by Malik Chibane, *Souviens-toi de moi* (1996) by Zaïda Ghorab-Volta, *Cour interdite* (1999) by Djamel Ouahab and *Wesh wesh, qu'est-ce qui se passe?* (2002) by Rabah Ameur-Zaïmèche. Others, including Belghoul, Fejria Deliba, Djabri, Youcef Hamidi and Malika Tenfiche, have to date only made short or medium-length films. Those who have been able to obtain funding for a first full-length feature film have usually worked in related aspects of the industry and/or first made a short film – the case of Yamina Benguigui, Djamel Bensalah, Ahmed Bouchaala, Bouchareb, Lyèce Boukhitine, Chad Chenouga, Karim Dridi[25] and Bourlem Guerdjou – or have already made their names from related professional activities, as with Charef (who had written the novel on which his first film was based), Rachida Krim (a fine artist) and Abdel Kechiche (an actor). Others obtained their first chance through co-directing, Kamel Saleh with well-known rap star Akhenaton, comedian Smaïn with white filmmaker Jean-Marc Longwal, and actress and screenwriter Zakia Bouchaala (formerly Zakia Tahiri) with husband Ahmed Bouchaala. Thus directors of Maghrebi origin operate within a range of filmmaking practices. For the most part, however, they are confined to relatively low budgets, many of their films draw on amateur or unknown actors (often family and friends), and at least five of the films addressed here feature the directors themselves in the principal role. Their desire for self-representation can be seen as symptomatic of their need for self-affirmation as both social and artistic subjects.

One of the key sources of funding for French cinema is the *avance sur recettes* (advance on box office receipts) provided by the CNC (Centre National de la Cinématographie). However, the CNC has no policy for promoting ethnic minority filmmakers, since this would run counter to Republican universalist principles. The *avance sur recettes* is used generously to support first films, but it generally privileges *auteur* cinema or mainstream 'quality' cinema, types of filmmaking which not many first time *beur* filmmakers can aspire to.[26] Television channels are another key source of funding for French filmmakers, and in recent years they have fostered both the work of directors of Maghrebi descent and television films addressing questions of ethnic difference.[27] Other more marginal sources of funding include the FAS (Fonds d'Action Sociale), which assists films purporting to promote inter-ethnic relations in France, and, more recently, the Conseils Régionaux, which seek to promote representations of particular regions. Given the difficulties of achieving funding, it is significant that a number of filmmakers of Maghrebi origin have themselves moved into film production, notably Aïssa Djabri and Farid Lahoussa[28] at Vertigo Productions, whose output includes Cédric Klapisch's *Chacun cherche son chat* (1996), Christophe Ruggia's *Le Gone du chaâba* (1998) and Mostéfa Djadjam's *Frontières* (2002) as well as Thomas Gilou's *Raï* (1995) and hit Jewish comedy *La Vérité si je mens!* (1997). Rachid Bouchareb's 3B Productions (with Jean Bréhat) has produced films such as Bruno Dumont's award-winning *La Vie de Jésus* (1997) and *Humanité* (1999) and Guerdjou's *Vivre au paradis* (1999) alongside Bouchareb's own films. One should also not underestimate the role of other cultural entrepreneurs of Maghrebi origin, such as Nacer Kettane at Radio Beur FM, and television presenter and filmmaker Yamina Benguigui, who is a sponsor of the proposed Beur TV channel.[29]

Although a significant number of filmmakers of Maghrebi descent have put together the funding to make feature films, they still have difficulty in getting them released and in attracting popular or international audiences.[30] As Hamid Naficy argues (Naficy 2001), exilic and diasporic filmmakers have an interstitial relationship to the film industry and, for *beur* filmmakers (who may be perceived as marginal to the French film industry), this often translates into small publicity budgets, very limited distribution and a lack of international sales.[31] As indicated in the filmography, some of their films have attracted fewer than 5000 spectators in France, whereas films on similar topics by majority white filmmakers (with a few exceptions) tend to achieve higher viewing figures. Although some also receive distribution on alternative festival and community circuits, as well as being screened on television, *beur*-authored films have rarely been incorporated into mainstream French filmmaking or invited to represent French filmmaking abroad.[32] To date the only really popular *beur*-authored films (with over a million spectators in France) are comedies, namely *Les Deux Papas et la maman* (1996) co-directed by Smaïn, *Le Ciel, les oiseaux . . . et ta mère* (1999) by Bensalah (a surprise hit starring comedian Jamel Debbouze, now one of France's most popular stars) and Bensalah's follow-up film *Le Raïd* (2002), though Charef and Bouchareb have achieved respectable viewing figures for one or two of their films, as have Dridi and Saleh (the latter in association with Akhenaton).

However, it is also the case that actors of Maghrebi descent have an increasingly active profile in French cinema and that their roles in mainstream cinema are increasingly varied. Although this issue is beyond the scope of this study, it is notable that stars like Jamel, Samy Naceri and Smaïn are able to attract large audiences, particularly through their roles in comedies, while actors like Sami Bouajila, Zinedine Soualem and Roschdy Zem have developed enviable filmographies in the work of a range of directors. Zem suggests that the possibility of *beur* actors taking on roles without being typecast for films about racism or immigration dates back to around 1993 (Zem 1998: 108). Like mixed-race actor Jalil Lespert, they are increasingly able to move between roles which are marked by ethnic difference and roles which are not. However, the picture seems to be less positive for female actors, despite a range of talented performers such as Fejria Deliba and Nozha Khouadra. Deliba has expressed her dismay at not being offered other unmarked roles like the one she enjoyed in Jacques Rivette's 1989 film, *La Bande des quatre* (Deliba 2003: 45). On the other hand, Rachida Brakni's success in Coline Serreau's *Chaos* (2001), seen by over a million spectators, was quickly followed by an unmarked role opposite Eric Cantona in Thierry Binisti's *L'Outre-mangeur* (2003). It is surely significant in terms of the history of representations that Naceri, first prominent as a hopeless *beur* drug-dealer in Thomas Gilou's *Raï* (1995), is now able to play unmarked roles, as in the *Taxi* series, which place him, if ironically, on the side of the law (figure 3).[33]

What I am most concerned with in this book, however, are films written (for the most part) and directed by *beur* filmmakers, and the extent to which their images and narratives, and the *beur* actors who embody them, can counter or, alternatively, penetrate and influence mainstream discourses on the nature of 'Frenchness'. Clearly this type of grouping runs counter to the desire of the film-makers themselves who, understandably, do not want to be labelled in terms of their ethnic origins, both for fear of being trapped into expectations of making films only about ethnicity and difference and because they expect their films to be judged according to their intrinsic, aesthetic merits. The label of *beur* film-maker also risks enshrining an essentialist notion of identity rather than recog-nising that identities are multiple, relational and shifting. Its validity is thrown into question by the difficulty of classifying directors of mixed-race origins such as Franco-Tunisian Dridi and Franco-Algerian Nicolas Boukrief (best known as a journalist for *Starfix*), who to date has not made films which address questions of ethnicity and identity. It is also challenged by the work of certain white direc-tors like *pied noir* Philippe Faucon, who has made at least two films, *Les Etrangers* (a 1999 TV film) and *Samia* (2001), which have some claim to being considered *beur* films because of their focus on *beur* characters and their sympathetic under-standing of the tensions and anxieties brought about by displacement and exile. I am therefore using the category not on the assumption of any essentialist dif-ferences between *beurs* and non-*beurs*, but rather on the supposition that, during the period covered by this book, individuals of Maghrebi descent (a heteroge-neous and permeable category) have experienced sets of social relations and discourses which potentially inflect their cinematic production differently from that of their white peers. The grouping of their films not only draws attention to their achievements but provides a perspective on the (changing) significance of ethnic difference at a particular period in French/film history.

3 Samy Naceri on the side of the law as Daniel, a Marseilles taxi driver, in *Taxi 2* (2002).

Hamid Naficy argues that films by deterritorialised people, among whom he includes the *beurs*, share a number of common features which he embraces under the umbrella term of 'accented cinema' (Naficy 2001). He, too, argues for the significance of authorship, pointing out that accented filmmakers are also 'empirical subjects, situated in the interstices of cultures and film practices, who exist outside and prior to their films', and expresses the view that their films 'signify and signify upon exile and diaspora by expressing, allegorising, commenting upon, and critiquing the home and host societies and cultures and the deterritorialized conditions of the filmmakers' (Naficy 2001: 4). They do so, he suggests, through an 'accented style', involving, for example, fragmented, multilingual and critically juxtaposed narrative structures, lost characters, themes involving identity and displacement, and liminal and politicised structures of feeling.[34] Such features would, theoretically, be equally applicable to films by displaced Maghrebi (and other) filmmakers, and chapter 12 tests out this proposition by comparing *beur*-authored films with films by émigré Maghrebi filmmakers working in France. The notion of an 'accented cinema' may also help to differentiate between *beur*-authored films which inscribe 'the biographical, social and cinematic (dis)location of the filmmakers' (Naficy 2001: 4) and films by majority white filmmakers, whose treatment of the (dis)location of others may be inflected differently because of their own more assured position in France.

The importance of *beur* filmmaking surely lies primarily in the shift it operates in the position of enunciation from which the dominant majority is addressed, focusing on minority perspectives which bring with them the potential for new strategies of identification and cultural contestation (Bhabha 1994: 162). For the postcolonial film critic, then, the textual operations of *beur*-authored films raise a number of questions. How do they reframe questions of ethnicity and identity in the context of Republican preferences for universalist, monocultural ideologies of Frenchness? What space do they make for *beur* subjectivities and agencies? To what extent do they challenge dominant perceptions of ethnic difference and disrupt or rework to their own advantage the use of stereotypes?[35] To what extent do they refuse and subvert the objectifying, othering eurocentric gaze of the white majority? Are they able to produce counter-narratives of nation which require the white majority to rethink their positioning? Do they offer narratives of mobility and transgression which break out of fixed identities? Are they able to introduce strategies which value difference, hybridity and transnationalism? The chapters which follow aim to address these questions by charting shifts and changes in *beur* filmmaking from the 1980s (chapter 1) through to the early 2000s (chapter 11), in part through a comparative study of white and *beur*-authored films.

Arguably, *beur* filmmaking can be divided between films which predate *La Haine* (discussed in chapters 1 and 2) and those that were made subsequently (the overlap with *banlieue* filmmaking is addressed in a separate section below, and foregrounded in chapter 4). Constructed through episodic realist narratives tempered with comedy and employing unknown or amateur actors, early *beur*-authored films differed from dominant French filmmaking of the 1980s and early 1990s, whose preoccupation with the *cinéma du look* and heritage cinema tended to avoid addressing 'reality' (Powrie 1997). Indeed, the first *beur*-authored films seemed, like the first *beur* novels to appear in the 1980s (Hargreaves 1991), to derive from the director's personal experiences and to offer firsthand, semi-autobiographical accounts of the *beurs*' lack of belonging (Fahdel 1990; Bosséno 1992). Having developed on the margins of mainstream French film culture, and in isolation from the theoretical debates which informed Black filmmaking in Britain in the 1980s, they do not offer examples of political avant-garde filmmaking strategies. Rather their naturalist style and low-key social realism have more in common with the work of Maurice Pialat or British filmmaker Ken Loach. Arguably, they constitute a strong plea for the recognition of difference, even as they stress the shared marginality of *beurs*, blacks and whites subject to the same, or similar, disadvantaged socio-economic circumstances.

At the same time, despite Farida Belghoul's short autobiographical fictions of the early 1980s, *beur* cinema was quickly identified with male-authored films about the problematic identities and aspirations of young heterosexual males (as in Djabri's *La Vago*), which evacuated or marginalised questions of sexual or gender difference. It is not surprising that troubled masculinity is a significant theme in most films by and about the *beurs*, given the need to counter the ways *banlieue* youth are demonised in dominant media discourses. However, the structuring absence of young *beur* women in *beur* and *banlieue* films has been challenged in the late 1990s by the emergence of women filmmakers of Maghrebi descent, whose films to date centre on women's lives. The question of gender difference is integral to the analysis of how *beur*-authored (and other) films reframe difference. It is foregrounded in particular in chapter 5, which compares Ghorab-Volta's construction of female *beur* subjectivity in *Souviens-toi de moi* (1996) with that of white filmmaker Anne Fontaine in *Les Histoires d'amour finissent mal en général* (1993), the first French feature film to centre on a *beurette*. It is also central to the analysis of the representation of minority teenage girls and immigrant women in chapters 7 and 10, and the exploration of masculinity in chapter 6. Differences in the ways in which gender is performed in these films highlight the significance of the gender and ethnicity of the filmmakers as well as of the characters in their relation to Frenchness.

Although *beur* films have been associated primarily with the subject matter of the *banlieue* and realist modes of filmmaking, filmmakers of Maghrebi descent have never been limited to such categories. Bouchareb's first films, *Baton Rouge* (1985) and *Cheb* (1991), were also road movies set for the most part outside France, and in the 1990s and early 2000s *beur* directors have increasingly tried to make their mark on mainstream filmmaking through the use of popular cinematic genres (or a postmodern mix of genres). In particular they have turned to comedy (as in Bensalah's *Le Ciel, les oiseaux . . . et ta mère* and Ahmed and Zakia Bouchaala's *Origine contrôlée*) and, most recently, big-budget action spectacle (as in Bensalah's *Le Raïd* and Dridi's *Fureur*). The question here is the extent to which the desire to appeal to a popular audience involves the suppression or marginalisation of ethnic difference (discussed in chapter 11).

From the mid-1990s, *beur* filmmakers have also turned to their parents' histories for inspiration, making period films which explore the experience of immigration in France in the 1960s and the 1970s from the point of view of Algerian immigrants and their children (see chapters 8 and 11). By reclaiming these histories, the *beurs* are challenging dominant French histories of the nation and working towards a valorisation of their own place within a multicultural France. In addition, there has been a move in both *beur* and non-*beur* filmmaking to claim new spaces away from Paris and its *banlieues* by focusing on aspects of the provinces not frequented by tourists, particularly the areas around Marseilles, Lyons and the North of France, which have also been the sites of immigration from the Maghreb (and elsewhere). A discussion of films set in the North of France in chapter 9 provides the opportunity for assessing the significance of places other than the city and the *banlieues* in the construction of difference, particularly on the part of white French filmmakers.

Significantly, a number of filmmakers of Maghrebi descent, notably Bouchareb, Charef, Dridi, Ghorab-Volta and Kechiche, have also made films which do not directly address the lack of belonging experienced by the *beurs*. However, their choices of topic generally evoke other forms of marginalisation and exclusion, as is the case with Charef's *Marie-Line* (2000), discussed in chapter 10, and Kechiche's *La Faute à Voltaire* (2001), discussed in chapter 12.[36] Such films can generally be seen as protests against intolerance and bids for inclusion within a multi-ethnic multicultural society.

Banlieue filmmaking

In a prescient article in the *Cahiers de la Cinémathèque* in 1994, José Baldizzone concludes his overview of cinematic representations of the *banlieue* from the 1930s through to the early 1990s by pointing out that 'No fiction film has yet invented a new style, a new mythology [for the *génération galère* – the 'generation in crisis'], as Duvivier, Prévert, Carné or Godard did for previous generations' (Baldizzone 1994: 80).[37] The following year, at a time of large-scale political protest in France, *La Haine* and its trio of *black-blanc-beur* youths dominated French cinema screens and, along with Jean-François Richet's *Etat des lieux*, Thomas Gilou's *Raï* and a number of less prominent *beur*-authored films, fomented debate about *banlieue* cinema as an emergent new genre (see chapter 4; Jousse 1995b; Tobin 1995; Reynaud 1996; Cadé 1999). For Michel Cadé, the *banlieue* has replaced the working-class as 'the frontier of social irreducibility, dangerous classes and salt of the earth'[38] (Cadé 2000: 72).

Precedents for *La Haine*, shot in the Parisian *banlieue* of Chanteloup-les-Vignes (see chapter 3), include Chibane's *Hexagone*, shot in the Parisian *banlieue* of Garges-la-Gonesse (see chapter 2), and various white and *beur*-authored films from the 1980s set on rundown working-class *banlieue* housing estates, such as Charef's *Le Thé au harem d'Archimède*, Serge Le Péron's *Laisse béton* and Jean-Claude Brisseau's *De bruit et de fureur*. As noted above, by the end of the 1980s the *banlieue* had come to refer not just to the suburbs, but more precisely to those *cités* (housing estates) linked with poor-quality social housing and high densities of immigrant and other disadvantaged populations. It is repeatedly evoked and stigmatised in the mainstream media of the 1990s through sensationalist headlines which associate it with social disorder and Islamic fundamentalism (see Bachmann 1994: 129; Ireland 2001: 69–70). The media's clichéd visions of the *banlieue* oppose 'center to periphery, cleanliness to filth, civilized to savage, native to foreign, and historical heritage to disquieting modernity' (Durmelat 2001: 118). They fail to take account of the majority of *banlieue* inhabitants who lead peaceful, hardworking lives, and serve primarily to erect scapegoats for the failure of successive governments to address the underlying causes of poverty, criminality and violence. Representations of the *banlieue*, like those of the *beurs*, are thus not to be understood in terms of transparent representations of reality, but as discursive constructs and sites of struggle for meaning.[39]

The cycle of films which led to the designation of the *banlieue* film are organised, crucially, around place, like the American Western. However, unlike the Western, which tends to legitimate the majority population's appropriation of spaces occupied by its perceived 'others', *banlieue* films seek to resist and contest the majority population's perception and control of the spaces in question. Their foregrounding of the voices of the disadvantaged suggests they have something in common with the 'hood' movies of early 1990s black independent cinema, and certainly American influences are evident in *La Haine, Raï* and *Ma 6-T va crack-er* (the white-authored rather than the *beur*-authored *banlieue* films). Crucially, though, these films avoid the construction of mono-ethnic ghettoes, emphasising instead the multi-ethnic nature of the French *banlieue* (and the inner city). In addition, their focus on issues linked to the contemporary *fracture sociale* (the perceived 'social divide') mark them in retrospect as a subset of films within one strand of what has since become known as the *jeune cinéma français* (Trémois 1997; Marie 1998; Prédal 2002), a label attributed to a new generation of filmmakers in the 1990s, including increasing numbers of women (see Tarr with Rollet 2001). A major feature of this set of films is the combination of poetic realism and documentary approaches to filmmaking with which they address issues of marginality and otherness.[40]

The prominence of the political in discussions of the *jeune cinéma français* is due in part to the role played by filmmakers in support of the *sans-papiers* (undocumented immigrants) in Paris, during and following their symbolic occupation of the churches of first St Ambroise, then St Bernard, and their brutal expulsion from St Bernard by the CRS (riot police) in August 1996.[41] (Seeking sanctuary in a church to make the case for their rights to citizenship obviously appeals not just to the secular tradition of the 'droit d'asile' but also to Christian beliefs in the sanctity of human rights.) Filmmakers (including Malik Chibane and Karim Dridi) signed a petition in February 1997 against the Debré bill on immigration, which made it illegal for French citizens to provide hospitality for those without the requisite papers. A short collaborative protest film, *Nous sans-papiers de France*, was shown at the 1997 Cannes Film Festival (see chapter 10). The public call to civil disobedience was followed in April 1998 by a further petition signed by 133 filmmakers, protesting against Jospin's failure to improve the situation and demanding the regularisation of the *sans-papiers*. It is not surprising that the political activism and solidarity these filmmakers demonstrated as citizens has in many cases been translated into films which centre on the excluded and the marginalised in France (not just immigrants and the inhabitants of the *banlieue*, but also the homeless, the unemployed, the working-class, the poor, and so on). A number of them have participated in various socially committed compilation films, including *Pas d'histoire! Douze films sur le racisme au quotidien*, released early in 2001, which included contributions from Benguigui and black filmmaker Fanta Régina Nacro. However, their actions also invite reflection on what sort of political filmmaking is possible in a postindustrial postcolonial society subject to the forces of transglobal capitalism.

Commentators on the *retour du politique* (the return of the political) in contemporary French cinema are agreed that there is now an identifiable body of films which provide a 'striking "political" portrait of a morally, humanly and economically disintegrating France'[42] (Prédal 2002: 125). However, there has been no return to the overtly political filmmaking styles and messages of the 1970s. And the perceived failure of traditional political institutions and practices has left a void which, for Martin O'Shaughnessy, is encapsulated in Hervé Le Roux's *Reprise* (1997), a documentary which sets out to recover the history of one of the women strikers at the Wonder battery factory in May 1968, and 'painfully trace[s] the dissolution of the narrative elements (the places, actors, projects, oppositions and temporalities) of one avatar of engaged cinema centred on the workplace and the organised working class' (O'Shaughnessy 2003: 191). As Michel Cadé points out, films about unemployment and the fragmentation of the working class have abandoned narratives of collective action in favour of individual protests or what he calls 'une solidarité de proximité' (the recourse to family or friends) (Cadé 2000: 70). Similarly, Francis Vanoye argues that the depiction of social disintegration often has as a corollary a (nostalgic) reaffirmation of social bonds (Vanoye 1998: 56). However, for Jean-Pierre Jeancolas (1997), the new emphasis in contemporary French cinema on the immediacy and proximity of the 'real' (what he calls 'le réel de proximité') is itself the sign of a political engagement, which, even if it cannot draw on the traditions of the organised or revolutionary Left, at least draws attention to the conflicts, actors and social structures which inform contemporary history.

Films associated with the *jeune cinéma français* which hint at a *retour du politique* are largely low-budget affairs which address aspects of everyday life, often using local or non-professional actors, local accents and location shooting, and often employing quite a physical, unpolished cinematic style.[43] A key aspect of their filming of the 'real', as in Bruno Dumont's *La Vie de Jésus* (1997), is the refusal of the places, spaces and characters which characterise mainstream French cinema, as well as a desire, typical of both *beur*-authored and *banlieue* films, to make visible the presence of ethnic minorities or other marginalised characters and engage with different narratives of Frenchness. The focus on alternative settings and spaces provides a particularly meaningful way of apprehending the 'realities' of life on the margins and the possibility of a politics of 'everyday life'. It also chimes with recent academic interest in cultural geography and the theorising of space in the construction of identity. In

1994 Homi Bhabha suggested that the postcolonial city 'provides the space in which emergent identifications and new social movements of the people are played out ... [and] the perplexity of the living is most acutely experienced' (Bhabha 1994: 170).[44] Representations of the multi-ethnic *banlieue* in films by directors associated with the *jeune cinéma français* provide a testing ground for theories of space and belonging, as does their choice of locations in the post-industrial North, discussed in chapter 9.

Adrian Fielder (2001), in his analysis of space in *La Haine*, draws on de Certeau's work in *The Practice of Everyday Life* (1984) to respond to Foucault's analysis of the ways in which the organisation of social space determines the distribution and circulation of bodies and relations of power (Foucault 1977). For de Certeau (1984), the city constitutes a textual system which attempts to identify, interpellate and regulate individuals, but which can be subverted, if momentarily, by the 'poaching' tactics of the oppressed. Fielder argues that if *banlieue* films 'explicitly thematize the many forms of territorial control to which *banlieue* inhabitants are subject, they also suggest that the characters are, in fact, capable of escaping and/or subverting that control (even if only temporarily)' (Fielder 2001: 276). Thus, on the one hand, the *mise-en-scène* of space in *banlieue* films emphasises the ways in which its protagonists are blocked and fenced in by their surroundings: typically, shots of anonymous high-rise flats and graffiti-covered walls block their horizon and imprison them in spaces of socio-economic deprivation, alienation and isolation. In addition, their occupation of transitional, anonymous public spaces, like the hallways in the blocks of flats, the surrounding outside spaces (often waste-lands), the bus stops and train stations from which they hope to depart, is shown to be subject to police and other forms of surveillance. On the other hand, they are also shown as on the move, momentarily escaping surveillance by transgressing borders and finding new spaces to appropriate (the cellars, the roofs, empty warehouses, and so on). The films' narratives thus set up an oscillation between forms of 'nomadism' (a term borrowed from Deleuze and Guattari, 1987) and state-regulated modes of occupying space. At the same time, as the repeated trope of travel to and expulsion from the city centre makes clear, the films ultimately demonstrate the characters' lack of a space to call their own (see Konstantarakos 1999).

The analysis of *banlieue* films in terms of their representation of the nomadic, opportunistic 'poaching' tactics of their otherwise oppressed and marginalised protagonists enables them to be read in terms of cultural, if not political struggle. The use of such tactics can also be related to Lefebvre's theories of festival and its challenge to oppressive social structures (see High-more 2002: 113–44). The first two films by Jean-François Richet, a Marxist who prides himself on hailing from (and still living in) the *banlieue*, lend themselves to such readings. *Etat des lieux* (1995), made, like some of the *beur*-authored films, outside the normal film industry circuits (in this case with money made by gambling his – and his co-writer's – dole money), charts the protagonist's resistances to authority and ends with a long sequence of joyful, secret, illicit sex (see chapter 4); *Ma 6-T va crack-er* (1997) culminates in a celebratory coming together of rap music and rioting (see chapter 6).[45] It may, then, be productive to approach *beur* and *banlieue* filmmaking with a set of questions relating to their use of space, bearing in mind that they seek to address mainstream as well as minority audiences. Do they reinforce the *banlieue* as a negative, homogeneous space, 'defined by an explosive cocktail of unemployment, poor housing, racial discrimination and lawlessness from which there appears to be no escape' (Hargreaves 1999: 117)? Do they challenge dominant constructions of the *banlieue* by representing it as a multi-layered site of difference? Do they offer examples of individual or group resistance to the state-sanctioned use of space?

To answer these questions, it is important to bear in mind that *beur* and white inhabitants of the *banlieue* – and filmmakers too – have a different relationship to place and space because of their different relationship to Frenchness. Whereas the majority white population may be cultural insiders and first-generation Maghrebis perceived as cultural outsiders, French people of Maghrebi descent are (still, at times) in a position of 'inbetweenness', displaced in relation to both French and Maghrebi culture. The question is whether their placelessness can be transcended, not just by the deployment of 'poaching' tactics (alongside their peers), but by the creation of alternative spaces beyond binary oppositions, which value hybridity. This book maps the struggle of *beur* filmmakers to construct what Bill Ashcroft describes as 'an effective identifying relationship between self and place' (Ashcroft, Griffiths and Tiffin 1989: 9, quoted in Ireland 1997), and suggests that their ways of reframing difference both reassure and disturb the nation's homogeneous image of itself.

Notes

The first eight chapters of this book were first written and published during the years 1992–2001, as I observed the development of *beur* and *banlieue* filmmaking in France. They have been modified here to reduce overlap between chapters, correct errors and standardise the use of vocabulary and dates; but otherwise they have been left substantially the same in order to reproduce the interest and pleasure in tracking a developing body of work. Where appropriate, notes have been added to make cross-references and draw attention to later developments. Dates of films given throughout are dates of release rather than dates of production. English-language titles are provided only for the principal films discussed. The translation of original quotations in French is my own.

1 One effect of this is that the INED (Institut National d'Etudes Démographiques) is unable to produce statistical information relating to the ethnic identity or immigrant origins of French citizens (Kédadouche 2002: 68; see also Tribalat 1995). In

2003, Michèle Tribalat suggested that the population of Maghrebi origin was 'about three million out of a total of fourteen million immigrants or people of immigrant origin' and dismissed the estimate of five million Muslims in France as having been 'pulled out of a hat' (Tribalat 2003). Clearly, without accurate statistical information it is very difficult to formulate effective policies targeting inequalities.

2 My focus on *beur* and *banlieue* filmmaking means that other important contributions to the representation of ethnicity and identity in contemporary postcolonial France are not addressed here, notably the work of *pied noir* and sub-Saharan African filmmakers and *auteur* filmmakers such as Claire Denis, Robert Guédiguian and André Téchiné.

3 For discussions of the meanings of the word '*beur*', see Begag and Chaouite (1990) and Durmelat (2001).

4 See Guénif Souilamas (2000: 33–40) for a critique of the eurocentrism at work in the use of the word Maghrebi (the Arabic root for which, ironically, means 'western').

5 See Begag and Chaouite (1990: 82) for a discussion of other terms used to refer to the *beurs*.

6 In 1991 Tribalat estimated that roughly 25 per cent of France's population was composed of immigrants or people with at least one immigrant parent or grandparent (Tribalat 1991: 43, 65–71).

7 The word Arab fails to distinguish the fact that many Algerian immigrants were Berbers from Kabylia.

8 Le Pen, a French army officer (and Poujadist deputy) during the Algerian War of Independence, was an uncompromising supporter of Algérie Française. He founded the Front National in 1972.

9 Benguigui's TV documentary, *Mémoires d'immigrés* (1997), documenting contemporary memories of immigration in the 1960s and 1970s, was a media event and achieved a theatrical release in 1998 (see Durmelat 2000).

10 This silence includes the shameful treatment of the *harkis* (Algerians who had fought on the side of the French), many thousands of whom were left behind to be massacred in Algeria.

11 There are signs in the new millennium that France is attempting to achieve some sort of historical closure through a formal recognition of some of the more negative aspects of its colonial past and a renewal of relationships with contemporary Algeria. In September 2001, President Chirac made a speech in homage to the *harkis* and their offspring (who are still unwelcome in Algeria); in October 2001, Bertrand Delanoë, the Socialist Mayor of Paris, laid an official plaque commemorating the Algerians who died in October 1961; and in 2003, Djazaïr, the Year of Algeria in France, provided an opportunity for discovering and celebrating cultural links with Algeria.

12 According to reports published by the Haut Conseil à l'Intégration (HCI), the unemployment rate of young people of immigrant origin in the most seriously affected areas has increased between 1990 and 1999 at approximately twice the national average rate for the same age range. For young women aged 20–24, the rate was 33 per cent (as opposed to 25.3 per cent) in 1990 and 39.5 per cent (as opposed to 28.4 per cent) in 1999. For young men aged 20–24, the rate was 23.5 per cent (as opposed to 14.8 per cent) in 1990 and 37.2 per cent (as opposed to 22.5 per cent)

in 1999. Furthermore, 31 per cent of young people of immigrant origin have no educational qualifications, compared with 14 per cent of those whose parents were born in France; 23 per cent of those with one parent born abroad achieve a further- or higher-education qualification compared with 40 per cent of other young people. Information cited in Mullier (2004).

13 In 1981, riots and hunger strikes in Vénissieux, a suburb of Lyons, spread to other French cities in what was called *l'été chaud* ('the hot summer'). In 1991, another 'hot summer' saw a succession of riots, notably in Sartrouville and Mantes-la-Jolie (and in Narbonne, by the children of *harkis*). Other riots have punctuated the 1990s and early 2000s, underlining the failure of successive governments to address the underlying causes.

14 'Déstabilisation des jeunes nés ou ayant grandi en France, privés de l'assurance de pouvoir y vivre durablement'.

15 The desire to possess and control the ethnic other by banning the wearing of the Islamic headscarf recalls the way French army photographers forced Algerian women to remove their veils in 1960.

16 '. . . le machisme des hommes de nos quartiers qui au nom d'une "tradition" nient nos droits les plus élémentaires'; '. . . une société qui nous enferme dans les ghettos où s'accumulent misère et exclusion'.

17 In 2002, two secretaries of state appointed to Jean-Pierre Raffarin's rightwing government, Tokia Saïfi and Hamlaoui Mékachéra, were of Maghrebi descent.

18 On the twentieth anniversary of the March of the Beurs in December 2003, Raffarin promised that a significant number of candidates of immigrant origin in the UMP (Chirac's Union pour un Mouvement Populaire) would be in a position to be elected at the March 2004 regional elections, a promise that he signally failed to deliver. The difficulties experienced by the *beurs* in local politics are explored in Jean-Louis Comolli and Michel Samson's documentary film *Rêves de France à Marseille* (2003).

19 *Egalité* ('Equality') is the name of an association of artists and intellectuals led, among others, by writer Calixte Beyala (herself of Cameroonian origin), to combat the inadequate representation of the black and *beur* population of France on television (Delesalle 1999: 98).

20 A reality TV show (the French equivalent to *Big Brother*).

21 A number of early short films and documentaries by *beur* filmmakers are available on video at the Forum des Images in Paris (if they include a Parisian setting).

22 See Fahdel (1990) and Dhoukar (1990) for overviews of the stylistic and thematic features of both short and feature-length *beur* films of the 1980s.

23 See Armes (1996: 141–9) for an overview of filmmakers of Maghrebi origin who began working in France in the 1970s but have not been associated with the *beur* movement, including Ali Akika, Mohamed Benayat and Okacha Touita.

24 In addition, Abdel Kechiche's second film, *L'Esquive*, came out in January 2004 and both Bourlem Guerdjou and Djamel Ouahab are preparing a second film. Actor Atmen Kelif is preparing to co-direct his first film with Lorant Deutsch.

25 Karim Dridi is actually of mixed-race (Franco-Tunisian) origin.

26 Nevertheless, according to Jean-Pierre Guerrieri of the CNC (4 February 2004), 50 per cent of films by *beur* directors have benefited from the *avance sur recettes*, while

another 10 per cent have received a (smaller) subsidy to help with postproduction costs.

27 Television films made for Arte by *beur* directors include Mehdi Charef's *Le Pigeon volé* (1995) and Malik Chibane's *Nés quelque part* (1997). Significant TV films include Olivier Dahan's *banlieue* film *Frères: la roulette rouge* in the 1994 Arte series *Tous les garçons et les filles de mon âge*, Romain Goupil's *Sa vie à elle* (1995) in the Arte series *Les Années lycée* (co-scripted with Ghorab-Volta), centring on a school-girl's decision to wear the Islamic veil, Daniel Vigne's *Fatou la Malienne* (2001) for France 2, the controversial but immensely popular exploration of a young Malian girl's rebellion against the imposition of an arranged marriage, and *Le Premier Fils* (2003) by Philomène Esposito, which explores a white woman's reunion with the mixed-race son she has not seen since he was a baby.

28 Lahoussa also made a number of short films in the early 1980s.

29 Benguigui assiduously promoted *beur* and Algerian women's filmmaking during the Year of Algeria (2003), and in December 2003 was made a Chevalier of the Legion of Honour by Jacques Chirac for her role as spokesperson for the population of Maghrebi descent.

30 For example, the only feature film to be made by novelist and documentary film-maker Amor Hakkar, *Sale temps pour un voyou* (1992), appears not to have received a theatrical release.

31 As a consequence of this, even when their films are released on DVD, they lack subtitles and so cannot be easily incorporated into film courses abroad.

32 In 2003, the London Film Festival included two films about the *beurs*, Jean-Pierre Sinapi's *Vivre me tue* and Christian Philibert's *Travail d'arabe*, and a film by an Algerian émigré working in France, Abdelkrim Bahloul's *Le Soleil assassiné*, but no film actually made by a *beur* filmmaker.

33 Naceri's character Daniel in *Taxi* (Gérard Pires, 1998), *Taxi 2* (Gérard Krawczyk, 2002) and *Taxi 3* (Gérard Krawczyk, 2003). See Hargreaves (2003) for a discussion of integrated casting in contemporary French cinema.

34 For the full list of features, see Naficy (2001: 4 and 289–92).

35 See Rosello (1998) for a brilliant analysis of 'declining the stereotype' in French culture.

36 For example, Charef's *Camomille* (1988) and *Au pays des Juliets* (1992), Bouchareb's *Poussières de vie/Dust of Life* (1994) and *Little Senegal* (2001), Ghorab-Volta's *Laisse un peu d'amour* (1998) and *Jeunesse dorée* (2002) and Dridi's *Pigalle* (1995), *Hors jeu* (1998) and *Fureur* (2003), as well as his documentaries *Citizen Ken Loach* (1996) and *Cuba Feliz* (2002). Bouchareb's films are particularly interesting. *Poussières de vie*, set in a brutal re-education camp in Vietnam, celebrates the rebelliousness and enterprise of a group of unwanted American-Vietnamese children, fathered by the GIs. *Little Senegal*, an inversion of the American roots narrative, follows the adventures of an elderly Senegalese man (the curator of the Museum of Slavery in Dakar), who travels to the United States to trace what happened to his family sold into slavery, and experiences the racism between African-Americans and Africans.

37 See Moinereau (1994) and other articles in *Cahiers de la Cinémathèque*, 1994, 59/60, for discussions of the *banlieue* in cinema prior to 1995. See also Vincendeau's

article on *La Haine* (Vincendeau 2000: 310–27), in which she distinguishes between an 'aesthetic' and a 'sociological' tendency in *banlieue* filmmaking, the 'aesthetic' tendency being evident in films by Godard, Rohmer and Blier, the more 'sociological' tendency in films associated with *beur* cinema. Arguably, Jean-Claude Brisseau's explosive account of white working-class alienation in *De bruit et de fureur* (1988) bridges the two.

38 'La frontière de l'irréductibilité sociale, classes dangereuses et sel de la terre'.

39 The inadequacies of any homogenising vision of the *banlieue* are exposed in François Maspero's *Les Passagers du Roissy-Express* (1990), a text describing his journey (with photographer Anaïk Frantz) to the Parisian *banlieues* served by the RER B suburban train line, which demonstrates their multi-layered historical, cultural and ethnic diversity.

40 See Konstantarakos (1998) for a critical discussion of the different strands of filmmaking encompassed by the label *jeune cinéma français*. See also Beugnet (2000a) for a positive account of how the *jeune cinéma français* constructs a different – non-voyeuristic, non-consumerist, but sensitive and attentive – look at otherness.

41 The *sans-papiers* were for the most part French residents affected by changes in the immigration laws which meant that their residence cards were not renewed.

42 '... le tableau politique" saisissant d'une France délabrée économiquement, humainement et moralement'.

43 There have been at least two attempts by white filmmakers to involve *banlieue* citizens in the construction of fictions about themselves, namely Paul Vecchiali's *Zone franche* (1996) and Christian Vincent's *Sauve-moi* (2000).

44 For studies of space in film, see for example Clarke (1997), Konstantarakos (2000).

45 Neither *Ma 6-T va crack-er* nor Richet's third film, *De l'amour* (2001), were well received by the critics, leading René Prédal to describe him as 'the Ed Wood' of new French cinema (Prédal 2002: 117). (I am indebted to Will Higbee for pointing this out.) See also Faroult (2004) for a discussion of Richet as a militant filmmaker.

1

Questions of identity in *beur* cinema: from *Le Thé au harem d'Archimède* to *Cheb*[1]

The theoretical debates informing British and North American analyses of the representation of 'new ethnicities' in popular culture have been largely absent from French discourses on race, immigration and national identity.[2] The French academy has remained impervious, if not hostile, to the development of critical theories on the construction of the subject which have fed the political agenda informing both cultural studies and women's studies. Feminists have noted with concern the failure of the French critical establishment to take on board some twenty years of feminist film theory (Vincendeau 1987). Still predominantly influenced by semiotic and auteurist approaches to film analysis, and indifferent to anything that smacks of 'ideology', film theory and film criticism in France have continued to marginalise issues around gender, sexuality, race and national identity.

Filmmakers from ethnic minorities in France are unlikely to find support for any openly political project in mainstream French cinema, especially if they turn for funding to state and industry subsidies, notably the *avance sur recettes* (advance on box-office receipts). A proposal must either show evidence of 'quality' (a sound script, a star cast) or potential as a self-expressive *auteur* film. There has been no equivalent to the British Film Institute or Channel 4 in the UK at a national level to give a boost to alternative filmmaking practices, and no equivalent to groups such as Sankofa or the Black Audio Workshop to provide practical and theoretical resources for aspiring minority filmmakers.

Nevertheless, from the late 1970s onwards, independent and community-based filmmakers from France's most visible ethnic minority group, the 'second generation' North Africans, began to produce a number of shorts and documentaries, both commercially and non-commercially. These films, mostly of a militant–informative nature, engaged with the conflicts and tensions of the immigrant experience in France, but were mainly dependent on alternative exhibition circuits. When in the mid-1980s 'second generation' filmmakers achieved popular successes with commercially made feature films, critics began to speak of a new phenomenon in French cinema, the *cinéma beur* or *beur* cinema. This chapter sets out to analyse how questions of identity and subjectivity are articulated in four *beur*-authored commercial feature films: *Le Thé au harem d'Archimède* (Mehdi Charef, 1985), *Baton Rouge* (Rachid Bouchareb, 1985), *Miss Mona* (Charef, 1987) and *Cheb* (Bouchareb, 1991). These questions cannot be addressed without locating the films in their socio-political context.[3]

The word *beur* is reputedly derived from Parisian backslang for *arabe* (Arab), and was in circulation within the immigrant community in the late 1970s.[4] Its hybrid form reflects the conflict of identity experienced by the newly visible 'second generation' (as they are still called). On the one hand, they owed allegiance to the culture of their Maghrebi (Arab or Berber) parents, who tended to maintain their original national identity, be it Algerian, Tunisian or Moroccan, and even to dream of the return to the homeland. They differed from the French in appearance, in their geographical location on the outskirts and in the ghettoes of French urban society, and in that their parents continued to practise their own language, customs and religion (Islam). On the other hand, despite their family backgrounds, they were also the products of the secular French education system, knew no other home but France, were often out of sympathy with their parents' values and had higher expectations than their parents of their future role in French society.

The tensions between the different sets of cultural roles and expectations were exacerbated by two factors, particularly for those of Algerian descent (the majority): conflicting nationality laws and the growth of racism. Whereas after independence in 1962, Algeria continued to consider the children of immigrants to be Algerian (and expected young males to do two years' national service in Algeria), the 'second generation' born in France also had the right to French nationality. Often against their parents' wishes, they had to claim that right (entailing a year's national service in France for young males) in order to get their national identity card. Additionally, as 'Arabs', as all those of North African descent were – and are – indiscriminately called, they were the primary targets of the increasingly hostile climate of racism in France, which came to the foreground in the early 1980s, as demonstrated by the spectacular rise of the extreme rightwing Front National, led by Jean-Marie Le Pen.

Racism against 'Arabs' in France is deeply entrenched in French society as a result of France's imperial past in North Africa and the relatively recent, long and bitter struggle for Algerian independence. It surfaced in the late 1970s and early 1980s as the 'second generation' became more visible, due to an increase in population combined with an increase in family immigration in the 1970s (primary immigration was halted by the French government in 1974 to combat unemployment). Immigrants found themselves the focus for French fears and anxieties about unemployment and law and order and, although after Mitterrand's election in 1981 some of the harsher tactics adopted by the previous government were dropped, there was a great deal of unrest among the immigrant communities as a result. The situation was exploited by the Front National in the municipal elections of March 1983, and there followed a wave of racist attacks in what became known as *l'été meurtrier* ('the murderous summer'). If the immigrant communities had pinned their hopes for change on the election of the Socialist Party, Mitterrand's policies in relation to immigration and racism were soon perceived to be vacillating if not ineffectual.

As a result, the *beurs* began to assert themselves in a more organised way. The late 1970s and early 1980s had already seen the development of *beur* theatre groups and other associations, and when the new administration granted immigrants the right of free association, a plethora of new community cultural organisations sprang up (working in film, radio, rock music and so on). There had also been some attempts to develop a youth-based antiracist movement through events such as 'Rock Against Police' in 1980. In 1983, the *beurs* organised a 'March against Racism and for Equality', which crossed France from Marseilles to Paris, where it was received by Mitterrand, and attracted 100,000 demonstrators (both French and immigrant). The media dubbed it the March of the *Beurs*, and for a short period the nation became sympathetic to the *beurs*' predicament. However, the movement quickly became fragmented. Convergence 84, the next national demonstration, was weakened by internal rifts and the autonomous *beur* movement was then dramatically eclipsed by a new rival organisation, SOS Racisme, set up in October 1984 under the leadership of Harlem Désir (of West Indian origin). SOS Racisme successfully mobilised a mass youth movement with its slogan 'Touche pas à mon pote' ('Lay off my mate'), but focused attention on bringing together a wide spectrum of political support to combat Le Pen, rather than drawing attention to the specific needs of the *beur*/immigrant communities.

The emergence of a putative *beur* cinema has to be seen in the context of this particular conjuncture of socio-economic and political circumstances. New popular cultural forms did not benefit from the underpinning of a strong, unified political *beur* movement, but rather emerged at a time of defiant yet defensive attempts to negotiate a recognition of the *beurs*' rights as French citizens and to create a climate of tolerance that would enable them to be more fully integrated into French society. Their precarious position was underlined when the Front National polled an exceptionally high number of votes in the 1986 elections and the Right was returned to power for a year of 'cohabitation' with Mitterrand, during which time the expulsion of lawbreakers to Algeria was reintroduced and immigrants' rights to French nationality came under threat. Although by the end of the decade, a number of *beurs* had organised to enter local politics, there were growing fears on the part of immigrants that the construction of 'Fortress Europe' (the Single European Market) would further prejudice their positions. Meanwhile, anti-Arab feeling in France was exacerbated by the first Gulf War, and the return of the Right in the elections of March 1993 was followed by a weekend of racist attacks and police violence. The introduction of hardline legislation limiting immigrant (and 'second-generation') rights to French nationality and citizenship was quick to follow.

Beur cinema also needs to be situated in relation to the representations of immigrants in circulation in mainstream French, 'first generation' and North African cinema. Critics reviewing the representation of immigrants in film in France share a common concern, which is voiced in article after article throughout the 1980s, that there should be no repeat of the 'miserabilism' which dogged the 'first-generation' films of the 1960s and 1970s, exemplified by Ali Ghalem's films *Mektoub* (1964) and *L'Autre France* (1974). By this, they mean realist films or melodramas which show Arabs as the wretched passive victims of French racism. The label was used to criticise Roger Hanin's well-intentioned *Train d'enfer* (1984), a dramatised reconstruction of a real-life incident when three French soldiers threw a North African from a train to his death.

The same critics have also been concerned that films should move beyond the stereotypes of Arabs which figure in certain French films of the 1970s and 1980s, where Arab roles are confined to the criminal underworld and associated with delinquency, drugs and violence, for example Bob Swaim's *La Balance* (1981) or Maurice Pialat's *Police* (1985). A few white-authored French films do in fact present narratives where a *beur* or immigrant character has, if not the central, then at least the second role, and a role which gives more recognition to the complexities and contradictions of the immigrant experience, in the manner of Michel Drach's *Elise ou la vraie vie* (1970). One or two films involve female *beur* characters, for example *Grand frère* (1982) by Francis Girod (involving an affair between a French criminal and a *beur* prostitute) and Gérard Blain's controversial *Pierre et Djemila* (a 1986 reworking of the Romeo and Juliet story); it is noticeable, though, that these roles confine the *beurettes* to the function of objects of sexual exchange. The theme of male friendship across ethnic divides, a major preoccupation of the ensuing *beur* films, is developed (if from a white French point of view) in *Tchao pantin* (1983) by Claude Berri and *Laisse béton* (1983) by Serge Le Péron. This latter film in particular prefigures the particular concerns of the first *beur*-authored feature films in its sympathetic construction of working-class youth culture and *banlieue* setting.[5]

Charlotte Silvera's *Louise l'insoumise* (1984) brings a rare female perspective to the problems of immigration, integration and identity, by foregrounding the point of view of a young schoolgirl at odds with her Jewish Tunisian family, now living in France. Until 1997, no *beur* women achieved the funding to make a feature film. However, the work of the independent filmmaker, Farida Belghoul, a militant activist in the *beur* movement of the early 1980s, provides an early alternative to both the forms and the topics of popular male-authored *beur* cinema. Both of her short films, *C'est Madame la France que tu préfères?*

(1981) and the formally innovative *Le Départ du père* (1983), explore the dilemmas of a young *beur* woman working out her identity in relation to her family. The first centres on a student living away from home to make the most of her independence but feeling guilty about lying to her family; the second features a dialogue between daughter and father, set in Algeria, as the daughter attempts to persuade her father to return to his family in France.

However, the film which most clearly heralded the popular *beur* films was *Le Thé à la menthe* (1984) by Abdelkrim Bahloul, a film which has been considered a *beur* film by critics in France, even though it fails to meet the basic criteria for a *beur* film as defined by Christian Bosséno, that is, 'any film directed by a young person of North African origin who was born or who grew up in France, usually featuring *beur* characters' (Bosséno 1992: 49). Bahloul is an Algerian émigré, who found himself unemployed in Algeria after studying film in France, and managed to achieve the *avance sur recettes* for a proposal for a short film, which he subsequently successfully transformed into a first feature. The central protagonist of his film is a young immigrant rather than a *beur*, and the film is structured around Hamou's attempts to find ways and means of staying in France, while his Algerian mother, having seen what is happening to him in the streets of Barbès, plans to take him back home to Algeria. There is a sense in which Hamou (Abdel Kechiche) draws on the stereotype of the Arab as delinquent, but the film transcends the limitations of such a designation by putting him at the centre of the narrative, humanising him and refusing to allow him to be seen as a victim. The film is characterised by its comic, light-hearted tone, and Hamou manages to retain audience sympathy through his appealing attempts at street credibility and because his delinquency is clearly compelled by his intractable socio-economic situation.

Le Thé à la menthe draws on a number of themes and sets a tone which account for its inclusion in the critics' construction of *beur* cinema.[6] It invokes the reality of urban French society through its choice of locations in the busy picturesque multi-ethnic streets of Barbès, it invites sympathy for the dilemmas of a young (male) immigrant who has little hope of getting a decent job and is forced to turn to street crime, and it vividly dramatises the conflict between two cultures and two generations through the energetic presence of Chafia Boudraa as Hamou's mother. Significantly, it omits to address head-on the legacy of France's colonisation of Algeria or the issue of racism in France, nor does it acknowledge Islam as a major factor in the construction of cultural difference. Young *beur*/immigrant women simply do not feature in the film and, on a more symbolic level, in its construction of the Maghrebi family it leaves out the figure of the father, a structuring absence which recurs in the later films. Where it differs fundamentally from the *beur* films which followed is in the implication that the return to Algeria is a real (if undesired and problematic) alternative. Not surprisingly, the film was read in a number of quarters as endorsing repatriation, a project actively supported by the Right in France at the time of the film's appearance.

Attempts to construct a corpus of *beur* films, and to provide a thematic and stylistic analysis of them, are to be found in a collection of articles in *Ciné-matographe* in 1985 and in *CinémAction* in 1990. Christian Bosséno's piece in *Popular European Cinema* reproduces the gist of these articles for an English-speaking audience. In his view, 'the chief interest of *beur* films is that by giving substance to a new component of French society and renewing the image of the immigrant in the French cinema they have galvanised the jaded imaginations of those responsible for mainstream productions' (Bosséno 1992: 51), a comment which suggests a lack of concern for the meanings of these films for the *beurs* themselves. Although the corpus may differ if Algerian filmmakers are included (for example, Mahmoud Zemmouri's comedies about immigration, *Prends dix mille balles et casse-toi* (1980) and *Les Folles années du twist* (1983), share certain themes and approaches with *beur* films), *beur* cinema as of 1993 is basically constructed out of twenty or so shorts and documentaries (mostly made in the early 1980s), *Le Thé à la menthe* (even though it is not technically a *beur* film) and the feature films of two *beur* filmmakers of Algerian origin, Mehdi Charef and Rachid Bouchareb. Even then, there is confusion over whether all of Charef's films can be considered *beur* films, since *Camomille* (1987) and *Au pays des Juliets* (1992) are not specifically concerned with *beur* or immigrant issues, while *Miss Mona* features an immigrant rather than a *beur*.

My concern here is with the ways in which questions of *beur* identity and subjectivity are articulated in *beur*-authored popular cinema, and I shall therefore confine my analysis to the two first specifically *beur* feature films, *Le Thé au harem d'Archimède* by Mehdi Charef and *Baton Rouge* by Rachid Bouchareb, both of which were relatively successful at the box office (*Le Thé au harem* also won the 1985 Jean Vigo prize and the César for Best First Film); and to the rather less successful follow-up films, *Miss Mona* by Charef and *Cheb* by Bouchareb. What sort of subject positions do these films make available for a multicultural French audience? How do the films represent and negotiate the tensions between the conflicting cultural identities available to their central protagonists? What is the significance of the insistent marginalisation of women in these male-centred narratives? Can differences between the first and second films be attributed, if tentatively, to the changing position of the *beurs* in French society?

Le Thé au harem d'Archimède/Tea in the Harem (1985)

Le Thé au harem d'Archimède (replacing the novel's even more exotic title *Le Thé au harem d'Archi Ahmed*) is a mischievous title. The film fails to deliver on its eastern promise: instead, the title turns out to be a play on words based on a schoolboy's miswriting of 'le théorème d'Archimède'. In the film's only flashback, motivated by the French youth's memories of his classmate's humiliation and revolt, black and white silent footage shows the young boy becoming the laughing-stock of the class, accompanied by the noise of an imaginary, old film projector. Charef turns the tables on his audience, in that it is the French who have difficulty understanding the *beur*-authored joke. Nonetheless, the film's attitude towards a French audience is ambivalent. Whereas the novel is dedicated to Charef's mother, Mebarka, 'even though she cannot read', the film ends with a dedication 'to Jean-Pierre' as the final credits roll. The film, then, though it foregrounds a *beur*'s story, is aware of its address to the (white, male) French spectator. Indeed, as far as Farida Belghoul was concerned, the eye of 'big brother' can be felt throughout the film (Belghoul 1985: 32).

The concern with addressing a mixed French audience is translated into the film's structure (as in the novel) through the construction of a variety of subject positions. The narrative centres on the adventures of a couple of eighteen-year-olds: Madjid, a *beur* (Kader Boukhanef) and Pat, his illiterate French friend (Rémi Martin). However, the loose episodic structure of the narrative, covering a week or so in the lives of people living on the ironically named Flowers Estate, allows other stories to be intercalated, particularly that of Josette (Laure Duthilleul), a single white mother who loses her job and is driven to attempt suicide, and Malika, Madjid's mother (Saïda Bekkouche), who not only holds her own family together, but also provides support for other women on the estate who are unable to cope. (Images of other immigrant families, potentially threatening to a white audience, are noticeably absent, however.)

The film is primarily interested in exploring Madjid's conflicts of identity, torn between the (unrealistic) expectations his mother has of him as an Algerian and his experiences on the streets of Paris with Pat. He is most often seen in the company of Pat and it is through the doubling-up of central protagonists with different ethnic origins, who nevertheless share the same underprivileged background (sordid housing estate, no job, no money, no prospects), that the film is able to provide points of recognition and identification for both a *beur* and a French audience. The pleasure in and solidarity of their good-natured, buddy-like friendship is represented through a series of shared experiences, including the crimes they carry out together (stealing, mugging, pimping), and moments of relaxation (drinking, going out with the gang, picking up girls). It is underlined by the sacrifices they make for each other: Madjid walks out on an admittedly boring factory job to join Pat who has been given the sack; and the film ends with a final shot of Pat gazing towards Madjid, the camera taking Madjid's point of view, as he gives himself up to the police to join his friend.

The film's basic message, then, is that there is no fundamental difference between *beur* and white French youth. They look alike (they are equally attractive, give or take Madjid's slightly darker complexion and black curly hair), they talk and dress alike, and they have the same tastes and the same problems (hence the film's international crossover appeal). Their delinquency is the product not of their respective racial origins, but rather of their deprived working-class background and the economic crisis. This theme is taken up by the role of the gang within the film, whose members hail from a variety of ethnic backgrounds, but who all live on the same housing estate and are jointly the victims of the violence and aggression expressed by the older generation of white, working-class males (figure 4). The generation gap is fundamental to an understanding of the social tensions informing the film: in a key scene, the local cinema auditorium becomes the site of youth solidarity, uniting rival gangs in the face of threats from the drunk middle-aged male (French) intruders.

At the same time, the film subtly positions the spectator to sympathise with Pat and Madjid's more reprehensible behaviour, by suggesting that their victims deserve what they get. For example, when they steal a wallet from a passenger on the metro, their victim immediately shows himself to be a racist by accusing Madjid of the theft (whereas it is Pat who has the wallet hidden); when Madjid entices a wealthy-looking gay man to follow him into a park, where he gets mugged by Pat, the victim can be seen as responsible for what happens to him by his treatment of the young *beur* as an erotic object; after Madjid feels sorry for Solange, the local lush whom they tout round the immigrant workers' huts for business, she justifies their abuse of her by spending all the money she earns on drink. These sequences are politically as well as morally ambiguous: the film is (perhaps unconsciously) shot through with images of French society as fundamentally corrupt and degraded, images which are at odds with the fact of (and desire for) integration into French society, presented through Madjid's friendship with Pat.

This reading is supported by an analysis of the film's obsessive handling of (hetero)sexuality and sexual difference. Pat and Madjid have a casually sexist attitude to women, which requires constant reinforcement through looking as well as acting. The fascination with the female other, combined with the commodification of the female body, is crystallised in the scene where they instruct the younger boys on the estate in how to treat Mado, the mentally retarded girl who lets them all fuck her. Femininity as both commodity and spectacle is a recurring theme – as in the scene when their former schoolmate Balou returns to the estate in a Mercedes, with the windows plastered with banknotes and a white French prostitute sitting on the back seat: as the gang surrounds the car and stares in admiration, Balou slowly parts the woman's legs. When Pat and Madjid have money, they go to the rue St-Denis to ogle at the prostitutes, or pick up French girls in a discotheque, or go back to the estate to screw Joséphine, a local housewife, before her husband gets back from work. With the judicious exceptions of Josette and Madjid's neighbour, Mme Levesque, both of

4 The multi-ethnic gang of *Le Thé au harem d' Archimède* (1985).

whom are inadequate mothers and the victims of violence perpetrated by
Frenchmen, and Anita, the token teenage girl in the gang (who utters occasional objections to the lads' macho behaviour and attitudes), all the French-
women represented in this film turn out to be sexually available 'slags'.

This is particularly shocking in the case of Pat's sister, Chantal, who is set up
early in the film as a potential love interest for Madjid (to his mother's despair),
but who turns out to be working as a prostitute in Paris. The scene in which
Madjid makes this discovery is crucially placed towards the end of the film.
Instead of sympathetically acknowledging the similarities between Chantal's
situation and his own, Madjid backs away, gets drunk, and abandons any further active role. As a result, when the police catch up with the gang and their
stolen car on the beach at Deauville (a location which invites comparison with
the ending of Truffaut's *Les Quatre Cent Coups*), Madjid is in a state verging on
catatonia, and is the only member of the gang to be caught. The development
of a love affair, or even simply a friendship, between the *beur* youth and the
French girl, is shown here to be an illusion. And by implication, so is integration into French society, not so much because of French racism, but rather
because the French turn out to be unworthy.

The film's negative coding of what it means to be French is also hinted at
through subtle differences between Pat and Madjid. Despite their ostensibly
shared attitudes to sex, the film contrives only to show (or hear) Pat having sex,
whereas Madjid remains visually 'innocent': partly out of choice (he decides

not to go to Joséphine's) and partly because of Pat's mischievousness (Pat lands him with the girl from the disco who is having her period!). Their attitudes to others are also significantly different. Pat mocks Madjid's father, whereas Madjid treats him with some sensitivity; Madjid feels sorry for Solange whereas Pat thinks she is putting on an act; Pat loses all interest in the girl with the period, whereas Madjid at least attempts to make conversation; and it is Madjid who helps his mother persuade Josette not to commit suicide. Madjid is also shown to be more intelligent than Pat, who cannot even read. And – very briefly – through the scene in the employment agency, the film allows that he may also be the victim of his conflicting identities (as an Algerian he is not entitled to a place on a training course to become a mechanic) and of institutionalised racism (he is refused the possibility of work in a driving school because of his allegedly poor eyesight, whereas a dim-looking French youth wearing thick-lensed glasses is ushered into the office). When Pat is given a chance to express his dreams, in a long monologue which takes place on the fateful car drive out of Paris, he reveals that his ultimate fantasy is to go to the Côte d'Azur with Madjid and get picked up by rich women looking for a bit of rough. In this context, it is perhaps not surprising that by the end of the film Madjid has opted out of any positive engagement with his surroundings.

Compared with the negative coding of the majority French community (not just through the female characters, but also through the adult males on the housing estate), the representation of the immigrant family is significantly more positive. The film opens with a sequence in which Josette brings her son Stéphane to Malika to be looked after while she goes to work. The music swells over her journey across the estate into the bosom of the immigrant family, where Malika is to be found dispensing warmth, sustenance and protection to her children and (later) to her husband, who has been reduced to the state of a vegetable as a result of an accident at work. Malika is the only character to maintain a connection with the past, continuing to pray to Mecca on a rug in her bedroom (mimicked by little Stéphane, but not by any of her own children), and listening to the Algerian music going round in her head while her family watches a line of French chorus-girls on the box. At the same time, scenes of her praying, or bathing her husband, position her in her difference through downward-angled shots through doorways seen from the point of view of others (Josette, Madjid). Friction between mother and son erupts each time Madjid returns home. Malika reproaches him for his failure to get a job, his failure to help her in the house and subsequently his drunkenness; but the only prospect she can offer for the future is to send him off to do his military service in Algeria to make him 'a real man'. The rift between them is represented by the breakdown in language, for Malika cannot speak French properly and her son cannot (or will not) understand Arabic, which has to be translated for the audience too by subtitles.

The film thus represents the young *beur*'s dilemma through the contrasting *mise-en-scène* and narratives of home and street, Malika and Pat (and Chantal). A brief, awkwardly inserted scene suggests that other, more politically aware identities might be available, when Madjid and Pat drop in on a rehearsal of a rather amateur agitprop play in which the *beur* actors protest about Arabs being murdered. But Madjid's trajectory towards being picked up by the police seems fairly inevitable, and even if the film's rejection of close-up shots, voice-over or introspective dialogue means that the character also remains slightly distanced, the spectator is moved to sympathy with his plight. The question of Madjid's identity is left unresolved.[7]

Baton Rouge (1985)

Baton Rouge was Bouchareb's first feature film, but he had already made four shorts, including *Peut-être la mer*, which was selected for Cannes in 1983, and worked for the television channel TF1. *Peut-être la mer* is about the unsuccessful attempt by two small boys to plan their 'return' to Algeria, a theme which he was to rework in *Cheb*. He was able to get the *avance sur recettes* for his screenplay for *Baton Rouge*, largely because of the prior box-office success of Bahloul's *Le Thé à la menthe*.

Baton Rouge, even more than *Le Thé à la menthe* and *Le Thé au harem*, plays to a crossover (male) youth audience for whom ethnic difference is represented as unproblematic. It is the story of three friends, one Frenchman (Mozart, played by Jacques Penot) and two *beurs* (Karim, played by Hammou Graïa, and Abdenour, played by Pierre-Louis Rajot), who dream of travelling to Baton Rouge in pursuit of the American Dream (inspired by a Mick Jagger song). After a series of sequences set in the suburbs of Paris, introducing the characters, and showing them doing various temporary jobs, a whimsical twist of fate allows the threesome to make their dream come true (figure 5). The plot follows their adventures in the United States as they journey south to Louisiana. Although they encounter obstacles aplenty, and are forced by lack of money into bumming train rides or stealing from a garage, they also bathe in the warmth of a more tolerant atmosphere than they have come to expect back in France: they get a ride in a bus with a choir of black gospellers and, more importantly, Mozart ends up falling in love with a black singer.

However, the two *beurs* eventually discover that there is no place for them in the USA either. Deported back to Paris, and fed up with still doing nothing but temporary work, in another unexpected (and unmotivated) turn of the plot the *beurs*, spurred on by Abdenour's little brother, finally get their act together. They form a collective to set up a burger bar, together with the people from the queue outside the Employment Agency. The film ends on a freeze frame of a happy well-dressed multi-ethnic group (rather like a Benetton advertisement)

5 The three friends dream of escape in *Baton Rouge* (1985).

stepping out towards the camera as they set about their new enterprise. It is authenticated by a final credit which reminds the audience that the 'California Burg' in Argenteuil was set up in 1981.

In this film, the young men want to get away from France because it does not offer them decent prospects in terms of employment. There are no direct references to racism as a motivation for their disillusionment (and no references in the film to any other wider political or historical circumstances). Indeed, as in *Le Thé au harem*, their shared tastes in music and fashion bring them together in an address to an international youth market. They are virtually indistinguishable from each other individually (apart from Mozart's blonde hair and saxophone) and the film seems thereby to want to prove that the *beurs* are as French as the French. In its *mise-en-scène* the film repeatedly uses the colours of the tricolour to draw attention to the question of French national identity as its backdrop, while Abdenour manages to convince the American girl visiting Napoleon's tomb that the names Napoleon and Abdenour both come from Corsica. The upbeat ending, with its vision of *beurs* finding a positive place in the French economy, remains an open one, leaving the spectator to speculate as to whether or not the project could ever succeed.

Unlike *Le Thé au harem*, *Baton Rouge* does not offer an alternative emotional centre based in the North African roots of the principal protagonists. All three youths are divorced from their family background, history and religion. All we know about Abdenour is that he has a young brother called Bruno, whom he is trying to prevent being sent to a foster home. Karim has a strict father, an Arab and a factory worker, who wants his son to get a proper job. His fleeting appearances inspire Karim to take action in his life, but his role could be that of any distant reproving parent. Rather than interacting with and rebelling against their parents' generation, the young people in this film are already unproblematically responsible for their own lives. They dream of US culture as an alternative to French culture, but this is shown not to be the answer to their predicament. Instead, they realise they must take their destiny into their own hands and find their place in France's enterprise culture. Not only does the film underline the importance of the slogan used during the demonstrations of the mid-1980s, 'J'y suis, j'y reste' ('I'm here to stay'), it provides a reassuring message for French audiences that the *beurs'* aspirations are no different from anyone else's.

Although the characters are constructed as unproblematically heterosexual, the film curiously avoids any sex scenes. Karim and Abdenour are allowed to be only mildly flirtatious (and Abdenour's relationship with the tourist lasts only until he meets her puritanical family in the USA). Mozart develops a sexual relationship, indeed a potentially explosive inter-racial relationship, but it is safely distanced and contained within the more tolerant and ultimately foreign US setting. The film fails to find a place for the representation of *beur* women.

The paradoxical construction of sexy *beur* youths, but no sex, in the two films considered so far may be attributed to the desire not to cause offence to a mixed audience, given the precarious state of race relations in France. Sex with French girls would be problematic for French youths, sex with *beur* girls would cut French youths out of the scene and also be problematic for the 'immigrant' community. But, more importantly, any form of sexual relationship for the *beur* youths (other than through the power relations of casual commodified sex) would risk calling into question their masculine *beur* identities, since a French girl would inevitably represent the oppressor, and a liberated *beurette* would challenge the traditional distribution of gender roles in an Arabo-Islamic family. In a world in which the *beurs* are trying to make sense of their conflicting identities, the representation of masculinity in these first *beur* films remains a last bastion of security.

Miss Mona (1987)

Miss Mona, Charef's second film, proceeds to offer a challenge to the masculine heterosexual identity of its protagonists. The film abandons the address to a crossover youth audience, and instead appeals to the audience's fascination with sexual ambiguity (like other French films of the 1980s such as Bertrand Blier's 1986 film *Tenue de soirée*). *Miss Mona* blatantly problematises issues of sexual identity and spectacle, and the spectacle that is foregrounded is that of male transvestism, announced by the film's garish poster showing Jean Carmet in drag. (It was Jean Carmet who played the infamous racist in Yves Boisset's *Dupont Lajoie* in 1974.)

In *Miss Mona*, the French male transvestites, prostitutes and homosexuals who people the film are viewed in part through the innocent eyes of Samir (Ben Smaïl), an illegal North African immigrant who in desperation forms a reluctant and uneasy alliance with the ageing Mona (Jean Carmet). Samir is desperate to earn money to send to his family back home and to get a false identity card so that he will not be harrassed by the police. Having lost his job in a ragtrade sweatshop, he is drawn first into prostitution, then into theft and ultimately murder, through aiding and abetting Mona. The film plays on the spectator's voyeurism through scenes which follow Samir's transfixed gaze as he pursues his odyssey towards degradation and despair. The camera withdraws from, and the toilet doors close on, Samir's first homosexual experience; but in the course of another job Mona gets for him, a naked Samir gazes impassively down through a glass ceiling at the grotesque client who is jerking himself off below; when he is rescued from the police by his partner in that job, he finds himself in a theatre, standing in the wings, peering in fascination through the curtains as the boy performs his striptease for the gay audience (and for us); and when the final theft (which leads to murder) is being planned, the spectator follows Samir and Mona's stare across the road at their victim, Mona's treacherous former lover and a successful transsexual. If *Le Thé au harem* constructed an image of a corrupt and degraded society through its representation of women and working-class, male adults, *Miss Mona* does something similar through the fascinated gaze it directs at transvestites and gays, who form practically all the French males in the film.

The film is regularly punctuated by a narrative strand which at first seems unrelated to the main plot, involving repeated shots of a metro train pulling into a station (a heavily phallic marker, and one which opens the film), and glimpses of the train-driver who at the end of the film is made responsible for delivering Samir to the police. The driver turns out to be Jean, Samir's first client, a lonely middle-aged gay who also appears in the gay striptease joint, and who spends much of his spare time looking for an idealised young partner through a dating agency. The significance of his role in the film's ending, however, is ambiguous, and his facial expression offers no guidance. Does he fail to help Samir get away because he simply does not realise what's going on? Or because he is both gay and a racist? Is it an unwitting, or a deliberate, act of betrayal of one oppressed, marginalised individual by another? Whatever reading one opts for, the representation of homosexuality in this film remains negatively coded.

Mona himself, however, is more ambiguously presented. Jean Carmet, in a much admired performance, appears in a series of female disguises: ageing prostitute, gypsy, Marlene Dietrich, housewife, Marilyn Monroe. He even appears at times dressed as a man. We see Samir silently watching him as he puts on his Dietrich outfit; and the scenes where he plies his trade in the Bois de Boulogne are shot from a very high downward angle, producing images reminiscent of security videos. Mona resembles a criminal specimen needing to be kept under observation. Nevertheless, an insert of Mona as Monroe skipping along the pavement suggests that the masquerade brings innocent pleasure even though it is followed by a scene in which Mona gets stabbed. Samir, and perhaps the audience too, comes to accept Mona for what he says he is, a lonely woman trapped in a man's body longing for a sex-change operation. By the end of the film Samir even helps Mona's childlike senile father, another transvestite, to put on his lipstick. Despite their 'perversity', Samir, Mona and Mona's father come to constitute a sympathetic alternative family, their intimacy encapsulated in a scene where they picnic in the sun together (and which contrasts strongly with the coldness which characterises Mona's meeting with his nearly blind, aggressive old mother).

The film builds up to an ironic climax, crosscutting between Mona in his canalside caravan with a bottle of champagne and Samir's forged papers, waiting for Samir's return, and Samir getting caught by the police in a routine check (figure 6). As with Madjid at the end of *Le Thé au harem*, Samir finds himself in the hands of the state, not because of the crimes he has actually committed, but simply for being in the wrong place at the wrong time, and the film encourages sympathy for Samir by emphasising how circumstances have driven him into crime. The film is thus as morally ambiguous as *Le Thé au harem*, but the process of change through circumstances is more clearly documented.

The film opens in documentary mode, establishing the wretched situation experienced by immigrants living and working in Paris. In Samir's overcrowded hostel accommodation (located near the ironically named Europe metro station), a man lies dying, and has to be buried in secret before the night is out. Immigrants are shown as perpetual victims, constantly hounded by the police, in images reminiscent of the 'miserabilism' of first-generation cinema of the 1970s. There is no doubt, however, where moral values lie. When Samir in despair tries to go to the mosque, he is too ashamed to enter. He has become corrupted by the corrupt society which surrounds him. He is finally damned when he enjoys a night of pleasure with the young gay dancer (underlining the film's fundamental homophobia), for the boy then robs Mona of his life savings before committing suicide on stage, and it is the need to replace this money which leads to the final crime. Having earlier agreed to act out the stereotype of the menacing violent Arab (his hand on the knife visibly shaking) to frighten one of Mona's clients into handing over his wallet, by the end of the film Samir has become truly violent, battering his victim to death to protect Mona from being recognised. Caught between the values of his Arabic

6 Samir (Ben Smaïl) gets caught by the police in *Miss Mona* (1987).

upbringing and the need to care for his family by surviving on the streets of Paris, Samir's identity as an innocent, upright Arab and as a heterosexual male have simultaneously been called into question. But it is the perverse, feminised French who are responsible for his downfall.

Cheb (1991)

Cheb is a Franco-Algerian co-production, shot in Algeria with the cooperation of the Algerian army, but not subsequently released for exhibition in Algeria. One of the scriptwriters was Abdelkrim Bahloul, director of *Le Thé à la menthe*.

Like *Le Thé au harem* and *Baton Rouge*, *Cheb* seems to be aimed at the youth market once more (*cheb* means youth in Arabic). Its main characters are two attractive young *beurs*, Merwan (Mourad Bounaas) and Malika (Nozha Khouadra), who have grown up in Roubaix. There are two fundamental differences from the two earlier films, however. First of all, even though the film is structured around Merwan's expulsion from, and then return to, France, the action of the film is set primarily in Algeria, with a few flashbacks to earlier events in France. Secondly, there is no central white French protagonist to generate interest and recognition for a white French audience. Instead, Merwan struggles alone with his problems for much of the time, and is joined only for the central section of the film by his girlfriend Malika. The isolation of the two *beurs* in what is for them, too, an alien environment manages both to stress what makes them different from a white French audience (the reasons for their presence in Algeria) as well as what makes them the same (their identification with French youth culture). As Duncan Petrie puts it, this is 'an exemplary post-colonial text, which asks fundamental questions of identity and belonging' (Petrie 1992: 7).

The film opens with a montage of documentary footage showing the demolition of high-rise flats, police violence, people in mourning, and political demonstrations against racism foregrounding the slogan 'J'y suis, j'y reste'. The sequence ends with a shot of a gun being pointed direct to camera, inviting the spectator to share the sense of fear and menace which informs the *beur* experience of living in France, and so to sympathise with the *beur* characters. The prologue cuts abruptly to starkly beautiful shots of the desert, before showing Merwan arriving in Algeria and being sent off to the army, having been deported after serving a prison sentence in France for theft. Despite the circumstances of his expulsion, Merwan's main objective is to find some way of returning to France. He himself does not question his identity. The narrative charts his attempts to escape from Algeria, by deserting from the army, travelling across the country with Malika in the hope of getting smuggled across the border (figure 7), and finally accepting the gift of a French passport from a young man from Nanterre who is trying to get out of doing his military service. The film ends with Merwan back in France, but ironically also back in the army. He has achieved his goal, but the price he has to pay for his French identity (at least temporarily) is the loss of his freedom and his individuality. The name on his uniform is that of his benefactor, Ceccaldi, whose origins can be traced back to an earlier wave of immigrants in France. Merwan does not join in the singing of the Marseillaise, and the film's ending continues to problematise his fate.

Malika's narrative fate is even less optimistic. Having come to Algeria on a visit to relatives in the hope of seeing Merwan, she discovers that her father has abandoned her with her uncle, removing her (French) passport, leaving her virtually a prisoner. Like Merwan, she is completely westernised. Her physical appearance – sunglasses, trendy clothes, aggressive stare – emphasises how totally out of place she is. To run away with Merwan, she is obliged to dress like a boy and cut her hair short. The film vividly demonstrates the conflicts between Malika's emancipated ideas about women's roles, and the puritanical and oppressive attitudes to women she experiences in Algeria. Even though she understands some Arabic, Malika insists on speaking French and wants only to return to France. She is aware that if she stays, she is likely to be subjected to an arranged marriage. When she is picked up by the police, her main hope is that Merwan will be able to contact her friends in the *lycée* back home, who can arrange legal help to get her out. However, the last image of Malika, an unmotivated insert punctuating Merwan's train journey back, shows her modestly

7 Malika (Nozha Khouadra) and Merwan (Mourad Bounaas) in *Cheb* (1993).

dressed in traditional costume, her face expressionless. Nightmare or reality? The status of the image is uncertain, as is Malika's future.

As with *Le Thé au harem* and *Baton Rouge*, the *beurs* are unable to seek assistance from their parents. Indeed, the rift between the two generations is particularly flagrant in this film. Merwan's parents, seen in flashback at his trial, do nothing to help him, while Malika's father and uncle actively prevent her from leading her own life. What is frightening about their experiences in Algeria is that they have no one to turn to for help. The culture is depicted initially as completely alien, whether it is men in the hostel in Algiers, crowds of Muslims praying in the streets, or country folk throwing stones at the couple when they embrace. Merwan has no understanding of Arabic, and no intention of learning any. He makes no effort to get to know the people or the places, and does not even appreciate the multi-ethnic 'family' which populates the taxi in which he crosses the desert. The magnificent desert scenery is merely a backdrop to his attempts to escape, and the only people he can communicate with are those who have some knowledge of French. The reactionary ideas of his friend in the army, Miloud, merely serve to underline how much Merwan wants to get back to France. Only when Malika has been taken away by the police does Merwan establish contact with a sympathetic Algerian who gives him hospitality, a job and the opportunity to loosen up a little, swapping his jeans for Algerian robes. Indeed, the Algerian constitutes a sympathetic and dignified father substitute (a unique character in these films), a man who is familiar with the two cultures and remembers the fight for independence. Just as many *beurs* in the 1980s began to rediscover their roots through seeking to understand the experiences of first-generation immigrants (exemplified in the 1991 commemoration ceremony of the shameful events of October 1961 when the French authorities rounded up and killed an unknown number of Algerian demonstrators), so Merwan discovers that his future depends on the assistance of his Algerian benefactor as well as his French one.

In its handling of sexuality and gender, *Cheb* acknowledges the problems of identity experienced by *beurettes* as well as by *beur* youths. Although there is no sex in the film, this seems to be less to do with preserving the masculinity of the male protagonist and more to do with emphasising the importance of choice as opposed to coercion in personal relationships, and in particular the woman's right to define her own identity (the couple spend the night together chastely at Malika's request). Even if this reserve is ultimately governed by a concern not to shock its Arab spectators, the film is unusual in French cinema in featuring a loving friendship based on equality between the sexes. But that, of course, does not necessarily make for a popular film, and it may be that Merwan and Malika, sexy though they are, are simply not sexy enough. Besides, *Cheb* suffers from the same failing as the other films in that Merwan is simply not given enough to say to enable the spectator to penetrate his inner world. Despite, or perhaps because of, a disorienting elliptical style which fragments the narrative, audiences are invited to witness the protagonists' conflicts of identity from a distance, rather than share them.

Conclusion

What do these four films have in common? All are *beur*-authored films, directed by filmmakers from France's most prominent (and most abused) ethnic minority group, which succeed in focusing critical and popular attention on the conflicts of identity experienced by individuals on the margins, torn between the need and desire to be accepted in French society and their North African ethnic origins. They all use a predominantly realist aesthetic, combined with features more characteristic of the art movie: episodic, occasionally elliptical narratives with endings that leave questions unanswered, and the expressive use of colour cinematography. In each case, the central characters lack introspection (through a general lack of close-ups, voice over and dialogue), leaving the spectator to interpret and respond to their conflicts of identity through the films' narrative strategies and *mise-en-scène*.

The male-centred nature of the four films is striking, particularly in *Miss Mona*, where the only woman character is Mona's aggressive, blind mother. Until *Cheb*, with its introduction of Malika and her problems, the films centre on male protagonists, where questions of identity are very much bound up with sexual identity. Samir's wretched position as an illegal immigrant is exacerbated by the loss of his masculinity as he is forced into homosexual acts which, initially at least, make him sick. In contrast, the central *beur* characters (like their white French friends) are heavily marked as young, attractive and heterosexual, even if they are jobless and in crisis (and even if their sex-appeal is not put to the test). They have a universal appeal because they lock into an international, masculine, heterosexual culture of youthful revolt, which elides ethnic differences and which would be jeopardised if their sexual identity were called into question.

Arguably, there are differences between the films which can be related to the political climate in which they were made. *Le Thé au harem* and *Baton Rouge*, made when the *beur* movement was at its height, take as their starting point a desire for and belief in the possibility of integration through the construction of already well-established friendships between *beur* and French youths. Socio-economic conditions are represented as the principal stumbling block to integration, and cultural differences are marginalised or erased (though less so in *Le Thé au harem*). The films refuse 'miserabilism' and minimise or omit references to racism and the legacy of the Algerian War. Even the representatives of oppressive state institutions are shown as relatively benevolent. The films set out to bridge the gap between *beur* and white French communities by offering French audiences a non-threatening and non-accusatory representation of ethnic differences. However, *Miss Mona* and *Cheb*, made after Mitterrand's first period of cohabitation with the Right, place their characters in more life-threatening situations and treat the topic of integration more pessimistically. *Miss Mona* was accused of 'miserabilism', and makes no attempt to minimise the hardships endured by the immigrant population in Paris, while French racism provides the starting point for *Cheb*. Rather than humour a French audience, these films articulate and document the problems of immigrants/ *beurs* quite explicitly, while at the same time distancing them through exotic locations: in the Parisian underworld and Algeria.

There are also certain similarities and differences to be traced along auteurist lines. Mehdi Charef's films betray both a fascination with and a disgust at aspects of French society. The films' recognisably French settings (the deprived rundown housing estate, the crime- and vice-ridden inner city), even given the occasional use of arty photography, are depressing: and there is nostalgia in both films for Arab culture as the site of positive values. As a result his films are fundamentally ambivalent, since the conflicts of identity facing his protagonists are virtually impossible to resolve. Madjid's trajectory leads to complete passivity, Samir's to degradation and murder: the endings in which they get picked up by the police have a certain ironic inevitability. Bouchareb's films on the other hand, despite being set either in the United States of America or in Algeria for most of the narrative duration, serve to demonstrate quite forcibly that the *beurs'* rightful place is back in France. They are more optimistic than Charef's films in that they present characters who are on the move, and who take initiatives to improve their situation. However, whereas *Baton Rouge* ends on a mood of multi-ethnic celebration, having suppressed cultural difference as an issue, *Cheb* seems to have regressed to a position of having to plead the case for integration, and is less convinced that it can be achieved. At the same time, although the importance of the Algerian background is initially denied, the film finally hints that a dialogue between the *beurs* and their Algerian forefathers may be possible.

This analysis suggests that the four *beur*-authored films are problematic above all in that, given the structure of French cinema and the composition of the French cinema audience, they address a French (or crossover) audience rather than a *beur* audience (unlike some of the earlier shorts and documentaries produced by and for the *beur* community). Even though the two later films may create spectator positions which are slightly unsettling for the French (losing in popularity as a result), only *Baton Rouge* can be considered empowering for the *beurs*, and then through a highly artificial ending and at the expense of suppressing cultural difference. The films do not challenge the processes of cinematic representation, and are curiously limited in the range of representations they offer. Their protagonists still inhabit a world of delinquents and victims on the margins of society, even if the films demystify the processes by which people come to assume (and in the case of *Baton Rouge* reject) those identities. Despite the notable successes of many *beurs* in moving into higher education, the arts, politics and business, the films lack narratives invoking characters in these positions (male and female), and also marginalise the representation of first-generation immigrants and Muslims. Given the small number of *beur*-authored films to have been made by 1993, these few take on the function of representing the *beurs* in general during this period, and there remains a gaping need for more pluralistic representations of the *beurs* in terms of both sexual and cultural difference. Without a wider-ranging set of representations, the term '*beur* cinema' risks serving as a sop to the liberal-critical conscience rather than as a productive category for a transgressive political cinema which would call French identity, as well as *beur* identity, into question.

Notes

1 The original version of this chapter was published as 'Questions of Identity in *Beur* Cinema: From *Tea in the Harem* to *Cheb*', in S*creen*, 1993, 34, 4, 321–42.
2 See for example Hall (1992a and 1992b).
3 This article was first written in 1993. See the introduction for an overview of the socio-political context from the perspective of 2004.
4 The first recorded usage of the word *beur* was at the end of 1981 with the appearance of Radio *Beur*, a local radio station in the Paris area (Hargreaves 1991: 29). Hargreaves' *Voices from the North African Immigrant Community in France* (1991) provides an invaluable account of *beur* writing in the 1980s.

5 *Laisse béton* is structured in part around the friendship between a white boy and a young *beur*. The focus on childhood in the *banlieue* is a theme later developed in Jacques Doillon's *Petits frères* (1999), in which the central character, a little girl from the city who runs away to the *banlieue*, is also white.

6 *Le Thé à la menthe* is also discussed in chapter 12 of this book, which addresses the contributions of émigré Maghrebi filmmakers to the reframing of difference in French cinema.

7 The actor himself reappeared in *Le Premier Fils* (Philomène Esposito, 2003), a TV film, playing the abandoned mixed-race son of a white French woman, who eventually becomes accepted and integrated into her (otherwise all-white) family as an adult.

2

Beurz in the hood:
Le Thé au harem d'Archimède and *Hexagone*[1]

The title of this chapter re-works the title of John Singleton's film, *Boyz N the Hood* (1991), one of a number of black independent films to emerge from the USA at the end of the 1980s, as a starting-point for examining the ways in which *beur*-authored cinema in France prior to 1995 was able to challenge dominant gendered understandings of ethnicity and identity through its representations of *beurs* in the *banlieues* of France. In particular I shall analyse *Hexagone* (1994), written and directed by Malik Chibane, the first of a new generation of *beur* filmmakers, comparing it with Mehdi Charef's earlier success *Le Thé au harem d'Archimède* (1985).[2] As filmmakers of the periphery, working on the borderlines where – according to Paul Willeman – 'the most intense and productive life of the culture takes place' (Willeman 1989: 28), both Charef and Chibane attempt to bring to the centre of French culture a concern with the hybrid identities of the *beurs*. In so doing they are also exploring the question of what it means to be French, testing out the permeability of French national identity and culture. As Chibane said in an interview with *Libération*, 'I would say that, broadly speaking, the *banlieue* has not changed since 1978 and the arrival of hard drugs. The only important difference is that now we are French'[3] (Chibane 1994). It is this difference, this recognition that *beur* identities have to be articulated in relation to Frenchness, which informs both *Le Thé au harem* and *Hexagone*. In comparing the two films, each produced at a significant moment in the history of postcolonial France, I shall be seeking to highlight shifts in the ways *beur* cinema addresses its audiences and can or cannot problematise the articulation of *beur* and French national identity in French cinema.

The development of *beur* cinema, described in chapter 1, led to speculation as to whether it could be appropriately described as a genre, a concept which might initially seem to be an empowering one. The adoption of the word *beur*, coined by the *beurs* themselves, signalled their active presence in the Parisian working-class suburbs, if not in the hexagon as a whole, and challenged the (continuing) dominant French misnaming of second- (and now third-) generation Maghrebis as 'Arabs' and 'immigrants'. *Beur* cinema similarly suggests both agency in the production of representations by this particular ethnic minority and a challenge to dominant representations of 'Frenchness' and 'otherness'. However, the term inevitably draws attention to the difficulties facing oppressed groups involved in identity politics. For how can *beur* cinema be empowering if it is grounded in an essentialist understanding of ethnic difference? Not only does it risk confining *beur* filmmakers to a cinematic ghetto, whose filmic expressions are largely understood as something different from – and lesser than – the cultural practices of majority French directors, it also risks constructing an audience who will respond to the films in terms of their positive or negative images of specific ethnic groups, rather than their potential opening up and problematising of the question of difference itself. While it may be of strategic importance at any given time to mobilise politically around particular definitions of identity, a fixed label leaves little space for understanding *beur* cinema, like the rest of French cinema, as the site of multiple and contradictory constructions of subjectivity and identity.

The interventions of *beur* filmmakers in the French cultural arena need to be seen in the wider context of discourses on ethnicity and national identity in French cinema as a whole. However, French film culture, like dominant French culture in general, lacks the will and the vocabulary for addressing identity politics. In the USA, the designation 'black' has now been replaced by the preferred term 'African-American', which at least recognises both the hybridity and the American-ness of those concerned, even if the 'whiteness' of the dominant film industry remains unnamed. In France, apart from a politically aware fringe movement like '*Black-Blanc-Beur*', which implicitly recognises the 'whiteness' of the dominant culture, the eurocentric discourses of majority French cultural productions are similarly ignored, and a term which fully recognises the hybrid Frenchness of the *beurs* without conflating the meaning of the word *beur* with either Arab, immigrant or Muslim – Maghrebi-French, for example – has yet to become acceptable. In French film culture, the problematic articulation of *beur* and French national identity was displaced in the 1990s by the focus on *banlieue* cinema, which allows white-French-authored and *beur*-authored representations of the *banlieue* to be grouped together without regard for the different discursive positions which they might be mobilising in relation to national identity. It is not insignificant that in the *Cahiers de la Cinémathèque*'s special issue on '*Cinémas et banlieues*' ('Cinemas and suburbs'), Michel Cadé's article on immigrants in the *banlieues* fails to take on board an understanding of the *beur* generation as having a different relationship with French national identity from that of first-generation immigrants (Cadé 1994). In this chapter, given the lack of alternative terminology, I shall use the opposing terms *beur/beurette* and white (or majority) French, not in any essentialist sense, but in order to leave the notion of an unqualified Frenchness open to a plurality of meanings.

Clearly, the combination of anti-Arab racism (fuelled in the early 1990s by Islamic fundamentalism and terrorism in Algeria), and the dominance of national French discourses favouring integration based on assimilation rather than multiculturalism (a debate raised to fever-pitch by the ongoing '*affaire des foulards*') circumscribe the ways in which *beur* filmmakers can address wider French audiences. Both *beur*-authored films and African-American films, like Singleton's *Boyz*, seek to give cultural visibility to oppressed ethnic minorities and claim authenticity for their films' representations of everyday life. But whereas Singleton (and others) have been able to use 'tougher, abrasive and quintessentially black elements' in their representations of underprivileged African-American communities (Biskend 1991: 6), *beur* filmmakers have been obliged to tread more carefully in the exploration of their hybrid identities. Their films use the medium not just to promote the visibility of the *beurs* in an address to what is, after all, a relatively small *beur* audience, but also to counter the negative stereotyping which informs mainstream media representations in their address to the wider French audience. In so doing, they tend to support the dominant model of assimilation (and thereby the suppression of differences) rather than investigating multiculturalism (and the recognition and acceptance of differences) as an alternative way forward for French notions of national identity.

As discussed in chapter 1, the production and success of Charef and Bouchareb's first films can be linked to the historical moment of the early years of Mitterrand's presidency, at the time of the growing visibility and media hyping of the *beur* generation, following the 'March Against Racism and for Equality' in March 1983. The slogans of the period 'J'y suis, j'y reste' (in response to the deportations of young offenders) and 'Touche pas à mon pote' (launched by SOS Racisme) touch on two fundamental issues for the period – the *beurs*' claim to rights of residency in France and the need to combat the growth of racism and the Front National. However, they also indicate the contradictions between a self-assertive *beur*-organised movement ('J'y suis, j'y reste') and the potential recuperation of the movement by wider interests (both speaker and addressee of the rather patronising 'Touche pas à mon pote' could be assumed to be white and male, while the notion of 'mon pote' neatly evacuates the question of difference in favour of an unproblematic concept of youthful fraternity). The suppression or marginalising of differences, and the desire for and belief in the possibility of integration through assimilation, inform Charef and Bouchareb's first films, which each construct narratives based upon friendships between *beur* and white youths with remarkably similar looks and desires. At the same time, the unquestioned privileging of a hetero/sexist version of masculinity in these films specifically prevents a consideration of gendered (and other) forms of oppression.

Charef and Bouchareb's second films are notably more pessimistic in respect of the fortunes of their main characters: the immigrant/*beur* protagonist remains fundamentally isolated, while the sympathetic young white French males of the first films constitute a significant new structuring absence. However, a more complex approach to questions of gender and sexuality is to be found. As noted in chapter 1, *Miss Mona* tackles the topic of homosexuality, transvestism and prostitution, while *Cheb* gives space to a young *beurette*'s crisis of identity and need for independence. In each case, the male immigrant/*beur* protagonist (and the spectator, too) is required to rethink accepted categories of gender as part of the film's narrative trajectory. These second films are decidedly less conciliatory towards a potential white crossover market and draw attention to the particularities of immigrant/*beur* experience and culture, and to the power of the state to make life intolerable for illegal immigrants, *beur* offenders and sequestrated *beurettes*. They can be read as signs of *beur* disillusionment with the antiracist alliances of the mid- to late 1980s; but at the same time their relative lack of popularity at the box office indicates that audiences were reluctant to confront the question of immigrant/*beur* identities from an uncompromisingly *beur*-centred perspective.

The situation facing *beur* cultural activists in 1994 was arguably even more problematic. The return of the Right to power in 1993, with its policy of curbing immigrant rights to French nationality and citizenship, its introduction of racist identity controls as a measure against fundamentalist terrorism and its provocative directive allowing head teachers to ban the wearing of the Islamic headscarf in French state schools, meant that Arabs, immigrants and Muslims – and, given the interchangeability of the terms, by implication the *beurs* too – were constantly being constructed by the media as 'other' to French national identity. Furthermore, the *beurs* continued to be scapegoats for majority French fears about unemployment, delinquency and drugs in France, as well as potentially being scapegoats for fears about AIDS. It would not be surprising, then, if representations of the *beurs* at this time returned to a rhetorical bid for integration through assimilation, by suppressing signs of difference.

In fact, Charef and Bouchareb's films of the early 1990s do not feature the *beurs* at all. Charef's follow-up films, *Camomille* (1987) and *Au pays des Juliet* (1992), focus on other forms of marginality in France, while Bouchareb's *Dust of life/Poussières de vie* (1994), addresses the topic of Amerasian children abandoned in Vietnam after the American withdrawal, and (like *Baton Rouge*) is aimed at an international/American audience. Abdelkrim Bahloul (the émigré Algerian director of *Le Thé à la menthe*) also takes a very different approach to ethnicity and identity in his second feature, *Un vampire au paradis* (1992). In this film, the story of Nosfer Arbi (Farid Chopel), a Maghrebi immigrant anxious to return to his native land and a would-be vampire, is interwoven with that of a white, bourgeois family's convoluted attempts to diagnose and cure their daughter's inexplicable outbursts of speech in Arabic. The film incorporates elements of fantasy, comedy, satire and romance, and ends with the young French girl and her Maghrebi male counterpart staring at each other in mutual fascination. It fails to deliver on its comic or satirical potential, perhaps because of the producer's insistence on highlighting the film's fantasy elements,[4] but it marks an interesting departure from *beur* cinema in its attempt to deploy popular genres.

In 1994 two younger filmmakers emerged to take up the challenge of representing the *beurs*: Malik Chibane, whose first film, *Hexagone*, is discussed below, and the Franco-Tunisian filmmaker Karim Dridi, whose first award-winning feature film, *Pigalle* (1995), focused on white marginality, but who announced that his second film would be about racism. The same year, Thomas Gilou, director of *Black mic mac* (1986) (and advisor to Chibane on the making of *Hexagone*) began shooting *Raï* with *beur* actors on location in Garges-lès-Gonesse, to the north of Paris.[5] The year 1994, then, presaged a second wave of films preoccupied with questions of ethnicity and identity in France. *Raï* (1995), Chibane's second film *Douce France* (1995), and Dridi's second film, *Bye-Bye* (1995), are all discussed in chapter 4. What remains to be seen is the extent to which these films continue to work within the generic constraints of *beur* realism and promote or challenge the possibility of integration through assimilation.

Hexagone/Hexagon (1994) and Le Thé au harem d'Archimède/Tea in the Harem (1985)

Chibane's *Hexagone* returns to the realism of earlier *beur* cinema but, because of its unusual production context, it has been described as 'the first film to be made by the *beurs* for the *beurs*'. Like Charef's *Le Thé au harem d'Archimède*, an adaptation of the director's semi-autobiographical novel *Le Thé au harem d'Archi Ahmed* (Charef 1983), *Hexagone* draws on firsthand knowledge and experience of life in the Parisian *banlieue* and specifically addresses the problems facing unemployed youths. However, Chibane was concerned less with telling his own personal story than with documenting the lives of the *beur* generation. One of four young people who created the community youth association IDRISS in 1985 to promote self-help among young unemployed *beurs* in Goussainville, he turned to filmmaking after the death of a friend who had contracted AIDS from an infected needle. 'It has become absolutely urgent to immortalise the generation we belong to; our cultural invisibility is increasingly intolerable' (Chibane 1994).[6]

Like Charef, Chibane had no prior training in filmmaking, having a *CAP d'électricien* and four years of unemployment behind him. But whereas Charef was sponsored by Costa-Gavras, Chibane set up his own production company and took six years to make *Hexagone*, facing problems in raising funding at every stage. The original script failed to get the *avance sur recettes*, and in the end the shooting of the film was financed through support from the local community, thanks also to technicians and a local amateur cast who were willing to work for free. The editing of the film was eventually funded by the FEMIS, and postproduction costs were secured by Bernard Tapie who, just two weeks before the Socialist Party lost power, pushed grants through from various Ministries. This film, then, was made outside the normal structures of the French film industry.

The lack of finance, as well as Chibane's lack of experience, are factors which leave their traces in the finished product. *Le Thé au harem* is a much more professionally finished film, more self-conscious and assured in its direction of the actors, its camera and editing techniques and its use of colour, music and sound. In contrast, *Hexagone*'s camera and editing techniques make it look and sound more like a home movie, and the film opts for a more low-key 'authentic' realism in its use of an amateur cast, its refusal of an extra-diegetic 'ethnic' music track and its restricted range of depressingly recognisable locations in Goussainville. The look and sound of the film are obviously important in determining its commercial appeal, especially if it is to attract a wide crossover audience. *Hexagone* enjoyed a certain critical success and achieved a reasonably successful first run for such a low-budget film (1,200,000 FF). It was screened in 80 towns in France thanks to the ACID[7] and released on video. However, Chibane was too immersed in his next project to get it subtitled for international distribution.

There are differences between the two films which are attributable to differences of funding and experience. But on the more fundamental issue of the representation of *beur* identities in France, a comparison of the narrative and audio-visual strategies used by the two films reveals both significant differences and significant similarities of approach. In the rest of this chapter I shall address these differences and similarities, in order to assess whether independent *beur* film production in the early 1990s was more able to problematise the notion of French national identity than was possible in the 1980s.

Both *Le Thé au harem* and *Hexagone* document the life of a working-class suburban community through an episodic narrative structure which interweaves the lives of a variety of characters. Various elements of *mise-en-scène* and plot are common to both: visually, the films privilege the exteriors and interiors of the blocks of flats and the other spaces frequented by the young people – streets, cafés, discos, trains and cars; narratively, both films include scenes foregrounding the effects of having no money or jobs, the tensions between *beurs* and their parents, and young people's attitudes to crime, drugs and sex.

In *Le Thé au harem* the narrative focuses primarily on the (mis)adventures of the duo formed by Madjid, a young *beur*, and his mate Pat, a young white youth, which lead straight into the hands of the police; but *Le Thé au harem* also engages with a variety of white characters, such as Josette, the single mother who attempts suicide, and the vicious Frenchmen living on the estate. In contrast, *Hexagone*'s fragmented multi-stranded narrative centres almost entirely on the thoughts and activities of a group of (mostly) unemployed *beur* youths and three *beurettes*. The narrative, which is loosely organised around the older generation's preparations for the festival of Eid, cuts between the lives of Slimane, his sister Nora and brother Samy, drug-dealer Karim and Samy's fellow drug-addict Paco, Slimane's friends Ali and Staf, and Staf's two sisters, one of whom, Nacera, is secretly Slimane's girlfriend. Although ostensibly dealing with similar basic situations and narrative structures, there is a fundamental shift between *Le Thé au harem* and *Hexagone* in the latter's focus on an almost exclusively non-white community and its incorporation of *beurette* voices. Chibane specifically refused advice to cut down on the number of *beur* roles, or create a role for a star actor such as Smaïn, and was criticised for the absence of white roles. His uncompromising *beur*-centred perspective was intended as a form of 'provocation'.[8]

The centring on *beur* characters does affect the way in which the film addresses its audience, as a comparison of the opening sequence of each film reveals. In *Le Thé au harem*, the credit sequence introduces the spectator into Madjid's home via the character of Josette, who brings her son to Madjid's mother to be looked after, while the following sequence introduces the local gang via the character of Pat. So Madjid is initially perceived as it were through white French eyes: first in bed, reluctant to get up, and then unsuccessfully attempting to repair his motorbike (figure 8). In contrast, *Hexagone* opens with a striking establishing shot which pans from a view of the open countryside to the sight of what appears to be a small town until the frame takes in the blocks of flats dominating the skyline. It is a shot which boldly displaces the cornfields and birdsong of *la France profonde*, placing the blocks of flats and the noise of planes at the centre, rather than the periphery, of the hexagon which is contemporary France. The film then cuts between children at play and a group of young *beurs* hanging about in the street outside the Maison du Développement Social du Quartier, an economical strategy for contrasting images of carefree childhood with the representation of the *beur* youths' problems of insertion into French society.

The opening sequence of *Hexagone* is accompanied by a voice-over (later identified with the character Slimane), voicing the speaker's feelings of emptiness and despair. The use of the voice-over was criticised in several reviews of the film, perhaps because the sound quality and intelligibility of the speech does leave something to be desired, perhaps because of the fact that it is not

8 Madjid (Kader Boukhanef) faces a crisis of identity in *Le Thé au harem d' Archimède* (1985).

initially attributable to a specific character. What the voice-over does, however, is to establish a discursive position emanating from the *beurs* themselves, which directly addresses the spectator as someone sympathetic to the *beur* predicament – 'vous ne trouvez pas?' ('don't you think?'), asks Slim – opening up the possibility of dialogue between spectator and speaker. Whereas Madjid is relatively passive and silent (and ends up in a virtually catatonic state), Slimane asserts his subjectivity through his appropriation of the soundtrack and his ability to comment on and express his feelings about the apparently hopeless situation he and his friends find themselves in. In *Le Thé au harem*, language is a source of conflict and misunderstanding which disadvantages the *beurs* – Balou did not understand what was meant by Archimedes' theorem and, like the white audience, Madjid cannot (or will not) understand his mother when she rages at him in (unsubtitled) Arabic. However, in *Hexagone* the *beurs* express themselves and communicate in a mixture of French, *argot*, *verlan* and Arabic, positioning the audience to accept such speech as the norm (even if the press release included a glossary).

The films' titles indicate a similar shift in self-awareness. *Le Thé au harem d'Archimède* still references the *beur* as 'other', even if the title is a joke at the expense of native French speakers. But *Hexagone* can be read as a claim for the *beurs* in the *banlieue* to be recognised as central to any conceptualisation of contemporary France. The film is not just an exotic representation of an underprivileged working-class ethnic ghetto, outside mainstream French experience, but rather an assertion of *beur* claims to citizenship, *à part entière*, regardless of ethnic difference.

This assertiveness reveals itself in a comparison of scenes in *Hexagone* which parallel scenes in *Le Thé au harem*. For example, at the ANPE (employment exchange), Madjid simply accepts that as the target of racial prejudice he will never get a place on a training course, whereas Slim and Staf devise strategies to overcome the disadvantages they face, getting Ali to forge them false diplomas and chatting up the girls working in the ANPE office. If Staf just makes a fool of himself, Slim persuades the *beurette* employee to take an interest in his case, and his prospect of a place on a course at the end of the film arouses some hope for his future (figure 9). Conversely, in parallel disco scenes, Madjid flirts with a white French girl apparently without any fear of racial discrimination, whereas Staf feels obliged to hide his ethnic origins from Annick, and is criticised by Slim for denying his identity. When Staf eventually opts to reveal the 'truth', he is rewarded with Annick's shamefaced smile. *Hexagone* is potentially more empowering than *Le Thé au harem* in its assumption that openness, and the recognition and acceptance of difference, is a better route to overcoming racial prejudice than dissimulation.

In fact, the debate around integration and assimilation is explicitly raised in *Hexagone* in a scene in which Chibane himself plays an uncredited cameo role.

9 Staf (Hakim Sarahoui) and Slim (Jalil Naciri), the sympathetic male leads of *Hexagone* (1994).

In the course of a night out in Paris, Slim, Ali and Karim decide to prepare themselves for racist hostility by acting not as 'hung-up, paranoid *rebeus*' but rather as 'self-confident *rebeus*... goodlooking lads'.[9] They still get turned away from their chosen nightclub because they are identified as 'Arabs', and spend the evening instead at a disco on the outskirts of Paris where, as a couple of *beurs* point out, the only whites are the French on TV! In a discussion with Thierry (Chibane), who sees no reason for the *beurs* not to be successfully assimilated into French culture like so many other immigrants before them, Ali argues that the *beurs* are still the victims of racism and need to assume their cultural difference and colonial past; and Thierry eventually concedes the argument.

However, if Ali asserts the importance of assuming *beur* history, culture and experience, Chibane as director takes care to confine the film's construction of *beur* identities within clear, acceptable limits. Both *Le Thé au harem* and *Hexagone* avoid dealing with really contentious issues and work to keep open the possibilities of integration through three principal strategies: they stress the ways in which *beur* lifestyles are similar to other young French people's lifestyles; they construct a sympathetic understanding of the role played by drugs and delinquency in the lives of the underprivileged; and they confine the representation of Islamic beliefs to the older generation.

Both *Le Thé au harem* and *Hexagone* are primarily male-centred youth films, concerned with the effects of mass unemployment on young men and exploring their strategies for survival. *Le Thé au harem*, however, foregrounds the

macho sensibility of its male protagonists and constructs misogynist representations of most of its (white) female characters; while *Hexagone* works to problematise unreconstructed male heterosexuality and constructs a relatively
progressive representation of the *beurettes*, making the film much more enjoy-
able for a female audience. True, it is Annick, the white girl, who is made to bear
the brunt of representing white racism (and Chibane has admitted that this
may be a weak point in the film's structure). But the film explores the economic
constraints and personal problems of the *beurettes* as well as *beur* youths,
including a scene in which Nora, Nacera and Nacera's older sister Yasmina (a
single parent) meet to chat about men, sex and marriage, in ways which would
be recognisable to most other young women. Nevertheless, it is noticeable that
their assumptions about the desirability (or otherwise) of virginity, arranged
marriages and inter-racial sex, for example, are articulated in a context which
suppresses more explosive and divisive issues like unwanted pregnancies or the
wearing of the *foulard*. And there is nothing in the street fashions adopted by
the *beurettes* which distinguishes them from other young French women.

Nacera's relationship with Slim provides an opportunity for suggesting that
the *beur* generation is freeing itself both from the strict Islamic moral codes of
their parents' generation *and* from the casual misogyny which informs *Le Thé
au harem*. Slim is forced to reflect on his behaviour towards Nacera, and Nacera
herself, despite the fact that she does not appear visually in the opening or closing sequences of the film, emerges as a forceful and independent-minded
young woman. Unusually, their relationship is seen from Nacera's point of view
as well as Slim's: it is she who takes the initiative in arranging their rendez-vous
and she who criticises the moral hypocrisy of the *beurs* in not taking issue with
their parents and voices the need to make an open commitment. Furthermore,
in a lovemaking scene which has no equivalent in *Le Thé au harem*, *Hexagone*
shows Slim not only being attentive to Nacera's needs, but also using a condom!
A 'new', more vulnerable *beur* masculinity is represented, too, in parallel bed
scenes, for whereas Madjid in *Le Thé au harem* simply loses interest when he
discovers that his partner has got her period, poor Staf finds himself unable to
make love to Annick for fear that his circumcision will give away his identity.

Despite its apparent liberalism and honesty in sexual matters, however, as a
realist film (and one which is therefore bound to be read as representative of
the community which it purports to represent) *Hexagone* could be criticised
for shying away from addressing controversial and contentious issues like
prostitution, homosexuality or AIDS among *beurs*. It chooses to privilege a
normative and unthreatening image of *beur* sexuality which wider French
audiences can relate to unproblematically: Nacera even says that it is Slim's *côté
yaouais* (his 'French side') which she finds attractive!

A similar sort of wariness can be seen in *Hexagone*'s construction of delinquency. Both films take care to represent drug abuse as self-destructive and

drug-dealing as reprehensible, but Chibane does not evoke the death from AIDS which originally inspired *Hexagone*. Instead, Samy quietly dies of what is presumably an accidental overdose, and Karim, the dealer, is picked up by the police. *Hexagone*'s stylistic and ideological refusal to foreground images of crime and violence makes it a very different film from the African-American films epitomised by *Boyz N the Hood* or, indeed, from *Le Thé au harem*. *Le Thé au harem* is structured through a series of petty crimes, and Madjid and Pat are constantly involved in acts of violence of one sort or another – they steal from a racist slob, pimp for a local prostitute, mug a gay guy, and burgle a tennis club changing-room in a wealthy suburb. Their crimes are justified by their economic plight (which is not of their own making), by the questionable morality of their victims, and by their own sympathetic nature (demonstrated by their inter-racial male camaraderie and their protection of the estate from drug dealers). So when they are finally picked up by the police for a crime they have not actually committed, the spectator is still positioned to feel sympathetic towards them. In *Hexagone*, in contrast, the principal characters display little signs of violence and the images of crime are toned down and even verge on the comic. Samy steals shoes and watches to pay for his drug habit, while Slim and Staf use Ali's false papers to try and get jobs. When Samy is caught shoplifting, the spectator is positioned to applaud both the way Slim rescues him and, after an awkwardly shot chase sequence, his own escape from the police (who in both films have an extremely low profile). But crime and violence are not represented as such a pervasive part of life in the suburbs as in *Le Thé au harem* or *Boyz N the Hood*. Whereas the aggressivity of *Boyz* can perhaps be read paradoxically as a measure of the director's sense of security about the African-American presence in American society, *Hexagone*'s reluctance to tackle drugs and violence outside of a conventional moral framework suggests that the *beurs*' presence in their Hood is one that still has to be very carefully negotiated.

In both *Le Thé au harem* and *Hexagone*, the representation of the parents' generation provides an opportunity for the *beurs* to distance themselves from the religious beliefs and cultural expectations of their parents. In *Le Thé au harem*, Madjid's mother may be the emotional heart of the community but she is also a devout Muslim who strongly identifies with Algerian culture and is unable to understand Madjid's problematic hybrid status. In *Hexagone*, the representation of Islam is relegated to the older generation's preparations for the festival of Eid and the religious rituals accompanying Samy's death. The film partially reverses the challenge to the traditional composition of the immigrant family constructed in *Le Thé au harem*: the mother figure (Slim's mother) is a superstitious woman, heavily dependent on her *marabout* (a Muslim holy man) and unable to comprehend what is happening to her family; while the father figure, who is marginalised or absent in the early *beur* films, here Staf's father (played by Algerian film director Mahmoud Zemmouri), is constructed as relatively tolerant and understanding in his relationship with his younger daughter. Such a shift in the representation of the family can be read as a sign of the film's desire to reassure French audiences both that the father's position has been normalised and that authoritarian relationships are giving way to more progressive ideas about women's roles. However, by clearly signalling that certain traditional elements of Maghrebi culture (belief in Islam, female virginity or arranged marriages, for example) have no significance for the younger generation, both *Le Thé au harem* and *Hexagone* are also signalling that, despite their hybridity, the *beurs* are really not very different from other young people in the audience they are addressing.

The endings of *Le Thé au harem* and *Hexagone* are indicative of their different emphases. In *Le Thé au harem*, when Pat opts to join Madjid in police custody, their inter-racial friendship – however problematic and limiting – is the only flicker of hope to emerge from an otherwise pessimistic narrative closure. *Hexagone*'s ending is apparently more open. Slim alone, suffering from a terrible headache, contemplates his current situation. His voice-over accompanies a fragmented montage sequence showing how his friends are now going their separate ways: Samy is dead, Karim is arrested, but Staf renews his relationship with Annick, Ali seems to have found a job, and Slim himself has a place on a training course and the opportunity to embark on a more honest relationship with Nacera. Arguably, *Hexagone*'s disjointed multi-stranded structure productively replaces *Le Thé au harem*'s closed narrative of despair with a recognition that, however limited and negative to date, the *beur* narrative can be a pluralised and individuated one. However, the film actually ends on a blank screen while Slim, still alone, having concluded that Nacera is the best thing that has happened to him, delivers the final line, 'After all, woman is the future of man, no?'.[10] Rather than a positive and empowering assertion of the *beurs*' active place in the Hood, this question suggests a rather uncertain retreat into an unproblematised and depoliticised private sphere.

Hexagone does more than *Le Thé au harem* to foreground both male and female *beur* subjectivities and so engage pleasurably with a *beur* audience. It moves away from the rather naive embracing of integration characteristic of the early *beur* films, and shifts the grounds of the debate onto a *beur*-constructed terrain. Nevertheless, the particular representation of *beur* identities foregrounded in *Hexagone*, despite or perhaps because of the film's evacuation of white French male voices, works even harder than *Le Thé au harem* to construct an image of the *beurs* which is culturally acceptable to a wider French audience, and which requires little or no shift in the dominant construction of 'Frenchness' beyond an acceptance of the visibility of *beur* faces and *beur* variants of the French language. The film suggests that the problems and aspirations of the *beurs* (male and female) are basically little different from the problems and aspirations of French working-class youth in general, merely exacerbated by racism, their parents' cultural expectations, and confinement to the ethnic ghetto. By making the case for assimilation rather than constructing *beur* subjectivities and identities as diverse and contradictory, *Hexagone* fails to problematise the dominant culture's construction of French national identity and its continuing marginalisation of those who wish to exercise alternative sexual, cultural or religious practices.

Notes

1 This chapter was first presented at a conference on French Cinema at the University of Nottingham in 1995. It was published in its original version as 'Beurz N the Hood: The articulation of *beur* and French identities in *Le Thé au harem d'Archimède* and *Hexagone*', *Modern & Contemporary France*, NS3, 4, 1995, 415–25.
2 Chibane was born in France in 1964, and is of Kabyle extraction.
3 'Je dirais que, en gros, la banlieue n'a pas changé, pas depuis 1978 et l'arrivée de la came. La seule différence importante, c'est que nous, on est français.'
4 Author's interview with Abdelkrim Bahloul, 15 September 1994.
5 According to a report in *Libération* (10 December 1994), during the shooting of *Raï*, several drunken amateur actors dressed as CRS (riot police) set up a blockade on the motorway north of Paris, and exercised an identity control on white French drivers, claiming: 'On a inversé le délit de sale gueule'. The actors were described as 'all Arabs' (and not *beurs*).
6 'Immortaliser la génération à laquelle on appartient devient une urgence absolue et cette invisibilité culturelle m'est de plus en plus insupportable.'
7 ACID stands for the Agence du Cinéma Indépendent pour sa Diffusion.
8 Author's interview with Malik Chibane, 12 September 1994.
9 'des rebeus complexés, paranos'; 'des rebeus qui assurent . . . de beaux gosses'.
10 'Après tout, la femme est l'avenir de l'homme, non?'

3

Ethnicity and identity in Mathieu Kassovitz's *Métisse* and *La Haine*[1]

Critics and historians of French cinema have marked out 1995 as the year of the *banlieue* film, the most significant of which was *La Haine*, directed by Mathieu Kassovitz.[2] *La Haine* won 27-year-old Kassovitz the Best Director Award at Cannes, was a major box-office success in France, was screened for Prime Minister Alain Juppé, and played to enthusiastic audiences in London, showing that there is an international market for French films which depart from the heritage blockbuster or the *intimiste auteur* film. *La Haine* takes as its topic the cycle of hatred and violence which tends to characterise relationships between young people and the police in the working-class suburbs of France. Given that the *banlieue* is also the principal location of France's marginalised ethnic minorities, cinematic representations of the *banlieue* cannot easily ignore the representation of ethnic differences, and in the case of *La Haine* the question of ethnic difference is specifically foregrounded through the choice of a *black-blanc-beur* trio of young people as its central protagonists. In this chapter, I aim to compare and contrast the representation of ethnicity in *La Haine* with the representation of ethnicity in Kassovitz's lesser-known first feature film, *Métisse*, made in 1993. *Métisse* is also centred on a trio of young people of different ethnic backgrounds, in this case *black-blanc-métisse*. But whereas *La Haine*, despite its exhilarating style, is primarily a pessimistic, realist film, *Métisse* is a light-hearted comedy with a happy ending. Superficially, then, these two films, made only two years apart, appear to offer diametrically opposed constructions of France as a multicultural, multi-ethnic society, *Métisse* promising hybridity and racial harmony, *La Haine* beginning and ending in violence, death and alienation. One of the links between the two films, however, is the privileged role of the white youth, and I want to suggest that this figure, potentially Kassovitz's *alter ego*, is structured into the films in such a way that, rather than representing a multi-ethnic society *per se*, they serve primarily to work through the relationship of white youth to France's ethnic minority others, first in a comic and then in a tragic mode.

To argue this point requires some clarification of Kassovitz's own relatively privileged background. Kassovitz himself is not a product of the *banlieue*. The son of film and TV director Peter Kassovitz, he shot his first Super-8 horror/sci-fi films at the age of twelve to thirteen and learnt his trade on the job, making a number of music videos and short films before writing, directing and acting in *Métisse*, for which he was awarded the Special Jury Prize and the Best Actor Award at the 1993 Paris Festival. (He also won the 1995 César for Most Promising Male Actor for his performance in Jacques Audiard's thriller *Regarde les hommes tomber*, 1994.) Clearly, he has been marked by his father's family origins and politics: Peter Kassovitz – who has made leftwing militant films, worked with Chris Marker and was in the *maquis* in Nicaragua – is of Jewish-Hungarian origin, and came to France in 1956 after the Soviet invasion of Hungary. (His own mother was a concentration camp survivor, and his father an anarchist and cartoonist who had lived in the Budapest ghetto and escaped from the Gulag.) But Mathieu Kassovitz has also been heavily influenced by the impact of African-American popular culture in France, and particularly rap music. He has affirmed that it was rap, when it was still an underground cult in France, which brought him into contact with people from a range of different ethnic backgrounds and made him aware of racism in France, and in particular of the way in which the police treated non-whites. His early short films already show an awareness of race issues and a critique of racism. In *Fierrot le pou* (1990), he plays a white basketball player who dreams he is Michael Jordan and scores successfully, but then realises he is really white and fails to score. In *Cauchemar blanc* (1991), the white protagonist dreams he is participating in a *beur*-bashing which is going wrong, then wakes up to find that the nightmare is really happening. These early films, then, suggest a fascination with black culture, a desire to 'be black', even, and a sense of guilt in relation to the *beurs* in French society. But above all they indicate an awareness that the multicultural and multi-ethnic composition of contemporary French society is an issue which needs to be addressed not ignored.

Given these preoccupations, it is not surprising that Kassovitz's filmic influences clearly include the work of black African-American director Spike Lee. Indeed, a number of critics have remarked on the thematic and stylistic similarities between *Métisse* and *She's Gotta Have It* (1986), and between *La Haine* and *Do The Right Thing* (1989). Nevertheless, Kassovitz is placed in a very different relationship to his material from that of Spike Lee in that he is not himself a black or *beur* filmmaker. Whereas Lee can be credited with opening up a new space for black independent American cinema, Kassovitz is following in the footsteps of a number of white and *beur* directors of the 1980s whose films had already drawn attention to life in the suburbs through narratives of youth disaffection and interracial male bonding (as discussed in chapter 1). The topics and settings of his films, together with their lively visual and verbal language and their use of (mostly unknown) black and *beur* actors, make them attractive and even empowering to most ethnic minority audiences. Nevertheless, as a privileged white director Kassovitz has been subjected to some criticism and accused, by Karim Dridi and rap group NTM (Nique Ta Mère) among others, of being a 'trendy Parisian' (*Parisien branché*) who is just slumming it in the *banlieue*, and whose representations of blacks and *beurs* are one-dimensional and inauthentic. The accusation of the white appropriation of black and *beur* culture is one that should be taken seriously. Kassovitz himself took pains to avoid being accused of exploiting the *banlieue* in the shooting of *La Haine* by involving the community in the filmmaking process, and has himself been critical of dominant stereotypical film and TV representations of blacks and *beurs* (as in Tavernier's 1992 film *L627*, where all the drug dealers are black), and of the United Colours of Benetton representation of race as a happy, unproblematic rainbow coalition. He has also clearly stated that he thinks second-generation *beur* filmmakers have their own films to make and that his film is only 'one vision among so many others'. Nevertheless, it is Kassovitz and lead actor Vincent Cassel who have reaped the greatest rewards of the film's massive and surprising success, while ethnic minority filmmakers and actors have yet to attain similar recognition. Are Kassovitz's films appropriating black and *beur* culture for a trendy white youth audience (albeit one which might be sympathetic to SOS Racisme), and in the process erasing real ethnic differences and social inequalities? Or are they attempting to cross boundaries and generate new hybrid identities which offer a challenge to dominant notions of French national identity? I shall attempt to answer these questions by examining the extent to which Kassovitz problematises and prioritises the identity of his two young white Jewish protagonists at the same time as he constructs an unproblematically shared urban and suburban multi-ethnic (male) youth culture, heavily influenced by African-American popular culture.

Métisse/Café au lait (1993)

In relation to *Métisse*, Kassovitz has acknowledged that the script was motivated by his personal anxiety as a liberal white male: 'Suppose my girlfriend went out with a black guy, would I call him a filthy bastard or a filthy black?' (Lallouette 1993).[3] The question is answered through a narrative focusing on a comic love triangle, triggered by the revelation that Lola (Julie Mauduech), the eponymous *métisse*, is pregnant but does not know which of her two lovers is the father. The lovers in question are, on the one hand, Félix, a working-class Jew who delivers kosher fast food by bike (played by Kassovitz himself), and, on the other, Jamal (Hubert Koundé), an African law student and the son of a diplomat. The plot follows the development of the initially antagonistic relationship between the two young men and the ups and downs of their relationship with Lola, and culminates with both men at Lola's bedside, the final frame centring on three differently coloured pairs of hands joined together. As Shohat and Stam argue, following Fredric Jameson (1986), 'films made in multiracial societies reveal a clear tendency toward "allegory" where "the personal and the political, the private and the historical, become inextricably linked"' (Shohat and Stam 1994: 230). *Métisse* is an allegory about the possibility of racial tolerance and integration, which depends not simply on the assimilation of the ethnic other, but on the overthrow of conventional attitudes to love, parenting, race and miscegenation. Lola refuses to choose between her two lovers and both men ultimately decide to join forces to support her desire for communal responsibility for the baby-to-be. In the tradition of comedies such as Coline Serreau's *Pourquoi pas!* (1977), *Trois hommes et un couffin* (1986) and *Romuald et Juliette* (1989), and Josiane Balasko's *Gazon maudit* (1995), Kassovitz uses the genre to question the centrality of the white heterosexual couple and the conventional white nuclear family. In its place he works through the trials and tribulations of a mixed-race *ménage à trois* (figure 10).

At the beginning of the film, each of the three main characters sports a religious emblem: Lola a cross, Félix the star of David, Jamal Fatma's hand. Since none of the young people practise their religion, these prove to be signs of cultural differences which are not an obstacle to their relationships. However, it is Félix's background which is given the most filmic space. Rather than taking whiteness for granted, Kassovitz situates whiteness in *Métisse* within a specific ethnic culture and history, that of the Jews, a pertinent reminder of the fact that France has always been 'a mixed-race country' ('un pays métissé') (Roze 1995: 10), and that racism has not been confined to blacks and Arabs. Félix's grandparents and great-aunt are the witnesses to the success of the *ménage à trois*, and these are the characters who most assert their ethnic specificity (celebrating the Sabbath, speaking Yiddish, dancing to Jewish folk music, and offering reminders about the holocaust), but who also give their blessing to the mixed-race triangle because of the civilising effects Lola has on Félix, and because despite their surface assertion of Jewishness, they are sympathetic to other peoples with a history of oppression. Lola's black grandmother is similarly supportive. (It is noticeable that the parents' generation is marginalised in this narrative: Lola's mother is in Martinique, Jamal's parents in Africa, and Kassovitz gives his own father the role of Jamal's boring University professor and Vincent Cassel's father the role of the sympathetic but ineffectual gynaecologist.)

At the same time as minimising the effects of ethnic and cultural differences, *Métisse* constructs a trendy multi-ethnic youth culture in which Félix, Lola and Jamal all participate in their different ways. The film opens and closes with a rap number by Assassin calling attention to the need to combat France's 'Fear of racial mixing' ('Peur du métissage'). The film's musical *métissage* associates Félix with rap, Jamal with jazz and Lola with the group Zap Mama (while in

10 Félix (Mathieu Kassovitz), Julie (Julie Mauduech) and Jamal (Hubert Koundé): the *black-blanc-métisse* trio of *Métisse* (1993).

his nightmare, Félix hears classical 'high art' music by white anti-Semite Richard Wagner). The film's *mise-en-scène* provides images of humorous but fundamentally harmonious racial interactions, be it in the streets, in the gym, on the basketball court, in the disco, in the lecture theatre, or in the hospital, to the extent that one might question whether racism is actually being effaced as a problem. Even in scenes of what could be read as racial antagonism, the exchange of insults reveals a basis primarily in sexual jealousy and insecurity. In fact, the initial antagonism between Félix and Jamal is based as much on class differences as on race. Félix, the Jew, speaks the language of the *banlieue* and comes from a relatively poor home background (brother and sister have to share a bedroom, and the *mise-en-scène* emphasises the overcrowding of their flat); Jamal, who speaks perfect French, is a wealthy, well-educated westernised African, living in a huge, elegant Parisian flat full of African artworks. This unexpected difference triggers some of the film's comedy. For example, the police treat Jamal with more respect when they discover who he is, class and wealth being more important than race in this instance. As the angry Félix says, 'We're losing our old traditions' ('Les vieilles traditions se perdent'). But it could be argued that by choosing a privileged middle-class black character rather than one who is more clearly rooted in a multi-ethnic contemporary France, Kassovitz avoids having to confront directly the everyday racial antagonisms within French society.

Furthermore, Kassovitz's fantasy of sexual and racial harmony is located in a *black-blanc-métisse* triangle which privileges white male subjectivity as well as the specificity of white ethnicity. The film could have opened with Lola discovering she is pregnant, or making the decision to have the baby despite not knowing who the father is, since these are the events which initiate the narrative. Instead, it opens with a stunning credit sequence of Félix riding through Paris on his delivery bike, a sequence which is an homage to Spike Lee as Mars Blackmon in *She's Gotta Have It*, but which also sets up Félix as the most important and entertaining screen character in the film. His rivalry with Jamal and his eventual decision to throw in his hand with Lola and Jamal is repeatedly represented as problematic, so that the character has more inner depth, and a greater narrative trajectory to effect, than the other two. Additionally, as the more 'unreconstructed' male, he has a more aggressive and energetic performance role, involving expressive verbal and body language and comic accident-prone behaviour. The most telling narrative twist, though, is the discovery that Félix is the biological father of Lola's baby, so the two men turn out not to have an equal investment in Lola's pregnancy. One cannot help wondering if Kassovitz's plot would have led to the same utopian outcome if Jamal had been allowed to be the biological father. It is notable, too, that the spectator is not required to confront the product of this transgressive mixed-race relationship since the baby (who in Félix's nightmare looks just like the adult Jamal) is heard but not seen, and is 'pink' according to the black nurse. The narrative confirms the white man's fertility and allows the black man only the dubious privilege of providing the material comfort of the *ménage à trois* and the baby-to-be. One might also note here that the film disappointingly fails to explore Lola's identity as a *métisse*. Her hybrid ethnicity functions primarily on a symbolic level, serving merely to constitute her as the appropriate object of desire for two men from different ethnic backgrounds.

Métisse, then, is a feel-good utopian fantasy, but one in which the reconciliation of racial, cultural, class and gender differences depends on a very schematic plot which doesn't bear too close a scrutiny in terms of realism and which, despite its fascination with and acceptance of the black and *métisse* ethnic other, ends up privileging the role and point of view of the white male.[4]

La Haine/Hate (1995)

The happy *ménage à trois* of *Métisse* does not include an Arab or a *beur*, but the greater realism of setting and topic of *La Haine*, Kassovitz's second film, requires the introduction of *beur* characters. *La Haine*, already in preparation at the time of the opening of *Métisse*, was inspired by a *fait divers*, the death of 16-year-old Makomé Bowole, a Zairean, who was shot in the head by a police inspector in a Parisian police station in 1993. Kassovitz was shocked at the lack of public outcry at this police *bavure*, compared with the Rodney King affair in the USA. He determined to make a serious social problem film, taking as its theme the relationship between youth in the *banlieue* and the police. The film was shot on location in the Cité de la Noe, Chanteloup-les-Vignes (Yvelines), an estate which consists of some 7,000 people from 64 different ethnic backgrounds, and involved 300 local people as film extras.[5] Kassovitz opted for a black and white documentary 'look' to the film to achieve an effect of harmonious, graphic realism which he felt would avoid the 'miserabilism' produced by the realistic use of colour.

In discussions of the film, Kassovitz avoided talking about ethnic differences, emphasising instead the commonality of experiences which unite young people on the estates. 'The problem isn't between Arabs and the police or between Blacks and the police, but between guys on the estates and the police ... It's not a question of race or colour, but a socio-economic and generational question' (Gaillac-Morgue 1995).[6] Furthermore, to avoid the hostility between youth and the police being interpreted along essentialist racial grounds, Kassovitz confronts the central *black-blanc-beur* male trio with a police force which includes a (rather unconvincing) *beur* police officer, and a white police recruit who is sickened by police violence. Nevertheless, *La Haine* has provoked contradictory readings with regard to its construction of a multicultural, multi-ethnic France. For *Le Figaro-Magazine*, the film provides evidence of the failure of integration, and the threat posed by ethnic minorities to French national culture (de Plunkett 1995). But for *Match de Paris*, the film's success is a sign that the *banlieue* is already being incorporated into French cinema's poetic realist tradition, 'In fifty years, we'll find it poetic and amusing. All these little *beurs* will seem so French' (Gaillac-Morgue 1995).[7] I would argue that Kassovitz provides a positive representation of inter-ethnic male bonding within an oppositional underclass youth culture (a theme reprised from the *beur* films of the 1980s), but that the question of racism and ethnic differences tends in the process to become marginalised, if not effaced. Rather, the film privileges the role of the white Jewish unemployed youth, who is already an unusual figure in representations of the *banlieue* (as Kassovitz has admitted).[8] A consideration of the casting points to an inbuilt inequality between the trio: Vinz, the Jew, is played by professional actor Vincent Cassel (son of Jean-Pierre, a close personal friend of Kassovitz, and Félix's brother in *Métisse*), while Hubert, the black, is played by the relatively inexperienced Hubert Koundé (Jamal in *Métisse*) and Saïd, the *beur*, is played by Saïd Taghmaoui, a friend of Cassel's, whose career was launched by Olivier Dahan's 1994 TV film, *Frères: la roulette rouge*.[9] Koundé and Taghmaoui both come from the sort of *banlieue* housing estate represented in *La Haine*. Not surprisingly, it was only Cassel's performance as the manic, posturing Vinz which won a nomination for the 1996 Césars.

The film emphasises what the three main characters have in common: their alienation as unemployed youths with no future and their hatred of the police (and of skinheads, one of whom is a cameo performance by Kassovitz himself). As in *Métisse*, there are no father figures to provide them with role models, and the *mise-en-scène* underlines the difficulty they have in taking control of their lives. Images of the estate emphasise the concrete slabs and looming walls which block their horizons, interior shots show how cramped and limited their private spaces are, and long takes point to the fact that the characters have nowhere to go and are going nowhere. Their estate is repeatedly invaded by the police (who break up the informal *merguez* barbecue being held on the rooftop, in itself an image of the overall solidarity of the multi-ethnic male community on the estate), the community gym where Hubert does his training is destroyed in the rioting, and the trio's night out in Paris is an unmitigated disaster. But the characters also share an exuberant use of language which (for some) is one of the principal pleasures of the film. Their hybrid speech, a mix of various forms of slang, popular idioms, Arabic and *manouche*, combined with *l'art de la vanne* (torrents of jibes and insults), is at times incomprehensible to the speaker of 'correct French' (the use of subtitles was rejected as a form of 'exoticism', but post-synchronisation was used to clarify certain *verlan* expressions, such as *il est bon ton teuchi*, meaning 'your shit is good'). So although on the one hand these characters have little to communicate beyond their alienation (they tend to forget the beginnings or endings of the stories they tell), on the other hand the 'dazzling inventiveness of the screenwriting' (Jousse 1995a: 34) with its crazy, rhythmic delivery, rather like French rap music, can be read as a positive marker of inter-ethnic integration, and of a symbolic resistance to dominant notions of Frenchness. By opening with Bob Marley's 'Burning and A-Looting Tonight', the film also yokes the characters' sense of injustice to a more universal struggle for minority rights.

Differences between the cultural and ethnic backgrounds of the characters are only briefly sketched in. Vinz comes from a Jewish family like the one depicted in *Métisse*, Hubert supports his heavily pregnant, single black mother out of his dope dealing, and Saïd tries, vainly, to keep a check on his streetwise *beur* sister (but there are no *beur* interiors in the film). Rather, the threesome are differentiated by their personal styles and temperaments (figure 11). Vinz is a nervy, edgy character, raging with suppressed violence, who models himself on De Niro in Scorsese's *Taxi Driver* (reminiscent of Jean-Paul Belmondo imitating Humphrey Bogart in Godard's *A bout de souffle*); Hubert is a stronger and calmer figure who has learnt to re-direct his violence into boxing; Saïd is their go-between, a milder, more ineffectual character with the gift of the gab but a tendency to get himself (and others) into tricky situations (as in the confrontation with Astérix the drug dealer). White skin privilege is recognised in the scene in which the police pick up Hubert and Saïd for questioning (and a

11 Vinz (Vincent Cassel), Saïd (Saïd Taghmaoui) and Hubert (Hubert Koundé): the *black-blanc-beur* trio of *La Haine* (1995).

beating), but don't immediately realise that Vinz is part of the group, and so allow him to escape. However, the Tarantinoesque episode set in the toilets in Paris can be read as an attempt to equate Vinz's cultural inheritance of injustice and oppression as the equivalent of the injustice and oppression experienced by blacks and *beurs* in contemporary France. In this scene, a little old man (played by Tadek Lokcinski, the Jewish grandfather in *Métisse*) tells the threesome a longwinded story about a man who goes for a shit and then dies of cold, having failed to get back on the train taking him to the Gulag. An apparently pointless story, it nevertheless serves to remind the audience of the horrors suffered by dissident East Europeans, including the Jews, and thus to provide Vinz with street credibility.

The narrative of *La Haine* also privileges Vinz's role. It is constructed through a series of desultory, loosely connected episodes in the lives of the three youths following the rioting on their estate, as they hang about, go on a (humiliating) trip to Paris and come back the next morning. However, the film combines documentary realism with a more classic suspense narrative based on Vinz's appropriation of a 9mm Beretta, phallic symbol *par excellence*, lost by a policeman during the rioting. Vinz threatens to take his revenge on the police if Abdel, the young *beur* they have beaten up, were to die. In other words, it is Vinz who generates the narrative tension and nudges them all along the path towards violence, while Hubert and Saïd try to restrain him. The suspense created by the presence of the gun is enhanced by the use of titles announcing the passing of time, and by the story told in voice-over at the beginning of the film of the man falling from a 50-storey building, telling himself at each storey 'so far so good' ('jusqu'ici tout va bien'). Even so, the violence of the film's ending comes as a shock. When the trio return to the estate and a chastened Vinz hands over the gun for safe-keeping to Hubert, the audience is quite unprepared for the sudden police *bavure* in which Vinz is casually, if accidentally, shot. As Hubert reluctantly takes over from Vinz, pulling the gun out and aiming at the policeman, it is Vinz's death which has to be avenged as much as Abdel's, and the white youth who replaces the *beur* as the film's tragic, romantic hero. Indeed, *La Haine* structures two *beur* youths into the narrative, only to use them in ways which deny them an active role. As the victim of the initial police *bavure*, Abdel has no further part to play. Compared to Vinz and Hubert, Saïd is an outsider, a witness to events rather than a participant. His eager look opens the film's diegesis (scanning the lines of police for the moment to make his mark, a graffito on the police bus: 'Nique la police') but his failure of vision closes it (he shuts his eyes in horror and the film fades to black as the last single gun shot is heard, leaving the audience to speculate as to who has pulled the trigger). In the circumstances his gleeful defacement of a poster announcing, 'The world is yours' ('Le monde est à vous') in favour of 'The world is ours' ('Le monde est à nous') is ironic rather than affirmative or hopeful.

La Haine's success is in large measure due to its timing. As Gérard Lefort put it, 'it hits the right spot in a country still groggy after the coronation of Jacques Chirac' (Reader 1995: 14), while *Time Out*'s critic referred to the 'liberating sense of a political sore finally finding legitimate filmic expression' (Charity 1995: 26). Picking up on the expression 'J'ai la haine', the film plays into a widespread sense of there being a crisis in French society, produced through the *fracture* between the estates and the rest of society and between unemployed youths and the police. But in addition it reaches out to a wider audience because of its appeal to a universal sense of the need to combat injustice. By implicitly harnessing images of an oppositional white/hybrid youth culture to the struggle against racism as well as against the police system, *La Haine* is a powerful antidote to international images of neo-Fascist white working-class male youths. From a minority standpoint, however, the marginalising of ethnic and cultural differences and the subordination of the black and *beur* roles in favour of the role of the white youth may mean that the film's value is more limited.

Just as Danny Boyle in *Trainspotting* (1996) has made a film which is unmistakably Scottish, yet at the same time challenges dominant notions of Scottishness, so Kassovitz in *Métisse* and *La Haine* is offering a substantial challenge to dominant notions of Frenchness. These first two films focus on representations of France's ethnic others, linked to a celebration of the impact of African-American popular culture on French working-class youth, and an evacuation or disparaging of French high culture. However, it is the figure of the white (Jewish) male which provides the main structuring interest of the films' narratives. True, this figure is able to take on a hybrid identity through the loosening of his ethnic cultural ties, his aspiration to be part of a multi-racial community, his adoption of the hybrid language of the multi-ethnic *banlieue* and his pleasure in black music. But this liberal integrationist vision is a one-way crossing of racial boundaries, and the complex hybrid identities of the ethnic others in these two films are much less adequately explored.[10]

Notes

1 This chapter was originally presented at a conference on 'Multicultural France' at the University of Portsmouth in February 1996, and published as 'Ethnicity and Identity in *Métisse* and *La Haine* by Mathieu Kassovitz', in T. Chafer (ed.) (1997), *Multicultural France, Working Papers on Contemporary France*, 1, University of Portsmouth, 40–7.

2 See chapter 4 for a discussion of the range of *banlieue* films made in 1995.

3 'Et si ma copine sortait avec un Noir, est-ce que je le traiterais de sale connard ou de sale nègre?'

4 See Sherzer (1999) for an exploration of 'France's ambiguous, contradictory feelings and attitudes towards identity and race: land of asylum or garbage can' (Sherzer 1999: 158) in *Métisse* and Coline Serreau's earlier 1989 film, *Romuald et Juliette*.

5 This estate has been used several times as a location, for example in *Les Enfants du désordre* (1989) by Yannick Bellon.

6 'Le problème n'est pas entre les Arabes et les flics ou entre les Noirs et les flics, mais entre les mecs des quartiers et les flics . . . Ce n'est pas une question de race ou de couleur, mais bien une question sociale, économique et générationnelle'.

7 'Dans cinquante ans, on la trouvera poétique et gouailleuse. Tous ces petits *beurs* feront tellement français'.

8 Kassovitz claimed he wanted to use a Jewish character for its folkloric interest, to please his grandmother, and also to prevent the story turning into a story of 'clans', but that a Portuguese character would have done just as well (Kassovitz 1995). Clearly, though, he also wanted to draw attention to the fact that white ethnicity is not monolithic, and that white minorities may also be oppressed groups.

9 *Frères*, a tense, imaginative *banlieue* drama which appeared in the TV series *Tous les garçons et les filles de mon âge*, also launched the career of Samy Naceri.

10 Since this chapter was written, there have been numerous analyses of *La Haine*, including Vincendeau (2000) and Forbes (2000). Kassovitz has also gone on to make other films. His violent third feature, *Assassin(s)* (1997), was not a critical success. Featuring the story of a professional white assassin who is seeking a son figure to whom he can transfer his skills, and drawing attention to the negative influences of TV violence, it moves away from *banlieue* realism whilst ending, chillingly, with a disturbed young *beur* as the new assassin. His fourth feature, *Les Rivières pourpres* (2000), was an extremely successful adaptation of a *série noire* novel, and Kassovitz now seems more interested in big-budget action movie spectacle than in personal *auteur* films. He has also continued to star as an actor, including in Jeunet's *Le Fabuleux Destin d'Amélie Poulain* (2001).

4

Beur and *banlieue* cinema in 1995[1]

The years 1994 and 1995 saw the first feature films of three new French film-makers of Maghrebi descent,[2] Malik Chibane (born in France in 1964), Karim Dridi (born in 1961 in Tunis) and Ahmed Bouchaala (born in 1956 in Algeria).[3] However, their individual voices have been obscured by critical discourses which either situate their filmmaking under the newly coined umbrella term *cinéma de banlieue* or associate it with Maghrebi, particularly Algerian, cine-matic concerns. The first strategy includes them within the broad domain of French cinema but renders their cultural differences invisible; the second excludes them as 'other' to French cinema proper. Both approaches refuse to recognise the specificity (or legitimacy) of cinematic perspectives generated by those whose hybrid or double culture makes them both insiders and outsiders in relation to dominant French culture. Insiders by virtue of being brought up in and resident in France, insiders also in the hybrid multi-ethnic youth culture of the *banlieue* (France's grim outer city housing estates), French people of Maghrebi descent are also outsiders, not just because of institutionalised state racism and the racism of those who target 'Arabs' and Islam as the scapegoats for France's socio-economic difficulties, but also because of the Republican definition of integration. As previously noted, Republican approaches to inte-gration assume that ethnic minority others must assimilate to the dominant culture rather than acknowledging and accepting minority cultures within a multicultural society, cultures which, given the historic relationships between France and its former colonies, also have a diasporic dimension. Theoretically, French people of Maghrebi descent are in a position to manoeuvre in and between 'territorial, local, diasporic, national and global cultures and identities', as Marie Gillespie describes the cosmopolitan state of mind of young British Punjabis in Southall (Gillespie 1995: 21). However, a *cinéma de banlieue* which represents the *banlieue* as just a 'melting-pot' of marginalised and excluded young people risks ignoring these multicultural dimensions. To cite Mireille Rosello, "'*La culture des banlieues*" is ... an interestingly de-ethnicized and de-essentialized paradigm of coalition between communities and a reassuringly reuniversalized entity for the dominant culture, the Republic' (Rosello 1998: 68). Cinematic representations of French people of Maghrebi descent, then, are significant to the extent that they recognise not just the right to integration but also the right to ethnic diversity.

Representations of France's postcolonial ethnic minorities have been largely confined either to the stereotypical, marginalised roles of dominant cinema or to the more subjective expressions of concern about the identity of second-generation Maghrebi immigrants, voiced in the handful of films of the 1980s known as *cinéma beur* (discussed in chapter 1). In the mid-1990s, however, Mathieu Kassovitz' stunningly inventive second film, *La Haine*, with its central *black-beur-blanc* trio of unemployed youths, brought the representation of the *banlieue* and the *fracture sociale* (the increasing disparity between haves and have-nots in contemporary French society) to the centre of the cinematic viewing experience (see chapter 3). In the same year, the multi-ethnic youth culture of the *banlieue* provided the setting for Jean-François Richet's *Etat des lieux* and Thomas Gilou's *Raï*, as well as for *Bye-Bye* by Karim Dridi, *Douce France* by Malik Chibane and *Krim*, a first feature film by Abdelkrim Bouchaala (whose previous work was in music videos and advertising). For the critics, this *cinéma de banlieue*, with its concern for social realities, not only formed part of the *jeune cinéma français* (Trémois 1997), but also seemed to establish a new, popular French genre (Konstantarakos 1999). However, the slippage from *cinéma beur* to *cinéma de banlieue* risks effacing the specificity of ethnic minority experiences and, indeed, the clear thematic links with the *cinéma beur* of the 1980s have been generally ignored.[4] For example, Yann Tobin in *Positif* refers back only to *Black mic mac* (Gilou, 1986), *La Thune* (Galland, 1991) and the later *Hexagone* (see Tobin 1995), while Thierry Jousse in *Cahiers du cinéma* mentions only *Laisse béton* (Le Péron, 1983) and *De bruit et de fureur* (Brisseau, 1988). At the same time, the unexpected success of *La Haine* limited critical consideration of the other five films. Yet, if *La Haine* and *Etat des lieux* emphasise the significance of the *fracture sociale* across ethnic lines and the commonality of experiences of a predominantly male underclass, the filmmakers of Maghrebi descent handle the same or similar material in rather different ways. This chapter examines the different representations of ethnicity and identity (and by extension, integration) in the six *banlieue* films of 1995, and establishes a comparison between the three white-authored films – *La Haine*, *Etat des lieux* and *Raï* – and the three films by filmmakers of Maghrebi descent – *Bye-Bye*, *Krim* and *Douce France*. It takes into account the narrative function and degree of subjectivity accorded to the characters of Maghrebi descent, the representation of the *banlieue* as a site of violence, the values ascribed to the culture of the parents' generation, and the construction of gender and sexuality.

La Haine/Hate, Etat des lieux/Inner City,[5] *Raï*

La Haine mobilises a trio of young men from different ethnic backgrounds – Jewish, black and *beur* – and insists on their common bonding within a hybrid oppositional youth culture, based on the language of the *banlieue*, music, drugs, petty crime, unemployment, hatred of the police and social exclusion, in a world where white, black and *beur* youths are all victims of police violence. The film follows the trajectory of the three youths through a day in their lives in which events spiral out of their control (figure 12). Nevertheless (as discussed in chapter 3), the characters of white Jewish Vinz (Vincent Cassel) and black boxer Hub (Hubert Kaoundé) are more fleshed out than that of Saïd, the *beur* character (Saïd Taghmaoui), and both have more significant roles in the narrative structure and final tragedy, where one is killed, the other about to kill or be killed. The ineffectual Saïd can only close his eyes in horror. *Etat des lieux* centres even more firmly on a white working-class character, Pierre (Patrick dell'Isola), though class solidarity across the racial divide is depicted through inter-racial encounters which are shot through with humour. The opening scene foregrounds a chorus of primarily black youths complaining direct to camera about their socio-economic situation, using a language inspired by Marxist rhetoric. Later, in a scene at Pierre's workplace, a workmate tells a long story about trying to get his friend Ahmed admitted to a nightclub and ending up in a brawl with the police. *Etat des lieux*, like *La Haine*, takes for granted the presence of ethnic minorities in the social spaces of the *banlieue* (and on the film's soundtrack), but gives more space to black youths than to youths of Maghrebi descent, and marginalises the latter in terms of its narrative concerns. In *Raï*, on the other hand, as the reference to raï music suggests, the *banlieue* is particularly associated with *beur* culture through a group of young, aggressive, predominantly *beur* males, which nevertheless includes Laurent (Tara Romer), a token white boy. The film centres on Djamel (Mustapha Benstiti), who has a job as caretaker of the local swimming-pool, his brother, Nordine (Samy Naceri), a drug addict, and Sahlia (Tabatha Cash), whom Djamel is in love with, the sister of the volatile Mezz (Micky El Mazroui). The spectator is encouraged to sympathise with Djamel, but Djamel's narrative trajectory is just as ineffectual as Saïd's in *La Haine*. He loses Sahlia because he does not understand her sexual desire and need for autonomy, he loses his brother whom he is unable to save from drugs, and when he finally throws in his lot with Mezz and the gang, in a climax of violence against the police, he does so out of despair rather than conviction.

The action of these three films takes place primarily in the sort of Parisian housing estate which is better known from television reports on crime and violence in the *banlieue*. *La Haine* opens with scenes of a riot transmitted by television. Its narrative then depends on the fate of Abdel, the hospitalised victim of a police assault, and the police gun found by Vinz, with which he plans to get his revenge if Abdel dies. A series of scenes show confrontations with the police and the abuse of police authority (even if this is mitigated by the presence of a Maghrebi police officer and a new recruit who is horrified by the violence). The film is sympathetic to its central trio who do not initiate violence, despite their macho posturing, whose resort to drugs and petty crime is a product of their impossible social situation, and whose justifiable anger does not merit the excessive police violence of the ending. The violence of the state is rendered even more explicit in *Etat des lieux* through a series of negative encounters between Pierre and various authority figures – his boss, the employee at the employment agency, the police – each of which leads to an explosion of anger (figure 13). Although, like Vinz, he is unable to change his worsening situation, he does not give in to it, and finds consolation in his political beliefs, his boxing, and in secret, explosive sex with his (white) friend's wife, shot in a protracted scene which brings the film to a close. In *Raï*, however, the youths (with the exception of Djamel) are more proactive in initiating violence, and the reasons for their behaviour are less clearly attributable to their desperate socio-economic situation. The film opens with the group operating a scam to steal money from a couple of naive white hitchhikers, proceeds through the activities of Nordine, in particular, to procure drugs (the film's most entertaining moments being provided by his theft of a racehorse actually destined for the knacker's yard), and ends with a fullscale riot, initiated by the youths in protest against the shooting of Nordine by a (white) policewoman, after he has been seen threatening the crowd in a shopping centre with a gun. However, Nordine clearly provokes his own death by insulting the

12 Trouble in Paris: the *black-blanc-beur* trio of *La Haine* (1995).

13 Pierre (Patrick dell'Isola) has a negative encounter with the police in *Etat des lieux* (1995).

policewoman and pretending to draw a gun on her (which the spectator knows he no longer possesses), and the ensuing riot therefore seems hardly justified, as Djamel at first acknowledges. Instead of underlining legitimate grievances (as in *La Haine*), *Raï*'s repeated scenes of muggings, shootings, car burning, looting and violence against the police risk playing into majority fears about mindless violence and aggression on the part of ethnic minority youths.

In *La Haine* and *Etat des lieux*, there is no representation of the family backgrounds or living spaces of the *beur* youths and no interest in first-generation immigrants. Saïd's continual intrusion into and ejection from the spaces of others demonstrate his lack of place in society. In *Raï*, however, the predicaments of Sahlia, Djamel and Nordine are attributable to the immigrant family rather than to their socio-economic situation. Mezz's honour depends on him preventing Sahlia from leading her own life, and Sahlia's resistance to marriage with Djamel, prematurely arranged according to tradition by the two mothers, leads her to walk out on her family and the estate. Djamel's superstitious mother favours her drug-addict son and relies on a fetish from a *marabout* (a Muslim holy man) to protect him from harm, while Nordine attributes his drug problem to his feelings of inadequacy at being expected to take over his dead father's place. Meanwhile, one of Nordine's attempts to procure drugs reveals an entire Maghrebi family involved in parcelling them up. *Raï* thus unapologetically attributes the alienation and violence of young people in the *banlieue* either to the immigrant Muslim family's outdated valuing of female purity, belief in arranged marriages and superstitions, or, alternatively, to their involvement in crime. Despite its foregrounding of the immigrant family, then, *Raï*'s representation of Maghrebi culture plays into the stereotypical prejudices of the majority culture and suggests that the only future for the second generation lies in leaving the *banlieue* (and Maghrebi culture) behind, like Sahlia, or sinking into violence, like Djamel.

In all these films, the masculinity of the central characters is in crisis. In *La Haine*, it is clear that the central trio are incapable of communicating with women, and the formation of the couple, mixed-race or otherwise, is not seriously entertained. In *Etat des lieux*, Pierre's wordless sex scene with his friend's wife may provide him with a sense of his identity as a man, but the black characters' relationships with women remain at the level of macho verbal posturing. Again, it is *Raï* which is most concerned with ethnic minorities and the representation of gender, but here again, the film plays into racist stereotypes. Above all, it suffers from the casting of a former porn star, Tabatha Cash, as Sahlia, and the decision to display her body as the object of a voyeuristic gaze. Her revolt against the patriarchal constraints of Maghrebi family life and Djamel's misplaced idealisation of her could have called into question conventional assumptions about masculine and feminine identities and gender roles. But a revolt which has Sahlia first try (unsuccessfully) to seduce Djamel, then sleep with Laurent, then erupt into the dance the gang has organised on the estate, wearing a blonde wig, tight skimpy skirt and thigh-high boots, smacks primarily of the fantasies of the film's white, male director. Sahlia is the only character able to leave the *banlieue* at the end of the film, but her role offers little hope for the formation of either the *beur* or the mixed-race couple.

La Haine and *Etat des lieux* are cinematically exhilarating films which express a healthy anger at the injustices and inequalities of contemporary French society, but they do not highlight the specificity of the situation facing second- and third-generation immigrants of Maghrebi origin in France. As for *Raï*, though it foregrounds this specificity, it does so in a way which, however unintentionally, plays into racist stereotypes of an alien immigrant culture spawning an irresponsible, violent youth culture. *Raï*'s representation of the *banlieue* can be usefully compared with Chibane's *Hexagone* (for which Gilou had been an advisor), which is also centred on two brothers, one of whom is a drug addict who meets his death, the other a dutiful son with a girlfriend who rebels against traditional Muslim family values (see chapter 2). *Hexagone* handles its subject matter in a sensitive, low-key, realist manner, allowing the central characters an unusual degree of subjectivity, and highlights the characters' problematic positioning in relation to both French and Maghrebi culture, rather than constructing Maghrebi culture as the cause of violence and alienation.

Bye-Bye, Krim, Douce France/Sweet France

Bye-Bye, Krim and *Douce France* address the situation of ethnic minorities in France through narratives which move beyond the semi-autobiographical bases of films such as *Le Thé au harem d'Archimède* and *Hexagone*. In *Bye-Bye*, Karim Dridi evokes the historic multi-ethnic Panier district of Marseilles through the eyes of two second-generation brothers of Maghrebi descent, Ismaël (Sami Bouajila) and Mouloud (Oussini Embarek), who are travelling south, prior to Mouloud being sent back to join his parents in North Africa. In *Krim*, Ahmed Bouchaala constructs a melodramatic world of obsession through the story of Krim (Hammou Graïa), who is released from prison for murdering his wife and goes back to Lyons after sixteen years' absence to search for his long-lost daughter (a story based on a *fait divers*, co-written with Zakia Tahiri). In his second film, *Douce France*, Chibane uses comedy to explore the inter-racial friendship of Moussa (Hakim Sahraoui), the son of a *harki*, and Jean-Luc (Frédéric Diefenthal), a white youth, and their relationship with three very different young Arab women. It is immediately noticeable that these films do not centre on the multi-ethnic gang of unemployed youths typical of many *beur* and *banlieue* films. In each case, the central (male) character of Maghrebi descent is older (aged thirty rather than twenty) and has put crime behind him. The films focus rather on interpersonal and intergenerational relationships within the Maghrebi community in France, and the central character's problematic relationship with French society.

In *Bye-Bye*, a series of flashbacks indicates that Ismaël is haunted by memories of the death of his handicapped brother in a fire for which he may have been responsible. His integrity, sensitivity and despair are rendered through a series of lingering close-ups, a relatively unusual technique in the construction of a character of Maghrebi descent. Ismaël is responsible for sending Mouloud back 'home', but the film first explores the brothers' family of relatives and experiences of life in Marseilles. Mouloud gets led astray by his cousin, Rhida, refuses to go back to North Africa, and gets embroiled with a local North African drug dealer as well as becoming the target of a group of racists, thanks to his spraying of graffiti on their car (figure 14). Ismaël drifts into work as a dockside labourer alongside his uncle, makes friends with his white workmate, Jacky (Frédéric Andrau), who saves him from drowning, but falls for Jacky's *beurette* girlfriend, Yasmine (Nozha Khouadra) and becomes the object of Jacky's abuse and Yasmine's contempt. He finally assumes responsibility for Mouloud, escapes with him from the drug dealer, and decides not to send him away. Having outstayed their welcome in Marseilles, the two homeless brothers set off in their 2CV, and the film ends on their reconciliation, even if the breakdown of their car means that they will have difficulty finding somewhere else to go.

14 Mouloud (Oussini Embarek) gets embroiled with a North African drug dealer in *Bye-Bye* (1995)

In *Krim*, the central character is a former boxer, who has spent sixteen years in prison for murdering his wife, sharing a cell with an older father figure (of uncertain ethnic origin), Eugène Parodi (Philippe Clay), his mentor and friend, an artist whose paintings represent his dreams for the future. On his release, he records the sounds and feelings of freedom to send back to Parodi, his experiences rendered through elaborate fragmentation of the image and the intercutting of unmotivated shots of a distressed young woman, who eventually turns out to be his niece, Nora (Elisabeth Rose). When Krim discovers that the block of flats where he once lived is due to be demolished and that his daughter has committed suicide, he cannot bring himself to tell Parodi the truth, and his tape-recorded lies cause a disillusioned Parodi to dismiss him as just '*un boug-noul*' (a racist term of abuse). Haunted by his past life and the loss of his daughter, he squats in the deserted flat and attempts to recreate the past, rejecting the friendship of a drunken white layabout, formerly his friend. Just as he is about to give up, his sister, Samia (Zakia Tahiri), asks for help with Nora, who has become a drug addict. Krim accepts the task, and tries first to force Nora, then to persuade her, to kick her habit. After a major setback, he is ready to abandon her, but Samia then confesses that Nora is actually his daughter, Yasmine. Krim's love for Nora enables her to pull through, and the film ends with Nora's voice-over on the tape to Parodi, who has at last regained confidence in his friend. Like *Bye-Bye, Krim* invests the second-generation immigrant of Maghrebi origin with a new sense of responsibility towards the younger generation, though the father–daughter relationship perilously resembles the traditional incestuous duo of classical French cinema (Vincendeau 1992).

Douce France operates in a different register from *Bye-Bye* and *Krim*. Moussa and Jean-Luc are able to transcend their condition as unemployed young men in the *banlieue*, thanks to a plot device in the opening sequence which has them discover a cache of stolen jewellery. Consequently, they are able to set themselves up in business, Moussa by taking over a bar frequented by North Africans (called L'Impasse), and Jean-Luc by setting up his solicitor's office in the back room. The film thus evades the pessimistic realism of more typical *banlieue* films, and is able instead to explore with humour the duo's interactions with the local community, and particularly with women. Jean-Luc tries to win back Souad (Séloua Hamse), a thoroughly modern young woman of Maghrebi descent, while Moussa sets his sights on her sister, Farida (Fadila Belkebla), who has chosen to adopt a strict Muslim identity. Moussa's pursuit of Farida, which requires him to frequent the mosque, is put at risk by the revelation that his mother has already arranged a marriage for him with an Arab girl from back 'home' (Algeria). When Myssad arrives, her sophisticated, liberated attitude confounds stereotypical expectations, and her decision to walk out on a marriage which is not based on love leads to the final sequence in which the three young women drive to the airport together, and Farida eventually throws away her headscarf. The ineffectual Moussa may be at an impasse, unable to stand up to his mother himself, but, as in *Raï*, the young women end up clearly rejecting the values and traditions of their parents insofar as they affect their lives as women. *Douce France* thus operates a significant shift from the male characters to the female characters as the agents of integration and change (figure 15).

In terms of cinematic space, these films extend the representation of a multi-ethnic France from the Parisian *banlieues* of St-Denis in *Douce France* to Marseilles in *Bye-Bye* and Lyons in *Krim*. But their *mise-en-scène* also foregrounds the domestic spaces of the Maghrebi family and refuses to focus on the *banlieue* as the site of violence and clashes with the police. In *Bye-Bye*, Ismaël finds himself at a crossroads, confronting the claustrophobic spaces of his uncle's apartment, the uncertainties of the workplace, the openness of the seascape where the ferryboat heads for North Africa, and the streets of Marseilles which are the site of drug-dealing, racist violence and sexual temptation, but also of a more utopian vision of a multi-ethnic working-class community, as in the scenes of the open-air dance and the marriage between a white woman and a black man.[6] In *Krim*, the wasteland of abandoned, decaying tower blocks represents the emotional disorder of Krim's mind, from which he manages to escape through his utopian vision of a little house in the country for himself and his daughter, as figured in Parodi's paintings and the brightly coloured wallpaper pattern of his daughter's bedroom, which he uncovers in the ruined

15 Competing images of femininity within the immigrant Maghrebi family in *Douce France* (1995).

flat. At the end of the film, Krim has left behind the city with its ex-cons and prostitutes, and the *banlieue* with its drunks and drug addicts, signs here of a degenerate white French culture, and the spectator witnesses with him the collapse of the ruined *banlieue* towers in glorious slow motion. Both these films end, then, with the characters of Maghrebi origin leaving the *banlieue* in search of a new way of life, however impossible. *Douce France* chooses another strategy to avoid the clichés of the *banlieue* film. Instead of impersonal tower-block settings, its characters live in small suburban houses or modern flats, and are seen at work, like Souad's father selling *merguez* outside the makeshift mosque and Souad herself working in a Quick burger bar. The film repeatedly draws attention to racism and ethnic difference as issues, but defuses them through comedy, as when the police shooting of a drunken immigrant becomes an opportunity for Jean-Luc to build up his business, or when a drunken Moussa finds himself accidentally in bed with a neighbour whose racist husband had earlier pulled a gun on him, or when Farida's sophisticated command of French leads to her teaching French to little Jewish children. Whereas the central characters of *Bye-Bye* and *Krim* can find no future in the *banlieue*, *Douce France* assumes that the *banlieue* can accommodate people of different ethnic origins and ends with Souad and Farida returning from the airport, hopefully in order to exercise some control over their lives.

These three films value the Maghrebi culture of the older generation, even if they also show that the second generation is capable of refusing or questioning aspects of that culture. *Bye-Bye* invests heavily in the sympathetic portrayal of the extended immigrant family, presided over by the silent but encouraging figure of the great aunt. In *Bye-Bye*, the uncle (unusually) has a job but still worries about the loss of his paternal authority, and the warm-hearted aunt helps her daughters with their homework and smokes the odd cigarette in secret. In contrast, the more rigid, authoritarian attitude of Ismaël's father, evidenced in his telephone calls, demonstrates why Mouloud refuses to go back to North Africa. The affectionate banter between the two brothers at the end of the film gives a positive image of youths of Maghrebi descent, whose family ties enable them to combat both racism and crime. *Krim* evacuates the older generation (Krim's parents apparently died of shame at his crime), and positions Krim as alone in the world except for the friendship of Parodi. But Krim desires to assume his position as head of the family, and berates his sister Samia for her acceptance of '*francaoui*' (French) values. (Samia works in a beauty salon, has dyed her hair blonde, and is eliminated from the narrative at the end, even though she dyes her hair black again.) *Krim* thus puts its trust not in adaptation and integration, but in the acceptance of traditional Maghrebi values, and the purifying of the new second-generation immigrant family is symbolised by the scene in which the father bathes the daughter in a tin bath outside the flats. In *Douce France*, Moussa spends his time trying, unsuccessfully, to escape from the influence of his violent *harki* father and his sick mother, who blackmails him into accepting her plans for an arranged marriage (in contrast to Souad, who leaves home to assert her independence from her parents). The community gathering for Moussa's wedding is primarily an excuse for local colour provided by the spectacle of traditional Algerian costumes and dancing. But the future of the second generation is shown, here, to depend on the refusal of traditional Muslim values, and Moussa's predicament is resolved by Myssad's rejection of a marriage which is not based on love. *Douce France* goes further than *Bye-Bye* in displaying the Islamic culture of the parents' generation (who have designed a mosque without minarets so as not to disturb the indigenous French), but it does so in order to demonstrate that this culture does not impede the process of integration among the second generation.

As in *La Haine* and *Raï*, the masculinity of the *beur* male is at stake in these films, given the impotence of their central characters, but the question of gender roles is addressed more extensively. *Bye-Bye* attempts to redeem Ismaël's impotence by allowing him to have sex with Jacky's girlfriend. However, Ismaël's inability to accept responsibility for his act leaves Yasmine in the thankless role of object of exchange between men, and the film ends on a regressive return to a 'safe' all-male world. In *Krim*, the overly masculine Krim, whose violence has already caused the death of his wife, avenges his powerlessness by having sex with and then humiliating a prostitute who had taken pity on him, and rejecting his French-identified sister. His possessive attitude towards his wayward teenage daughter is a sign of his inability to enter a world of adult sexual relationships, even if the film itself endorses the formation of the father–daughter couple. In *Douce France*, Moussa is assumed to be capable of forming a heterosexual relationship, but there are no images of the couple and he is last seen discovering Myssad's absence. However, *Douce France* is different from the other films in that the female characters provide the film's narrative impetus and the final image shows Souad, literally, in the driving seat.

Conclusion

The differences between the two sets of films discussed here are significant. The white-authored films express the anger and alienation of young people in the *banlieue*, regardless of their ethnic origin, and focus in particular on violence and hostility between male youths and the police, a violence which is even more pronounced in Richet's follow-up film, *Ma 6T va crack-er* (1997) and, in a more stylised form, in Kassovitz's *Assassin(s)* (1997). The films by directors of Maghrebi descent are careful to avoid or defuse scenes of confrontation with the police and other authority figures, and are more interested in exploring individual problems of identity and integration, and addressing changes within the Maghrebi community in France, including the question of women's place within that culture. This does not prevent them from reaching different conclusions. Whereas integration is considered possible in *Douce France*, it is far more problematic in *Bye-Bye* and *Krim*. And while *Douce France* consolidates the theme of inter-racial friendship and signals the importance of women in the process of integration, both *Bye-Bye* and *Krim* refuse inter-racial friendships (apart from Krim's ambiguous relationship with Parodi) and seek to contain the female characters they construct.

   Nevertheless, even if *Bye-Bye* and *Krim* are pessimistic about the integration of the *beurs* in France, it is clear that the three films considered here are more sensitive to questions of ethnicity and identity than the first three films. Without them, the representation of characters of Maghrebi descent would remain marginalised or even invisible (as in *Etat des lieux*), undeveloped (as in *La Haine*) or verging on the stereotypical (as in *Raï*). Their more diverse, individualised and challenging representations show the importance of ethnic minority contributions to the representation of contemporary France as a multicultural society. The shared hybrid culture of young people represented in white-authored *banlieue* films should not mask the significance of ethnic difference, and the difficulties it presents for an assimilationist understanding of integration, as demonstrated in *banlieue* films by filmmakers of Maghrebi descent.

Notes

1 An earlier French version of this chapter was presented at a conference on 'New French Cinema' at Roehampton Surrey University in 1998. An earlier English version was published as 'Ethnicity and identity in the "cinéma de banlieue"', in P. Powrie (ed.), *French Cinema in the 1990s: Continuity and Difference*, Oxford: Oxford University Press, 1999, 172–84.

2 At the time of writing this article, the use of the word '*beur*' was becoming problematic. I have therefore adopted the more acceptable phrase 'of Maghrebi descent' throughout most of this (and subsequent) article(s). However, it should be noted that Karim Dridi is actually of mixed-race (Franco-Tunisian) origin and for this reason also does not like to be identified as a *beur*.

3 Dridi and Bouchaala both came to France as children. Unlike Chibane, Dridi has a professional background making films for industry, Bouchaala in making advertising films.

4 The notion of *beur* cinema as a genre seems to have disappeared from critical vocabulary, and has in any case enjoyed little currency with *beur* filmmakers who have been afraid of being ghettoised by the label.

5 The American title is geographically inaccurate but translates the way in which the *banlieues* are identified with disadvantaged ethnic minorities.

6 For a more detailed analysis of space in *Bye-Bye* see Higbee (2001a).

5

Beur women in the *banlieue*: *Les Histoires d'amour finissent mal en général* and *Souviens-toi de moi*[1]

If dominant French cinema has tended to maintain the hegemony of a white, patriarchal, eurocentric understanding of Frenchness, voices from the periphery, particularly those of filmmakers of Maghrebi descent, have turned French cinema into a site of struggle for constructions of French national identity based on the realities of France as a multicultural, multi-ethnic society. One of the most original voices to intervene in this arena was that of Zaïda Ghorab-Volta, a young woman of Algerian descent, whose first semi-autobiographical film drew attention to the androcentricity of previous representations of ethnicity and identity in France. This chapter analyses the ways in which gender, ethnicity and identity are articulated in Ghorab-Volta's *Souviens-toi de moi* (1996) by comparing it with a more commercially oriented film also centring on a young Maghrebi-French woman, Anne Fontaine's prize-winning comedy drama *Les Histoires d'amour finissent mal en general* (1993). A comparison of the positions of identification and desire which these two films offer their audiences may offer some insight into the ways in which dominant constructions of femininity and Frenchness can and cannot be challenged by the hybrid status of the young woman of Maghrebi descent.

In the course of the 1990s, there was a proliferation not only of *banlieue* films (as discussed in chapter 4) but also of comedies involving ethnic difference and films by a new generation of filmmakers which take for granted a multi-ethnic social background. However, even after two decades of settlement in France of the families of immigrants from the Maghreb, there were relatively few representations of young *beur* women. The majority of these films figure an ethnic minority presence primarily through black or *beur* males or black females, as in *Métisse* (Mathieu Kassovitz, 1993), *J'ai pas sommeil* (Claire Denis, 1994), *La Haine* (Kassovitz, 1995), *Etat des lieux* (Jean-François Richet, 1995), *En avoir (ou pas)* (Laetitia Masson, 1995), *N'oublie-pas que tu vas mourir* (Xavier Beauvois, 1995), *A toute vitesse* (Gaël Morel, 1996), *Chacun cherche son chat* (Cédric Klapisch, 1996), *Les Trois Frères* (Les Inconnus, 1996) and *Les*

Deux Papas et la maman (Smaïn et Longwal, 1996). Films offering a secondary role for a young woman of Maghrebi descent tend either to subordinate the female role to the drama of the white central male character, as in *Le Cri de Tarzan* (Thomas Bardinet, 1996) and *Le Plus Beau Métier du monde* (Gérard Lauzier, 1996); or to construct her as object of desire and punish her for attempting to assert her autonomy, as in *Bye-Bye* (Karim Dridi, 1995) and *Krim* (Ahmed Bouchaala, 1995). In *Raï* (Thomas Gilou, 1995), the young *beur* woman is accorded a significant narrative strand to explore her problematic identity, but Gilou's casting and direction of former porn star Tabatha Cash highlights her primary function as exotic, sexualised object of desire. In *Salut cousin!* (Merzak Allouache, 1996), the independent young woman of Maghrebi descent is given just the briefest of cameo appearances in order to undermine stereotypical expectations that she must be a prostitute (see chapter 12). Only Malik Chibane's *Hexagone* (1994) and *Douce France* (1995) construct complex secondary roles for their sympathetic independent-minded young *beur* women characters without simultaneously exploiting them as objects of the gaze or containing them through the structuring of the narrative. *Les Histoires d'amour finissent mal en général* and *Souviens-toi de moi* stand out, then, as the only feature films prior to 1997 to take the way in which a young woman of Maghrebi descent negotiates her identity as their central preoccupation and to explore female subjectivity through relatively complex characters who enjoy some narrative agency.[2]

As well as negotiating a place for themselves within a fundamentally male-dominated French cinema industry, films which centre on realistic representations of young French women of Maghrebi descent need to situate themselves in relation to Republican discourses on assimilation as the route to integration, and to orientalist discourses, islamophobia and anti-Arab racism, the products of centuries of French colonialism. Novelists[3] and sociologists[4] have documented the frustrations and conflicts experienced by young women who are at odds with the traditional Arabo-Berber-Islamic culture of their parents' generation, with its insistence on male authority, female virtue, arranged marriages and women's destiny as wife and mother (a patriarchal culture which is reproduced in a number of the films cited above). But while young women's aspirations for autonomy may mean that they have much to gain from integration into French society, their ability to integrate is made difficult by their desire to retain affective links with their parents, often through acceptance of aspects of their parents' culture, and the widespread rejection they continue to face on the part of the majority culture. Young *beur* women, then, are doubly oppressed as female within Maghrebi culture and as female and ethnic other within dominant French culture. With some exceptions, they lack social, political and economic power, and are normally constructed by the French media (in relation to issues such as the *foulard* affair[5] and reports on sequestrations in

Algeria and female runaways) as victims of Islamic fundamentalists or traditional Maghrebi culture rather than as agents of personal and social change.

If identities are best understood as not given and unified but relational,
produced through changing social conditions and processes of affiliation and
differentiation (Woodward 1997), then the interest of *Les Histoires d'amour
finissent mal en général* and *Souviens-toi de moi* lies in the way they negotiate the
contradictory relations in which their central protagonists are implicated. To
what extent do these films enable their women characters (and by extension their
audiences) to acknowledge and reconcile the different elements of their problematic gendered and bicultural heritage? To what extent do they suggest that
gender roles and Frenchness are not natural or given but subject to change?

Both *Les Histoires d'amour finissent mal en général* and *Souviens-toi de moi*
are first feature films by young women who began making films without professional training (Fontaine, who grew up in Portugal, was a dancer and actress
who wanted to write; Ghorab-Volta, who was born in Clichy, the fifteenth child
of Algerian immigrants, was a social worker). *Les Histoires d'amour finissent
mal en général* received the *avance sur recettes* (advance on box office receipts),
was shown at the Cannes Festival and won the Prix Jean Vigo (the first film by
a woman ever to do so). It is a low-budget romantic comedy, aimed at a mainstream audience, using little-known actors and starring Nora, herself a young
woman of Maghrebi descent, who had just completed her acting training when
cast in the central role of Zina. For Fontaine, the choice of a *beur* heroine was
a way of dramatising and intensifying the romantic dilemmas facing any lively,
ambitious young woman, and there is no reason to suppose that the choice of
subject matter (written with the assistance of Claude Arnaud) is invested with
personal or political commitment. In contrast, *Souviens-toi de moi* (which
actually has a running length of only 59 minutes) was the product of some nine
years of labour outside the normal modes of professional cinematic production, an indication of the difficulties faced by ethnic minority filmmakers in
getting funding.[6] Devised by Ghorab-Volta in 1987, it was refused the *avance
sur recettes* and shot on a shoestring budget at weekends with a cast of amateurs
and Ghorab-Volta herself in the central role of Mimouna. A very personal film,
given semi-autobiographical authenticity by the filmmaker's screen presence,
it received a limited release in 1996 to some critical acclaim, but assured itself
a place on the festival circuits and in community-centre screenings. Its very
existence is a tribute to Ghorab-Volta's refusal to be excluded from French film
culture and her determination to give expression to the experiences of women
like herself.

Despite their different conditions of production and exhibition and despite
the different class and ethnic backgrounds of the two women filmmakers, the
two films share a considerable number of common elements. Neither film is
informed by the debates about ethnicity, identity and representation which have

underpinned much independent black filmmaking in Britain and America.[7] Rather, both films address a majority audience by minimising issues relating to Islam and racism and refusing spectatorial positions based on 'miserabilism' or the call for political activism. Both films choose a narrative structure which centres on a young *beur* woman in a vulnerable, formative position between school and settling down, and explores how her identity is constructed through her interactions with others. Both avoid the narratives and iconography typical of male-authored *banlieue* films centred on streetwise male youths, unemployment, crime, drugs, violence and confrontation with the police. Instead, they focus on female-centred interpersonal relationships, articulated through the presence of a geographically mobile independent-minded female character who lives in the Parisian *banlieue*, is alienated from her parents, has French friends and an unrewarding low-paid job, and is engaged in an impossible relationship with a French man. In each case, the young woman survives, but the formation of a permanent, successful, integrated mixed-race couple, potentially symbolic of the coming together of French and Maghrebi cultures, is denied. Despite these common elements, however, there are considerable aesthetic and ideological differences between the two films, which I shall now analyse separately.

Les Histoires d'amour finissent mal en general/Love Affairs Usually End Badly (1993)

In *Les Histoires d'amour finissent mal en général*, Zina, an usher in a Parisian *boulevard* theatre and would-be actress, is engaged to be married to Slim (Sami Bouajila), a serious-minded young taxi driver who is studying to be a lawyer; but she falls in love with Frédéric (Alain Fromager), the quixotic young star of the play. Slim and Frédéric are from different ethnic backgrounds, but they also differ in terms of character and aspiration, the *beur* representing (unusually) a secure but dull suburban existence, the white Frenchman representing romance, the city and the unknown. The plot explores Zina's fractured identity through her geographical, cultural and affective oscillation between the two men up until her wedding day, when her inability to choose between the two means that she eventually loses them both. But the film avoids ending on a melancholy or pessimistic note by having her hitch a lift to Marseilles with a third man who turns out to be a musician. Although the camera centres primarily on Zina, allowing the spectator to share her predicament until the moment she disappears from view, it also works to create a more judgemental spectator by the way it foregrounds the negative reactions of her lovers and friend (her gay neighbour Philippe) to her impulsive and apparently perfidious behaviour.

The film begins by establishing Zina's place within the urban and suburban landscape, but then gradually works to undermine it. In the opening sequences a carefree Zina takes the train back to the *banlieue* or walks through the streets of Paris accompanied only by her Walkman. As the film progresses and she finds it increasingly difficult to juggle her relationships, however, her mobility becomes more and more circumscribed and dependent on others, be it in Slim's taxi or on the back of Frédéric's scooter; and the film ends with her departure in the unknown young man's car. Similarly, at the beginning of the narrative, despite serious financial problems, Zina has a flat of her own (her family has gone back to live in Algeria). However, her move into Slim's flat as the wedding date draws near and the fact that Frédéric has no room for her in his theatre dressing-room accommodation mean that at the end of the narrative Zina is homeless and penniless. Her aspirations to a stage career are shattered when she is refused a part in the chorus in a forthcoming musical because 'there are no *beurettes* in rock music'. And she gets little consolation from Philippe, who accuses her of only ever thinking about herself. In terms of narrative structure, Zina's aspirations for something more than a conventional *banlieue* existence with her *beur* fiancé seem doomed to failure.

Zina's inability to make a commitment to Slim can be interpreted as a form of revolt against both conventional gender roles and her Maghrebi background. Despite his modernity and intelligence, Slim is a possessive young man who is not supportive of Zina's desire for a career. And although Zina's family has been carefully evacuated from the narrative, leaving Zina apparently free to make her own decisions about her life, Slim himself is inextricably associated with his traditionally dressed mother, Zina's future mother-in-law, who buys them the matrimonial bed, supervises the purchase of Zina's wedding dress, and sleeps beside Zina on the night before the wedding. Her attempt (in Arabic) to persuade Zina of the future pleasures of pregnancy precipitates Zina's hurried departure in search of a now reluctant Frédéric. So Zina's rejection of Maghrebi culture is overdetermined by being mapped on to a rejection of a dull, traditional domestic existence as wife and mother.

However, the alternative offered by her affair with Frédéric is also problematic. Frédéric's feelings for Zina are initially generated by the fascination she exerts from her position as 'other' in terms of gender, class and ethnicity (he wants to know where she comes from and is intrigued by a visit to her apartment). But he feels unable to introduce her to his family, fails to help her in her career as he had promised, and is ultimately unwilling to make a commitment to her, blaming the breakdown of their relationship on Zina's fickleness. So the film does not allow Zina to reject her Maghrebi origins in order to integrate successfully into the majority culture. Rather it punishes her for her reluctance to make an impossible choice and then leaves her, temporarily at least, somewhere on the margins of French society, belonging nowhere and still desperately trying to find her place (figure 16).

The somewhat pessimistic structure of the narrative is mitigated by Zina's seductive appearance in a range of contemporary Western youth fashions and

16 Zina (Nora) tries to find a place for herself in *Les Histoires d' amour finissent mal en général* (1993).

the energy with which Nora interprets and performs the role. Zina's ability to project herself into others, as when she imitates a man snoring in the opening sequence or mimics a posh nurse to impress the theatre impresario, suggests that she is infinitely able to adapt and re-invent herself. Yet this adaptability, rather than being a positive asset in the postmodern, postcolonial condition, can be interpreted as a way of covering over a fundamental lack of identity. For Zina's sense of herself as a liberated human being ('I'm my own man now!' she says to Frédéric) is contradicted by her drive to seek security through marriage with Slim and her desire to seduce others, including Philippe and his boyfriend, to achieve a sense of self-worth. Forced to confront her contradictory desires at the moment of the wedding ceremony in the Town Hall, Zina's fractured identity is expressed through the rip in her wedding dress, a rip which leads to her walking out. But despite a touching image of a disconsolate Zina collapsed on the bridge between the suburbs and Paris, the film does not allow either Zina or the spectator time to reflect on the implications of her rejection of and by the men she claims to love. Instead it imposes a light-hearted but reactionary resolution which fixes Zina's identity as the seductive but fickle female 'other', and allows her to survive only at the cost of having her voice drowned out by that of her male saviour. So the film both recognises and dismisses her problematic identity as a young woman of Maghrebi descent.

Souviens-toi de moi/Remember Me (1996)

Souviens-toi de moi does not have the same tightly plotted narrative drive as *Les Histoires*, but rather uses a loosely episodic, discontinuous narrative structure in which key moments are marked by a poignant string-based original music score. The action of the film takes place over a few weeks in the course of a summer during which Mimouna and her parents go on holiday to Algeria. It begins by charting Mimouna's anguished state of mind but, in contrast to *Les Histoires*, ends with Mimouna having acquired a new inner strength as a result of her experiences, even if her material situation remains problematic. The different facets of her fractured existence are articulated through her interactions with a variety of characters – lover, mother, father, brother, sister, workmate, girlfriends and Algerian cousins (to whom the film is dedicated) – which combine to build up a complex, syncretic portrait of the contemporary young woman of Maghrebi descent.

From the beginning, Mimouna's experiences are embedded within the context of the immigrant Maghrebi family. After tracking shots leading the spectator into the *banlieue* setting, the film opens with a close-up of the *couscous* being kneaded by the mother. The mother's appearance in traditional dress, her use of Arabic rather than French, her restriction to the domestic sphere, her preoccupation with traditional domestic tasks and her deference to her authoritarian husband explain the westernised daughters' revolt against conventional women's roles in Maghrebi culture. But Ghorab-Volta also uses close-ups of the mother and shots of the isolated father to invite the spectator to share in and sympathise with the parents' lack of communication and inability to understand what is happening to their family (one daughter has run away, another is planning to). The harrowing scenes of conflict between mother and daughters are rendered in a naturalistic semi-improvised acting style (*à la* Pialat) through fixed frames and long takes, with the mother speaking in Arabic, the sisters shouting back insolently in French (figure 17). The scene in which the father insults his son Hamid for failing to get a job and keep his sisters under control is equally distressing. However, the film also includes a long sequence which foregrounds the sympathetic relationship between the two sisters. And Hamid's refusal to accept a traditional male role usefully calls into question one of the last (if disputed) vestiges of masculine privilege which is frequently reproduced in other *banlieue* films.

For the first forty minutes, the film cuts between the emotional scenes in Mimouna's home and scenes involving her dying love affair with Jacques, her dead-end job, and her female friendships. As in *Les Histoires*, the young *beur* woman turns to a relationship with a (white) Frenchman for an alternative sense of identity and self-worth. But Mimouna's exchanges with Jacques also end in shouting and screaming as Jacques, who no longer loves her as he used to, explains that he does not want her to be dependent on him and explicitly refuses the role of surrogate father figure. Mimouna is aware that her hysterical attachment to him is damaging, and by the end of the film has decided not to see him again (whereas in *Les Histoires* Zina is abandoned by Frédéric). Mimouna also has the courage to walk out of her job in a canteen (having told her parents that she works in a hospital), refusing the identity that such unrewarding, low-paid work confers on her. But she finds comfort and pleasure in the company of her (white) female workmate and her (white) female friends, sharing complaints with them about life in general and about men in particular (though, like Zina in *Les Histoires*, she is accused of only ever thinking about herself). Her inter-ethnic friendships are the strongest markers of her ability to integrate into French society (whereas in *Les Histoires*, Zina's friendship with Philippe is ambivalent), and the final images of the film show her walking with her girlfriends by the river, sharing gossip about the holidays. Whereas Zina finally gets evacuated from the narrative, soundtrack and *mise-en-scène* of *Les Histoires*, at the end of *Souviens-toi de moi* Mimouna is an unmistakable visible and audible presence in the urban environment.

Ghorab-Volta chooses to locate the last twenty minutes of the narrative in Algeria, where Mimouna also discovers warmth and pleasure in the company of her Algerian cousins (a discovery which contrasts with Zina's negative references to her experiences in Algeria in *Les Histoires*). This section includes scenes

17 Conflict between mother and daughters in *Souviens-toi de moi* (1996).

which invite the spectator to understand the choices and sacrifices Mimouna's parents made in emigrating to France and to sympathise with their disappointment and pain, themselves caught between two cultures. But it primarily functions to enhance Mimouna, who comes to wear traditional dress and use a few words of Arabic. Unable to express herself in her normal abrasive way, she sits and listens as the camera pans across the group of young women talking, enjoying their animated discussion of arranged marriages and criticisms of men's roles in Algerian society, which allow her to appreciate the benefits of living in France. On her return, though the future may be uncertain (no job, no boyfriend, no obvious improvement in her relationship with her parents), Mimouna herself has increased in confidence, a phenomenon which can be attributed both to female solidarity and to her new acceptance of her cultural heritage (figure 18). *Souviens-toi de moi* thus offers a more empowering ending than *Les Histoires*, and presents Mimouna's identity precisely as something changing and in process, the result of interactions between Mimouna and her roots and Mimouna and the circumstances in which she finds herself.

Conclusion

The ways in which these two women's films inflect the *banlieue* film are to be welcomed in that they give visibility and a voice to a central young *beur* woman

18 Mimouna (Zaïda Ghorab-Volta) and friends in *Souviens-toi de moi* (1996).

character, a phenomenon which is still relatively unusual in French cinema.[8] Both films represent the predicament of the young woman of Maghrebi descent torn between two cultures and uncertain about her identity and her future, and both films invite the spectator to sympathise with that predicament, which remains unresolved. Neither film seeks to address the spectator directly through the use of subjective voice-over or direct address to camera. However, whereas *Les Histoires'* use of a conventional classic narrative may leave the spectator relatively undisturbed, the spectator of *Souviens-toi de moi*, already interpellated by the film's title, may be unsettled by its fragmented narrative, its placing of the camera at close range and its apparently spontaneous style of acting.

Where the two films also differ is in their exploitation of the women's relationships with their peers. *Les Histoires* privileges Zina's problematic relationships with men, rejects the figure of the Maghrebi mother and the culture that she represents, denies Zina support from her gay male friend, and ignores the possibility of female friendships (though there is a very brief cameo appearance by Ghorab-Volta). *Souviens-toi de moi*, however, contrasts Mimouna's problematic relationships with her parents and her lover with the close relationships she enjoys with her sister, her French friends and her Algerian cousins (though not, it should be noted, with other young black or *beur* women). Thus, on the one hand Ghorab-Volta's film is more strongly focused on the issues facing young women of Maghrebi descent through its exploration of Mimouna's Algerian cultural heritage, a heritage which problematises the possibility of integration through assimilation and is too casually brushed aside in *Les Histoires*. And on the other, it invites the spectator to share in the construction of an identity based on intercultural solidarity between women, itself a comparatively rare phenomenon in contemporary French cinema.

In conclusion, then, an analysis of these two representations of young *beur* women in French cinema of the 1990s highlights the ideological work of cinema with regard to questions of gender, ethnicity and identity. *Les Histoires*, the more commercially oriented film, ultimately defers to a majority audience by condemning the young *beur* woman to marginality in terms of both her gender and her ethnicity, leaving her unable to establish an autonomous identity through her relationship with either Maghrebi or French culture. Whereas the more committed *Souviens-toi de moi* suggests that the young woman's refusal of conventional gender roles and her syncretic acquisition of aspects of both French and Maghrebi culture can lead to a different sort of social solidarity and belonging.

Notes

1 An earlier version of this chapter was presented at a conference on 'Entertaining Ideologies and European Cinema' at Keele University in 1997. It was originally published as 'Gender, Ethnicity and Identity in Contemporary French Cinema: The Case of the Young Maghrebi-French woman', *Iris*, 1997, 24, 125–35, and re-printed in Farid Aitsiselmi (ed.) (2000), *Black, Blanc, Beur: Youth Language and Identity in France*, University of Bradford: Interface, Bradford Studies in Language, Culture and Society, 5, 83–93.

2 There have been a number of documentaries and short films by *beur* women film-makers, for example Fejria Deliba's prize-winning short *Le Petit Chat est mort* (1992), which explores the problematic relationship between mother and daughter from the daughter's point of view. Mention should also be made of *La Nuit du doute* by Cheikh Djemaï (1989), which dramatises the anguish experienced by a young woman of Maghrebi descent torn between her white French boyfriend and her family and friends. *Sa vie à elle* (1995), a TV film directed by Romain Goupil and co-scripted by Ghorab-Volta, sensitively explores the identity of a schoolgirl of Maghrebi descent who chooses to wear the veil. Since 1996, Rachid Bouchareb has directed *L'Honneur de ma famille* (1997), discussed in chapter 9, which focuses on the inter-ethnic friendship between two young women – one *beur*, one white – while Abdelkrim Bahloul's third film, *Les Soeurs Hamlet* (1998), addresses the problematic identity of two mixed-race teenage sisters, brought up by their (white) mother and separated from their Algerian father.

3 The experiences of young women of Maghrebi descent have been evoked at length in numerous semi-autobiographical novels of the 1980s and 1990s. For an early study, see Hargreaves (1991).

4 See for example Wallet, Nehas and Sghiri (1996), Guénif Souilamas (2000), Flanquart (2003). See also Djura (1993) for a lively and thoughtful account of
   Maghrebi-French women's experiences in contemporary France.
5 The controversial suspension of three Muslims girls from their state school in 1989
   for the wearing of the Islamic headscarf (the *foulard* or *hijab*) generated an acri-
   monious debate about the role of Islam in France in relation to Republican secular
   institutions such as the state education system. See Hargreaves (1995: 125–31). See
   also Dayan-Herzbrun (2000). In 2003, the wearing of the Islamic headscarf in
   school became a key political issue, leading in February 2004 to the passing of a
   controversial law banning all 'ostentatious' religious symbols in school, a law interpreted by many as a sign of anti-Muslim racism (see Nordmann 2004).
6 Malik Chibane had to overcome similar difficulties in the making of *Hexagone.*
7 See for example Mercer and Julien (1986) and hooks (1989).
8 See chapter 7 for a discussion of *Samia* (2001) and *La Squale* (2000), made after this
   article was written.

6

Masculinity and exclusion in post-1995 *beur* and *banlieue* films[1]

The 1995 phenomenon of the *banlieue* film in French cinema was associated with the advent of a new generation of filmmakers (born in the late 1950s and 1960s) whose films, not unproblematically, have been grouped under the label of *le jeune cinéma français* ('young French cinema') or *la nouvelle Nouvelle Vague* ('the new New Wave') (see Trémois 1997; Chauville 1998; Marie 1998; Prédal 2002).[2] Many of these filmmakers demonstrated a newfound concern with documenting social realities, including the anger and frustration suffered by those who find themselves socially excluded, a concern which was also manifest in their support of the *sans-papiers* (see Powrie 1999: 10–16). Whilst a number of their films about the alienation of contemporary youth centre primarily, and more conventionally, on the existential angst of the (white) privileged bourgeois or intellectual classes (such as Cédric Klapisch's *Le Péril jeune*, 1993; Xavier Beauvois' *N'oublie pas que tu va mourir*, 1995; Pascale Ferran's *L'Age des possibles*, 1995; Arnaud Desplechin's *Comment je me suis disputé. . . (ma vie sexuelle)*, 1996), a significant body of both *beur*- and white-authored films have continued to focus, like *La Haine*, on disadvantaged youths from the deprived *banlieue* housing estates or inner-city ghettos in France. At a time when rightwing discourses relating to France's postcolonial others continue to encapsulate the fears and anxieties of the majority white population, the representations of such marginalised masculinities are of crucial significance.

Like the first *beur* films of the 1980s and most of the *banlieue* films of 1995, *La Haine* foregrounds a group of disaffected, unemployed working-class youths at an age when they would normally aspire to adult masculinity. Typically, the young protagonists, here a *black-blanc-beur* trio, find it difficult if not impossible to assert their masculinity in socially acceptable ways. Arguably their socioeconomic deprivation combined with an apparent lack of any acceptable paternal role models (a common trope of both *beur* and *banlieue* films) prevent them from assuming an active role in society through work, a family, and a place of their own. Instead, they seek to protest at their emasculation though an overaggressive but ultimately self-defeating performance of phallic masculinity. As Vincendeau notes, they are actually 'anomic, helpless and hopeless. Their aggression . . . is random and self-defeating . . . [they] stay at home in a state of perpetual childhood' (Vincendeau 2000: 323). At the same time, in contrast to American black-gang crime films (Albert Hughes' *Menace II Society*, 1993, for example), films such as *La Haine* tend to emphasise the commonality of underclass experiences of the *fracture sociale* ('social divide') through peer-group solidarity, regardless of ethnic differences. They thus underline the significance of class and social exclusion in the performance of masculinity. However, whilst the focus on male bonding may, within a limited context, produce positive images of cross-race integration, it risks effacing not just female experiences (or the experiences of older inhabitants of the *banlieue*) but also the specificity of ethnic minority experiences and the possibility of alternative performances of masculinity.

I argued in chapter 4 that there were in fact considerable differences of emphasis between white and *beur*-authored *banlieue* films, the former foregrounding cross-race male violence, the latter more concerned with how individual ethnic minority (*beur*) youths confront and negotiate problems of identity and integration in a social context in which they are excluded on grounds of both class and ethnicity. In this chapter I want to examine whether similar differences can be found in post-1995 *beur* and *banlieue* films. I am therefore going to compare the construction of masculinity and violence in two chronicles of life in the ghetto, *Ma 6-T va crack-er* (1997) and *Comme un aimant* (2000), the most obvious successors to *La Haine*, and in the 1999 hit comedy *Le Ciel, les oiseaux . . . et ta mère*.[3] *Ma 6-T*, a second film by Jean-François Richet, is set in Richet's home *banlieue* estate of Beauval-Collinet in Meaux, to the east of Paris (where he still lives, as does his co-writer, actor and cousin, Arco Descat C.); *Comme un aimant*, a first feature co-written and co-directed by Kamel Saleh (a *beur*) and Akhenaton (the stage name of Philippe Fragione, star of Marseilles rap group IAM, who is of Italian immigrant descent), is set in the Panier district of Marseilles (like Karim Dridi's *Bye-Bye*, 1995). In contrast *Le Ciel*, a first feature by Djamel Bensalah (a *beur* from Saint-Denis, to the north of Paris), displaces its *banlieue* youths into the alien setting of the ultra-white bourgeois seaside resort of Biarritz. Arguably, the shift in setting enables the mechanisms of masculine performativity and male bonding to be rendered more transparent.

There are certain resemblances between the three films on the level of theme and style: the foregrounding of a disadvantaged young male peer group of diverse ethnic origins, a loosely structured episodic plot rather than a goal-oriented linear narrative, location shooting, the periodic use of a handheld camera, the lack of glamorisation of the principal protagonists, an emphasis on the youths' at times impenetrable *banlieue* slang, the expression of macho yet largely impotent attitudes towards women, and the conspicuous absence of family life (a factor which distinguishes these films from earlier *beur* films). Where they differ is in terms of genre. The first two aim for a degree of realism, drawing on 'authentic' settings (the *banlieue* housing estate, the inner-city ghetto) and a cast of amateur actors, friends and acquaintances of the director(s), who also perform in the films themselves. They both focus on large, loosely formed gangs of unemployed males whose anger and frustration at their continuing marginalisation from mainstream society, itself a form of emasculation, drives them deeper and deeper into violence and confrontation with the police. *Le Ciel*, however, is a teen/summer holiday comedy of manners, set far from the *banlieue*, which centres on a smaller number of protagonists, one of whom is played by Jamel Debbouze, who has since become a hugely successful stand-up comedian and comic actor. Its plot, such as it is, studiously avoids the physical, criminal violence which structures *Ma 6-T* and *Comme un aimant*, channelling the youths' aggression in particular into their use of language. Like *La Haine*, *Le Ciel* also incorporates a critical reflection on the stereotypical way the media construct youth and violence in the multi-ethnic *banlieue*, for which by implication it aims to offer an alternative.

My argument is that, despite commonalities in their constructions of testosterone-fuelled underclass youths, the representation of disempowered masculinity in these three films is inflected in ways that relate to the cultural background and ethnic origins of their directors. Although Richet's racialisation of the *banlieue* expresses solidarity with those who are persistently discriminated against, its use of violence risks making a negative impact on majority French audiences; in contrast the incorporation of white ethnicities in the two *beur*-authored films marks a bid for integration and is accompanied by a less alienating use of violence. In their address to a mainstream audience, they indicate more clearly than *Ma 6-T* that their protagonists' aggressive masculinity is a way of compensating for exclusion that masks an inner vulnerability.[4]

Ma 6-T va crack-er/My C-T is Gonna Crack (1997)

In *Ma 6-T va crack-er*, Richet, a self-proclaimed Marxist, constructs a male-centred fantasy of revolution in the *banlieue*, culminating in a climactic rap-accompanied battle between the youths and the CRS riot police, who are represented in Manichaean fashion as the irredeemable class enemy. Paradoxically, the violence is introduced in a prologue sequence centred on white actress Virginie Ledoyen (to whom the film is dedicated), who is shot direct to camera with a little girl by her side, waving a red flag and then loading a Kalashnikov, against a background of images of international revolution and a rap accompaniment. The sequence ends with her pointing handguns at both her head and heart and closing her eyes (followed by a fade to black and the

sound of an offscreen gunshot). Reprised near the end of the film, this excessive image of potentially self-destructive female violence can perhaps best be
read as a sign of the film's political confusion, glamorisation of violence, and
inability to imagine a constructive vision of the postrevolutionary future.

The film has no clear linear narrative and deliberately makes little attempt
to establish its multiple male protagonists as individuals (Masson 1998: 115).
Shot mostly in the public spaces in and around the depressing blocks of flats
and local shopping centre, the youths' aggression derives from the fact that
they are both confined to the estate (there are no scenes shot outside the *banlieue*) and unsettled there (they are regularly disturbed by the police or rival
youths). The film revolves around two particular mixed-race gangs – one
school-age (principally Arco, Malik and Mustafa), one older (principally Djeff,
JM, Pete and Hamouda) – both of which are actively involved in violence, petty
thieving and hostilities with the police. The tone is set in the opening scenes as
Arco and friends get temporarily expelled over violence at school and the older
youths are involved in altercations with their rivals over drug payments. The
two gangs are linked by the fact that Djeff and Arco (played respectively by the
director and his co-writer) live in the same flat and jointly set fire to a litter bin
which they throw down onto a police patrol car. The film suggests that the
younger boys turn to their elder brothers as role models rather than to parental
or other authority figures. Parents are noticeably absent from the diegesis and
the authority figures who take their place – the white, female head teacher, the
black gym teacher, older residents on the estate – are openly mocked and their
advice in favour of restraint ignored.

The violence comes to a head on the night of a hip-hop concert, intercut
with shots of the rappers protesting about the state of the estate and the role
of the police, and defiantly affirming their masculinity, 'We're guys who never
give in' (*'Nous sommes des gars qui ne lâchent rien'*). For some twenty minutes
the film builds up tension (or tries to) through relentless crosscutting
sequences. First it cuts between three of the younger gang setting fire to a car
outside the supermarket (venting their frustration at not getting in to the concert) and an American-style shoot-out between the rival older gangs outside
the concert. Then, when Malik is shot dead by the police (a *bavure* which
recalls the starting-point of *La Haine*), it cuts between the mass of rioting
youths (smashing up and setting fire to cars and telephone boxes) and the
arrival of the CRS in force and in full riot gear. And finally, it cuts between the
battle with the police – with the youths hurling petrol bombs and setting a
policeman on fire – and the rappers whose rap number carries the message
that 'sedition is the solution' (figure 19). The interminable accumulation of
violence and destruction, occasionally tempered by clichéd slow panning
shots, may be intended to give the audience cathartic pleasure along with the
sounds and rhythm of the rap music, but the effect is rather to emphasise

19 The battle between *banlieue* youths and the CRS in *Ma 6-T va crack-er* (1997).

Richet's deadening use of violence as designer spectacle, despite his claims to the contrary (Masson 1998: 115).

Ma 6-T thus constructs an over-extended, reactionary image of phallic masculinity in the *banlieue*, based on the belief that underclass youths should never show signs of weakness and that violent action, preferably with a gun, is the only way of countering disempowerment. The film celebrates such violence by piling up mini-narratives in which criminal activities go unpunished and encounters with aggressive law officers (including a white woman) often lead to the police being overpowered (a shot of a poster advertising the left-of-centre weekly *Le Nouvel Observateur* displays the headline, 'The estates where the police no longer dare go'!). The screen becomes invaded not just by the police but by increasing numbers of virtually interchangeable angry youths who share the same looks, language, gestures and actions. Clearly Richet wants to minimise racial or ethnic differences in order to foreground the youths' potential as a revolutionary class (and the end credits list his acknowledgement to Engels, Marx and Eisenstein, among others). However, the lack of differentiation between individual protagonists, or between criminal violence and violence against the police, means that there is little possibility of establishing identification or sympathy for a mainstream audience.[5] Richet ends the film with a coda sequence set in another *banlieue*, where a *beur* motorcyclist gets shot dead when he fails to stop for the police. Presumably he wants the audience to react to yet another representation of unjustified violence on the part of the representatives of the bourgeois state by starting a riot; at the same time, the image of yet another death also seems to acknowledge the hopelessness and ineffectuality of that position, and the film's final message, the reproduction of Article 35 of the Declaration of Human Rights claiming the right to insurrection, reads like wishful thinking rather than a call to action.

In fact, there are moments of respite in the violence when a more sympathetic image of masculinity damaged by social exclusion and dysfunctional families struggles to surface. At several points, the film shows the youths sitting around talking about their lack of communication with their parents, their lack of hope for the future, their feelings of being invaded and persecuted by the police, and the need for revolutionary change. However, the failure of the youths' relationships with women, a trope for their impotence in the wider world, is extremely troubling. Despite their macho talk, no sexual relationships are shown on screen, and their occasional interactions with women demonstrate the powerlessness underlying their aggression (unlike *Etat des lieux*, which ends with a scene of frenetic sexual intercourse).[6] Whenever Djeff and JM try to chat up a passing woman, they can only do so through verbal bullying and physical harassment. In each case the woman is capable of putting them in their place, though only by accepting a degree of unwanted physical contact. The film seems implicitly to recognise the inadequacy of such behaviour by suggesting that none of the youths is able to progress beyond a state of prolonged adolescence (the scene in which they plan the shoot-out takes place in a children's playground). But at the same time it also celebrates their aggressive masculinity through the aestheticisation of their subsequent violence, and offers no alternative vision of their future beyond the imagined purification brought about by burning and rioting. Unfortunately, as Will Higbee (2001b: 202) has argued, such imagery risks contributing to the 'already exaggerated media representation of the disadvantaged urban periphery as the site of violence and delinquency which warrants the repressive police presence'.

Comme un aimant/*The Magnet* (2000)

Comme un aimant differs from *Ma 6-T* in its initially humorous tone, its use of space, and its more obviously differentiated and individualised protagonists. The film centres on a group of eight young men in their mid-twenties, all either of Italian or Maghrebi immigrant descent. It is set mainly in the narrow streets of the Panier district where its protagonists grew up and hang out (punctuated by shots of the bench and bar where they congregate, as well as of patrolling police cars), but it embraces the whole of Marseilles, linking the *quartier* to the city in a way which is very different from the geographical anonymity of *Ma 6-T*. The film's setting underlines the economic insecurity and social (and also racial) exclusion suffered by its young male protagonists, who regularly leave the area to find something to do (have some fun, make some money), but find themselves frustrated and disillusioned (unable to get the girls or carry out their crimes successfully, suffering from racial hostility, and discovering that the Mafia and even the younger kids have more of a place in the city than they do). They are drawn back to the Panier like a magnet (the title comes from a rap number in IAM's 1993 album),[7] but their inability to move on (or grow up) draws them into a spiral of violence which leads to tragedy and pathos rather than to the revolutionary anger which fuels *Ma 6-T*.

The film begins light-heartedly with a sequence in which Santino (Titoff) drives past the sea in a red sports car and tries (unsuccessfully) to chat up a passing young woman. It is followed by sequences demonstrating that Santino and his friends are fundamentally likeable lads looking for a good time, rather than hardened criminals. First they sell boxes of stolen video-recorders to a couple of black guys, all but one of which contain nothing but stones. Then they try to gain access to a nightclub (a typical trope of *beur* and *banlieue* films), which they eventually manage by paying the black bouncer to kit them out in fancy (more feminised) clothes (though their summer clothing of shorts and short-sleeved T-shirts already gives them a softer, more feminised look than the combat-style sports clothing worn by the youths of *Ma 6-T*).[8] As the film progresses, however, their actions produce increasingly serious repercussions, and the spaces of the Panier become dominated by shots of railings and other signs of imprisonment. (They also get captured 'on screen', either as images of police cars are seen on, or reflected on, the television, or because of a video surveillance screen.) Houari's mistake in blurting out their address to the guys they have conned leads to Cahuète spending a couple of nights in jail; Christian is hit by a car when trying to steal a handbag and badly damaged, both mentally and physically; Fouad is shot dead by a security guard when he attempts an armed robbery; and Kakou and Houari are arrested in a robbery which has been set up by a police informant. In a parallel narrative strand, Santino's frustrated attempt to get in with a gang of older Mafiosi leads not just to him getting badly beaten up for not returning the money he owes, but also to the demise of Brabra and Sauveur, who attempt to avenge him: Brabra's fate remains unknown but Sauveur is shot dead on the pavement in cold blood. So the film's narrative structure demonstrates the young men's inability to handle crime and violence, producing a very different inflection on masculinity from that of *Ma 6-T*.

The spiralling towards tragedy is punctuated by sequences detailing the failure of their relationships with women and with their families, giving them a solidity and individuality lacking in the more undifferentiated figures of *Ma 6-T*, and also allowing female figures to play a slightly more significant role. For example, feckless Sauveur (Akhenaton) is rejected by his *beurette* girlfriend, Soraya, to the applause of other women in the street, and evicted from his home by his angry Italian immigrant father, who accuses him of 'not being a man' because he has not got a job; he takes shelter in a cellar, through the barred window of which he is befriended by a little Bosnian girl refugee. Brabra, Fouad and Kakou are unable to make out with the French girls with whom Brabra arranges a date, despite their intense preparations, and Brabra discovers that the girl he fancies votes for the Front National. Fouad is gently reproached for his constant absence by his Algerian immigrant mother, but is so destabilised by her death that he gets himself shot trying to hold up a jeweller's shop. Santino is forced to pay back the mob by stealing a cheque from his beloved Italian immigrant grandmother, and is left humiliated and in tears.

The exception to this pattern is Cahuète (Saleh), the most intellectual of the group (he is seen holding a copy of Dante's *Inferno*) and also the most settled and mature (he has a stable relationship with a supportive *beurette* girlfriend, whose flat is lined with shelves of books). Able to keep his cool when he is held for questioning (although the spectator shares his nightmare fantasy of being shot by a sadistic policeman), he speculates about giving up a life of crime, but can see no acceptable alternative. The film ends on what appears to be an apocalyptic revenge for what has happened to his friends. He drives off in an unattended petrol tanker, spreads petrol through the streets of Marseilles, sets the petrol alight, and then drives high above the city to watch it burn (the shots of fire filling the screen mirroring shots in *Ma 6-T*). However, a close-up of Cahuète closing and re-opening his eyes cuts back not to fire and destruction but to a view of the city intact. The violence proves to have been merely imaginary, and the last image of Cahuète's impassive gaze suggests that it is his ability to redirect his anger into fantasy (like Saleh, the actor–director) that makes him the lonely, silent survivor.

The film's shift from a light-hearted opening to a more serious, elegiac ending is underlined near the film's end by a silent slow-motion flashback sequence showing the group of friends as happy, carefree youths messing about in the sun and the sea. A sense of nostalgia is also promoted by the soundtrack (a hybrid mix of rap, pop and classical music by Akhenaton and classical composer Bruno Coulais, which draws on 1970s soul music as well as Italian and Corsican popular songs). Dedicated to 'Alhassan and other friends who have disappeared', the film's protest at the fate of a lost generation recognises that its dream of revolt against injustice is just a fantasy. Rather than uncritically celebrating youthful male violence as a way of compensating for social exclusion, like *Ma 6-T*, *Comme un aimant* demonstrates its inadequacy. Yet at the same time it, too, has little to offer as an alternative and, arguably, the youths fail because their softness and incompetence forces them to give way to the superior performances of masculine violence demonstrated by the police and the Mafia.

Le Ciel, les oiseaux . . . et ta mere!/Boys on the Beach (1999)

Le Ciel, les oiseaux . . . et ta mere! draws its humour from the displacement of the *black-blanc-beur* male group typical of the *banlieue* film into an alien and potentially hostile setting. The opening pre-credit sequence, set in an underground car park in St-Denis, shows a trio of school-leavers fabricating a video documentary about a *banlieue* drug dealer, played by their classmate, Mike (Julien Courbey), who obligingly re-does his lines wearing a hood and smoking a joint to look more 'authentic'. Their film fools the judges and wins them a holiday in Biarritz, leaving spectators to anticipate that *Le Ciel* itself will offer alternative representations of *banlieue* youth. Indeed, the film self-consciously distances itself from drugs and violence and interactions with the police. Instead it offers the spectacle of three rather pathetic, penniless youths – Youssef (Jamel), the *beur*, Christophe (Lorent Deutsch), the 'white', and Stéphane (Stéphane Soo Mongo), the 'black' – who arrive in Biarritz with the rather over-optimistic hope of picking up lots of girls and little to their credit except a video camera and an extraordinary propensity for *banlieue* slang. Bensalah claims to have been looking at the films of Scorsese, Coppola and De Palma for inspiration for a filmmaking style that would 'tear the generation of my little twelve-year-old sister away from American films' (Médioni 1999: 103). But this film has little to offer his sister in its focus on male bonding, its casual misogyny, and its evacuation of ethnic minority girls and women.

Like *Ma 6-T* and *Comme un aimant*, *Le Ciel* has no clear goal-oriented narrative drive. It consists of a series of loosely linked episodes in the day-to-day lives of its protagonists, humorously punctuated by their clumsy, amateur video footage (and occasionally by other inserts: a 1950s promotional film of Biarritz, a supermarket surveillance screen, fish-bowl shots through the flat door's spy-hole, clips of pornographic and Hollywood films, and the final self-reflexive end credit sequence in which Youssef/Jamel jokes that, 'We could be in a film'). Suffering from a lack of funds and sexual know-how, the lads spend their time aimlessly hanging around watching television, messing about in the kitchen, shopping, lying on the beach, playing with their video camera, and moaning about the boredom of life in Biarritz. At first, they attribute their inability to attract girls to their lack of money (they get moved on from the sofa they are sprawling on in a nightclub because they cannot afford a drink); later, when Mike joins them and suggests pretending to make a video documentary about young people on holiday, their plans for seduction are foiled because his car runs out of petrol. More significantly, they repeatedly refuse the invitation of Lydie (Olivia Bonamy), a Parisian girl in the neighbouring holiday flat, to join in a game of volleyball on the beach. The image of *banlieue* youth constructed here is thus primarily one of enforced domesticity, passivity and sexual inadequacy, enhanced by their unthreatening, youthful appearance: three of them are small and thin, including Youssef who also has a damaged arm (and writes home to his Mum), and Stéphane may be large but he is also soft and the most domesticated of the four (figure 20). In addition, the film draws attention to Youssef's vulnerability to racism, first when the concierge gives the key to Christophe rather than him (he calls her Mme Mégret, after the Front National politician), then in his confrontation with a bus conductor (Sam Karmann) who, having asked him for his nationality when his ID card clearly indicates that he is French, then imposes an unjustified fine. It thus demonstrates the youths' lack of belonging, contrasting them with the posh (white) '*Biarritziens*' like the 'surfers' to whom Youssef constantly refers.

Instead of resorting to physical violence to deal with their exclusion, the youths use their video camera and their potentially offensive language as a way of asserting their presence and their masculinity. Their group solidarity is clearly based in part on shared anxieties about their sexuality, emphasised by their sexist comments and sexual slang. It is also reinforced by their anti-Semitism, evident in Youssef's dislike of Steven Spielberg and refusal to see the Jewish-centred hit comedy *La Vérité si je mens!*. However, the film also offers a critique of this position through Youssef's budding relationship with the unbelievably patient and forbearing Lydie. Youssef is at first unable or unwilling to

20 The passivity of the *black-blanc-beur* trio in *Le Ciel, les oiseaux ... et ta mère* (1999).

respond to Lydie's interest in him and admit his attraction to her and, after a fanciful game of Scrabble in which they appear to be getting closer, he recoils when he notices her Star of David. When Lydie angrily accuses him of racism, Youssef responds by pointing out that people in Biarritz will not mix with him and his friends (her two girlfriends being a case in point), reducing her to silence and tears. However, the narrative ends with Youssef pursuing her to the airport to return the eggs he had borrowed and give her his phone number in Paris, a scene that duly ends with a kiss. The audience is invited to believe that Youssef's racist and macho posturing is just a defensive bluff and that he has been won over to romance with a woman who is also vulnerable to racism. At the same time, the potentially threatening theme of cross-race sexuality is defused by the deferral of sexual gratification to an uncertain future.

The deconstruction of the rhetoric of macho masculinity underpinning male bonding is reworked in the activities of Christophe, who is goaded by his mates to chat up Christelle (which he does by imagining himself in the role of a Hollywood movie star, a sequence which is shot in black and white and heavily accented English). Unexpectedly successful, Christophe is the only one of the group actually to have sex (Stéphane does not go near a woman, and ugly Mike's insensitive attempts to chat up women regularly meet with disaster). However, his affair brings about the group's disintegration, since he is too ashamed of his friends to introduce them to Christelle, and Stéphane, who is already fed up with Youssef's 'platonic affair' with Lydie, feels so let down that he decides to leave. Christophe attempts to retrieve the situation by claiming that his relationship with Christelle is just a holiday fuck, but when Christelle overhears and walks out on him, he is genuinely upset and can no longer function happily within the remaining trio. Clearly their adolescent male bonding is dependent on their ability to score and scorn women, not to have relationships. The film ends with them setting off for Paris in silence, having broken the video camera, leaving open the question as to whether it is possible for underclass male bonding to survive the intrusion of the feminine and the transition from adolescence to maturity which such a relationship implies. Arguably, then, the film moves towards a critique of their boorish behaviour, exposing it as a masquerade covering over their sexual anxieties (as in the repeated taunts about Christophe and Mike still being virgins). At the same time, however, it also invites the spectator to enjoy their casual misogyny, in particular through the sparky irreverence of Jamel's virtuoso verbal performance.

Conclusion

Like *La Haine*, these three films each articulate a multi-voiced, cross-race protest at the ongoing exclusion of underclass male youths from the pleasures and stabilities of mainstream society. Nevertheless there are significant differences between them. *Ma 6-T va crack-er* offers images of 'hard' masculinity and a narrative of increasing, excessive and, to some extent, successful violence. Arguably, such a narrative is only possible in a film by a white director, because it risks endangering the precarious integration of France's ethnic minority others by constructing them in stereotypical fashion as threatening and dangerous (though it does also single out *beur* youths as the principal victims of police violence). *Comme un aimant* and *Le Ciel, les oiseaux . . . et ta mère*, the two films by *beur* directors, offer images of a 'softer', less threatening masculinity and use strategies which defuse or avoid scenes of confrontation and violence, injecting comedy, putting more focus on individual dilemmas (including the experience of racial hostility), and stressing the difficulties of gaining a purchase on the world, be it through crime (as in *Comme un aimant*) or through amorous adventures (as in *Le Ciel*).

All three films use the sexual impotence of their young male protagonists as a trope for their lack of agency in the wider world. Despite the vociferous assertion of their heterosexuality, the youths in question are generally unable to work through their Oedipal trajectory and achieve adulthood by forging mature, satisfactory sexual relationships. Furthermore, their inability to form a couple seems to be a precondition of the cross-race male bonding which informs these films, rendered explicit in *Le Ciel*, but implicit in the other two films in their repeated demonstrations of the youths' failure to engage adequately with women. Yet in contrast to *Ma 6-T*, both *beur*-authored films gesture towards other possibilities for their *beur* protagonists, be it through Cahuète's self-containment and survival in *Comme un aimant* or Youssef's last-minute realisation in *Le Ciel* of the potential permeability of the boundaries of sex, class and ethnicity. Thus, if post 1995 *banlieue* films about disadvantaged youths seem disturbingly unable or unwilling to envisage alternative, more mature and empowering performances of underclass masculinity, it is nevertheless the *beur*-authored films, with their stake in integration, that offer a more nuanced view.

Notes

1 An earlier version of this chapter was first presented at a conference on 'Exploring Masculinities and Film' at the University of Newcastle in 2001, and published in P. Powrie, A. Davies and B. Babington (eds), *The Trouble with Men: Masculinities in European and Hollywood Cinema*, London and New York: Wallflower Press, 2004, 110–19.

2 As Myrto Konstantarakos (1998) has argued in her review of the literature, however, these films are far from constituting a homogenous grouping.

3 Another film of interest in this context is Djamel Ouahab's *Cour interdite* (1999), a low-budget but artful, stylish black-and-white *film noir*, shot in a series of deserted streets and courtyards with a cast of non-actors, and a narrative organised around gang rivalry, drugs and violence. Ouahab, a self-taught filmmaker, himself plays the central character, Illyr, who is finally caught by the police when trying to find out what has happened to his friend Paco. The film displays a very pessimistic, black vision of the future of disadvantaged youth, embodied in the point of view of Illyr's sad mother, whose oldest son is already in prison, and who is trying to protect her youngest son, Claquette, whose dream of New York opens the film. (The actor playing Claquette subsequently died in a fight at a party.) The film took six years to make, and was financed in part by Luc Besson's father.

4 These differences were reflected in their distribution. *Ma 6-T* was withdrawn from general distribution because of fears of incitement to violence, whereas *Le Ciel* was selected for international distribution as part of the Martell French Cinema Tour of the UK in 2000.

5 This contrasts with *beur* films such as Malik Chibane's *Hexagone* (1994), where the protagonists are individuated through a wide variety of social interactions (see chapter 2).

6 Richet's third film *De l'amour* (2001) centres on mixed-race couple Marie (Virginie Ledoyen) and Karim (Yazid Aït), but disappointingly turns into a very crude rape revenge film rather than a study of a mature inter-racial relationship.

7 The image of the magnet (*l'aimant*) is as fatalistic as the image of the fall from a high building in *La Haine*.

8 Their fundamental harmlessness is also embodied in the figure of Kader, a simple-minded gentle giant.

7

Grrrls in the *banlieue*: *Samia* and *La Squale*[1]

If the cinematic *banlieue* is constructed as a site of difference, plurality and otherness, the *banlieue* film, as discussed in chapters 4 and 6, is also primarily concerned with articulating the crisis in young *beur*, black and/or white under-class masculinities. With few exceptions (see chapter 5), the visual texture of the *banlieue* film gives preference to spaces represented as male domains. The women who inhabit them are generally silenced, relegated to minor or secondary roles, and/or constructed through stereotypes. Two white-male-authored films of the early 2000s, however, focus on girl power in the *banlieue*: *Samia* (Philippe Faucon, 2001) and *La Squale* (Fabrice Génestal, 2000). *Samia* is an adaptation of Soraya Nini's 1993 novel, *Ils disent que je suis une beurette*, co-written with Nini herself and based loosely on the author's own experiences of growing up. *La Squale*, Génestal's first film (which was nominated as such for the 2001 Césars), originated in a project initiated by the head teacher of a secondary school where Génestal was a teacher, and features two young ethnic minority women, a *renoi* (black girl) and a *beurette*. Co-written with Nathalie Vailloud (and others), it developed out of the testimonies of adolescents regarding the practice of *les tournantes*, or gang rapes, in the *banlieue*.[2] Both films thus draw their topics indirectly from lived events and use a strong cast of non-actors and location shooting. Moreover, despite obvious differences – *Samia* is a realist chronicle of growing up in an immigrant Algerian family, *La Squale* a more melodramatic action narrative dependent on the tropes of the *banlieue* film – both received positive critical reviews underlining their perceived authenticity.[3] Yet both also generated controversy, *Samia* because of its negative construction of the traditional immigrant Algerian family,[4] *La Squale* because of its shocking indictment of *banlieue* life.[5] Bearing these criticisms in mind, I want to examine how relations of power are inscribed in the spaces of the *banlieue* they project, and what connections can be traced between their spatial and sexual politics.

Feminine spaces in cinema have conventionally been coded, as Elisabeth Mahoney points out, as 'enigmatic, silent and the negative Other, but also as a "support or precondition" of the masculine and social' (Mahoney 1997: 173, quoting from Grosz 1995: 50). The spaces of the city available to young ethnic minority women in mainstream French cinema are doubly othered by the legacy of colonial stereotyping. City streets and public spaces are frequented by transgressive, sexualised women, from the Maghrebi prostitute of *Grand frère* (François Girod, 1982) and the exotic, drug-addicted dancer of *Clubbed to Death* (Yolande Zauberman, 1997) to the black and Maghrebi prostitutes of *Gamer* (Zak Fishman, 2001) (figure 21). In contrast, domestic spaces contain the victims of the oppressive patriarchal Arabo-Islamic sex/gender system, from the tragic heroine of *Pierre et Djemila* (Gérard Blain, 1986) to the sister who needs rescuing in *Chaos* (Coline Serreau, 2001). Thus, representations of the spaces occupied by young women of immigrant origin, aimed primarily at a majority French audience, tend either to exoticise the ethnic other or, as Deniz Göktürk argues in relation to the representation of Turkish women in German cinema, to construct 'hypocritical narratives of rescue, liberation and Westernisation' (Göktürk 2000: 66).

Nevertheless, as discussed in earlier chapters of this book, a growing number of films of the 1990s challenged the absence of young ethnic minority women in the city as the subjects and agents of history and change. In Malik Chibane's *Hexagone* (1994) and *Douce France* (1995), young women of Maghrebi descent occupy public spaces without being reduced to stereotypical roles. And young *beur* women are the principal protagonists of Anne Fontaine's *Les Histoires d'amour finissent mal en général* (1993), Zaïda Ghorab-Volta's *Souviens-toi de moi* (1996) and Rachid Bouchareb's *L'Honneur de ma famille* (1997), while a Maghrebi woman is the heroine of Rachida Krim's *Sous les pieds des femmes* (Tarr 2000). These women-authored films foreground hitherto marginalised female subjectivities and identities and in the process contest women's place within both the domestic and the public spheres.

It is notable that both *La Squale* and *Samia* focus on teenage schoolgirls and their quest for identity at the awkward, vulnerable moment of the transition from adolescence to adulthood. Representations of the adolescent girl in mainstream French cinema have often been associated with the display of the nubile female body as the object of the spectator's gaze, and this is certainly an issue in *La Squale*. However, in both these films the feisty teenagers are the principal subjects of the narrative, actively seeking their place in the world by defying dominant configurations of gender and space, both at home and in the outside world. *Samia* does so through a realist representation of the eponymous heroine's conflictual relationship with her immigrant Algerian family (the film is set and shot in the *banlieue* of Marseilles). *La Squale* (the 'shark', a slang expression for a girl warrior) does so more problematically through a female revenge narrative that allows its teenage heroine momentarily to appropriate the male-dominated spaces of the Parisian *banlieue* (shot in part in Sarcelles). Both films

21 Béatrice Dalle as the exotic, drug-addicted dancer in *Clubbed to Death* (1997).

end by transporting their protagonists into transnational spaces of female solidarity and potential self-realisation. But it is a matter of concern that they identify the oppressive immigrant *banlieue* family and the patriarchal violence of young men of immigrant origin as the chief obstacles that stand in their way. Although both Génestal and Faucon in interviews attribute violence towards women to the pressures of an impossible socio-economic situation (including long-term unemployment and institutional racism), *La Squale* in particular fails to embed its narrative within the wider French social context.

Samia (2001)

Samia begins with a scene that neatly encapsulates its heroine's problematic place in French society. It is set in a school classroom, and the camera focuses on fifteen-year-old Samia (Lynda Benahouda) as she is subjected to careers counselling from a (white) teacher who suggests that, if she gets poor results, she might be advised to train as 'une employée de collectivité' (a technical euphemism which clearly hints at a dead-end job as a cleaner). Sullen but not inarticulate, Samia responds sardonically by pointing out that she already does this sort of work at home. The scene draws attention to the hierarchies of power that configure this institutional social space and hints at the connection between Samia's ethnicity and her unsuccessful schooling; at the same time it establishes Samia as a bright, rebellious teenager with a critical voice and an uncompromising attitude. In the following scene, Samia's older brother, Yacine (Mohamed Chaouch), materialises in front of her in the street in order to make sure that she returns home without delay. The juxtaposition demonstrates the 'inbetweenness' of Samia's life, torn between and restricted by both (white, French) social expectations and her (Algerian) family's patriarchal traditions. The rest of the narrative is concerned with her revolt against the more restrictive aspects of her culture of origin and her struggle to find a new place for herself both within the domestic sphere and without (figure 22).

The film's principal setting is the *banlieue* flat that constitutes Samia's family home, which is immediately coded as 'other' to a majority audience. As Yacine says, 'This isn't America, it's *le bled*', a reference to Algeria confirmed by the way Amel, one of Samia's older sisters, quickly changes out of her mini-skirt before entering. Its 'foreignness' is emphasised by the visual presence of the large Algerian family (three adults, eight brothers and sisters), the use of Arabic, the foregrounding of Algerian furnishings, costumes and food, the rituals associated with Ramadan. In the first scene of family life, the camera displays the family listening to the prayer broadcast by Radio Soleil before starting their meal. The atmosphere is dominated by respect for (and fear of) the father, a sick man in need of hospitalisation whose fragile body is marked by years of exploited labour. Paternal authority is in turn vested in Yacine, the oldest son, and marked by the close, physical filming of his abusive treatment of his sisters whenever they step out of line. The oppressiveness of family life is also conveyed through the presence of the mother (Kheira Oualhaci), a large, bulky woman in traditional dress, who attempts to moderate her son's excesses but spends most of her time dragooning her daughters into doing the domestic chores and lamenting their reluctance to accept the family's traditional way of life. In such an enclosed, claustrophobic environment, Samia can never find a space of her own, even when she just wants to linger alone on the balcony with its view of the mountains.

Samia vociferously challenges the family's traditional demarcation of gender roles and objects to the restrictions on her freedom and mobility. In particular, she condemns Yacine's violent exercise of patriarchal authority, referring to her brother as the GIA (Groupe Islamiste Armé)[6] and repeatedly criticising her mother for supporting him. The lack of a space for negotiation between Yacine and his sisters becomes clear after an agitated scene in which Yacine beats up Amel for having a white French boyfriend. Amel feels she has no choice but to leave home, helped by Samia and her other sisters who smuggle out clothes for her. Subsequently, after the celebration of an Algerian wedding (an addition to the source novel which allows *pied noir* director Faucon to introduce a touch of local colour), Samia tells her mother and other women of her mother's generation that she will never get married and that she has no

22 Samia (Lynda Benahouda) and friend long for autonomy in *Samia* (2001).

desire to spend her life cooped up with children and a slave to men like them. Though the space of the family home is not impermeable to Western influences and female pleasures (the younger sisters dance to rock music in their room, while wearing western clothes and laughing at their mechanical belly-dancing doll), Samia continues to perceive it as a form of prison. Her attitude is fundamentally different from that of the beleaguered Yacine, for whom it constitutes a refuge from the outside world. As he tells the brother who suggests that he should find another way of expressing his identity, there is no other place for people like him in France. The film thus suggests that Yacine's otherwise excessive (and unacceptable) assertion of authority over his sisters needs to be understood within the context of a hostile, racist French society.

Unlike *La Squale* and other *banlieue* films, *Samia* refrains from constructing the external spaces of the *banlieue* in stereotypical fashion as the site of masculine violence and delinquency and instead hints at the atmosphere of racial tension that disempowers young people of immigrant origin. For example, Samia is subjected to verbal abuse at the bus stop, a (white) woman moves away from her on the bus, and Amel is treated in a condescending manner at the supermarket where she works. More importantly, the film clearly illustrates Yacine's disempowerment, first when he is refused an interview over the phone as soon as he gives his name, then when he intervenes to protect a youth being manhandled by the police and nearly becomes the target of police violence himself. However, for Samia and her sisters, the main source of violence in the outside world is Yacine's insistent policing of their activities (an obsession criticised by two young dyed-blonde women of Maghrebi descent, who hail Yacine from a car they are driving and tell him what they think of him). And, in fact, Samia is represented as successfully able to occupy a range of spaces in and around the *banlieue*, going shopping, roller-skating by the sea, dancing at a multi-ethnic concert and watching the boys play football. She trades insults with the racist youths at the bus stop and actively inscribes her subjectivity in the city by writing 'SAMIA LA BOSS' in the condensation on a bus window. However, her autonomy is fundamentally challenged when she gets home late after playing truant from school with her sister Naïma. After spending the day by the sea swimming and talking with her friends (including a boy who fancies her), Samia has to face Yacine's violent reaction and makes her definitive stand against her family's archaic patriarchal values.

The scene of the gynaecological examination that Yacine imposes on his sisters (another episode which does not feature in the source novel) raises the question of how the camera films the ethnic minority female body. Before Samia rebels against being examined, the spectator witnesses Naïma being forced to lower her trousers and pants and open her legs for the white male doctor to inspect her. The act is represented not through voyeuristic shots of Naïma's body, but through over-the-shoulder shots expressing her vulnerability and humiliation, focusing on the doctor's medical apparatus, the shining of the spotlight and the wielding of the speculum. The scene criticises the way in which Algerian family honour is invested in female virginity, but also represents the white-authorised virginity test as a violation of the female body. Samia's refusal to be examined or touched by others is linked to her refusal to be objectified by others, and the film shoots her active, energetic body accordingly, without subjecting it to an objectifying or eroticising gaze. Her claim to the integrity of her body is thus linked with her attempt to establish herself as an active, independent subject.

Samia's rebellion, which could have ended in tragedy, brings about a potentially optimistic narrative resolution. Exhausted by all the beatings and quarrels, Samia's mother undergoes a change of heart and makes the unprecedented decision not to tell Yacine. Instead, as she and Samia are about to leave on the ferry to Algeria for the summer, she warns him that on their return there is to be no more violence. *Samia* thus finds the solution to the oppression of women in active female solidarity within the immigrant family, and suggests that the older generation, too, is capable of change.[7] However, it is notable that this change can only take place away from the *banlieue*, in the transitional space of a boat that is actually heading for a country where women are perceived as even more oppressed. As the film cuts back from Yacine standing alone on the quayside to Samia enjoying the feel of the wind in her hair, Samia's freedom of movement appears to be achievable only at the expense of the traditional immigrant family and immigrant youths.

La Squale/The Squale (2000)

La Squale differs from *Samia* in representing the impact of girlpower on the communal, external spaces of the city as much as within the domestic sphere. The film opens with a pre-credit sequence which establishes the *banlieue* as the imagined site of masculine lawlessness, a wild space isolated from French society at large, where women have no place except as the victims of wayward young men's desire for domination. The spectator is invited to witness, with horror and fascination (accompanied by the music of Cut Killer), the seduction of a young, gullible *beurette* by handsome, smooth-talking black gang-leader Toussaint (Tony Mpoudja). Set first in the graffiti-sprayed, underground spaces of the grim, concrete estate where the young people congregate, then in Toussaint's private den, an overturned lorry container on a nearby patch of wasteland, the sequence sets up Toussaint both as an object of desire (the girl, Leila, has fallen for him; his peer group look up to him) and as the subject of sadistic, criminal behaviour (the vicious beating up of Leila's cousin/minder by the rest of his gang and the gang rape). Though the rape is not directly visualised, the sequence ends as Toussaint brands the screaming Leila with a signet ring inscribed with the letter 'S' (standing for Suleymane, his inspiration, a legendary gang leader from the *cité*). A close-up shot exposing Leila's naked, tortured flesh invites a voyeuristic, sadistic gaze that challenges expectations of a woman-centred film. However, *La Squale* subsequently works through the ways in which two young women challenge the conventional masculine disposition of space, Désirée (Esse Lawson), the 'squale' of the title, and her rival Yasmine (Stéphanie Jaubert), the more conventional, studious *beurette*.

The key to the two young women's attitudes and behaviour lies, as in *Samia*, in the representation of the immigrant family. Désirée is first seen when she appears in the school corridor, the camera panning up her athletic, androgynous body, aggressive expression and dyed-blonde short-cropped hair. Challenged by a mixed-race gang of similarly tough, aggressive young women, she establishes her credentials as the 'squale', the imagined daughter of Suleymane, by beating up a youth who pesters them in the girls' cloakroom (figure 23). However, her delinquent behaviour can be explained by the representation of her home life. Her hardworking but bitter and vindictive mother treats her with a mixture of violence and neglect, leaving her no food, punching her for stepping out of line, and driving her to spend the night outdoors. The home setting demonstrates Désirée's defiance of her mother (she sets fire to the hairdo her mother is giving a client) but also exposes her vulnerability as she sets out to acquire an alternative family in the *cité*. She seduces Toussaint because he resembles the photograph she has stolen from her mother, which she (wrongly) imagines to be that of her unknown father/Suleymane. And she looks fondly at babies and children, longing to create a loving mother–child

23 Désirée (Esse Lawson, top right) and her mixed-race girl gang in *La Squale* (2000).

bond by having a child of her own. Désirée's transgressive behaviour is thus tempered by a desire for a more conventional femininity, and although she is able (rather unconvincingly) to make her peace with her mother as soon as she reproduces her mother's mistakes – getting pregnant and then being aban- doned by her lover – the final stage in her rebellion against her mother is her decision not to have an abortion. In *La Squale*, then, the heroine's problematic performance of femininity is clearly attributed to the inadequacies of the single-parent black family.

Yasmine's position within the immigrant Maghrebi family is equally prob- lematic and raises the same issues as in *Samia*, namely, the abuse of patriarchal authority by Maghrebi men and the consequences for young women of the investment of Maghrebi family honour in female virginity (figure 24). How- ever, it is represented here in an even more oppressive way, since Yasmine lacks any sisterly support. Her father is absent (and is presumed never to be coming back), her bed-ridden mother is unable to cope and expects lonely Yasmine to undertake all the family chores, and in the absence of parental authority her violent older brother, Redouane, not only treats her like a domestic slave (and encourages her little brother to do likewise) but also invades the space of her bedroom to check on her at night. Yasmine's desire for a relationship with Tou- ssaint is clearly attributable to the need to escape family pressures, even though her trust in his feelings for her turns out to be as misplaced as Leila's. Her response to getting raped by him is to rebel against her place within the family

24 Yasmine (Stéphanie Jaubert) suffers from the abuse of patriarchal authority in *La Squale* (2000).

as the dutiful daughter, shouting at her mother, defying Redouane by pouring his drink on to the tablecloth, and offering the necklace given to her by her mother to help Désirée get an abortion.

La Squale, then, represents the immigrant families of the *banlieue* in a very negative, highly stereotypical way, through cold, enclosed spaces, non-existent fathers, dysfunctional mothers, and brothers who assume the worst aspects of an abusive patriarchal authority. However, whereas restrictive cultural traditions and/or an unloving family may account for the young women's need to rebel, Toussaint's overly vicious performance of masculinity cannot be so easily understood. Although Toussaint lacks a father, his indulgent mother and abrasive, self-confident older sisters provide him with a relatively untroubled, comfortable home background. Since the film does not take the trouble to attribute his violence to his exclusion from mainstream French society, his behaviour (like that of all the other young men) risks being 'naturalised' either as part of his ethnic minority male persona and/or as a perverse reaction to an over-feminised domestic space and/or as the inevitable product of the gloomy *banlieue* housing estate, shots of which regularly punctuate the narrative. Thus, whereas Désirée and Yasmine can both be read as positive figures of rebellion for majority audiences, Toussaint is simply represented as the monstrous 'other'.

Like other *banlieue* films, *La Squale* contains scenes in which the marginalised figures of the periphery attempt to escape the confines of the *banlieue* and establish their presence in the city centre. Early in the film, Désirée and her girl gang take a trip to the Champs-Elysées where they gleefully invade and trash an elegant beauty shop. Their exuberant behaviour briefly challenges the white middle-class occupation of the city centre and calls attention to the white-centred nature of the beauty industry (one product is called 'Porcelain'). Later, Yasmine and Toussaint hold a romantic tryst in the folly of the Buttes-Chaumont, overlooking Paris. In this pastoral urban space where Toussaint is no longer a figure of authority, Yasmine perceives him as a different, gentler person (whereas back in the *banlieue* she becomes his victim). The opening up of the familiar cityscape to alternative voices and experiences is a trope typical of the *banlieue* film, but *La Squale* is unusual in focusing on the way the city is (fleetingly) empowering for young ethnic minority women, rather than on its exclusion of young ethnic minority men.

However, the city centre does not offer the young women a permanent place of refuge, and the film is more obviously concerned with Désirée's attempt to make a place for herself in the male-dominated spaces of the *banlieue*, which she does not through her girl gang but, more conventionally, through her association with Toussaint. Désirée first sees Toussaint trying to kiss Yasmine beneath a tree in the open spaces of the *cité*, and manipulates him into claiming her as his girlfriend by taunting him about Yasmine and attracting him by her sensuous disco dancing. After they become lovers, she is admitted to the spaces he controls (his bedroom, his wasteland den and gangland headquarters) and assists him in a drugs heist (though she nearly messes it up by going to get a drink for the baby whose pram is used to transport the drugs). The fragility of her position becomes evident when she catches Toussaint, the father of her unborn child, in his den in the act of raping the vulnerable, more conventionally 'feminine' Yasmine, and she gets badly beaten up when she attacks him with her knife. However, once she realises that Toussaint is a brutal, lying rapist who will never fulfil his promises to her, she takes the law into her own hands. Entering into male terrain both literally and metaphorically, she makes his gang think, wrongly, that he stole their drugs haul, and leads them to him, getting her revenge on him by engineering his death in his own gangland headquarters.

Nevertheless, Désirée's role as active narrative agent is frequently undermined, not just by the way her narrative is embedded in that of Toussaint, but also by the way in which she is shot. Despite her androgynous appearance, ability to wield a knife and willingness to match violence with violence, she is constantly defined by the sexualisation and objectification of her body. When she first spends the night with Toussaint, the camera frames her eagerly stripping off as soon as she enters his bedroom. Similarly, when she seduces him for the last time knowing that he has betrayed her – and does so by taking charge and holding him down on the bed – unnecessary close-ups of her heaving buttocks and thighs, as well as full-frontal nudity, invite the spectator to see her not as a young teenager taking control of her life, but as an exotic object of the gaze. Furthermore, this scene also confirms her as an archetypal, duplicitous female, since she betrays Toussaint by planting the drugs under his bed immediately after making love to him. However, the film's framing of the black male body is even more pernicious. In two scenes, Toussaint's taut, muscled body is rendered abject and inert. When Leila's brother, Samir, beats him up in the gym and forces Yasmine to watch, he is stripped naked, covered in piss and (off-screen) sodomised with a bottle; at the end, as Désirée looks on, he is knifed in the stomach by his erstwhile sidekick, Anis. The film thus suggests that the young women's quest for equality and social justice can only be achieved through the humiliation or suppression of the ethnic minority male.

The murder of Toussaint by his equally violent peers provides the dramatic climax that enables Désirée and Yasmine to make their peace, and it is Yasmine who persuades Désirée that an abortion will give her a better chance of getting out of the ghetto. The film's final scene cuts abruptly (and improbably) from the cemetery to the beach at Brighton, where the two young women frolic in the sea together and Désirée laughingly declares that she will only have an abortion if it's a boy. The ending thus leaves open the choice between abortion and motherhood, focusing instead on the pleasures of cross-race female friendship. Yet the only space of freedom and independence that *La Squale* offers its teenage rebels is one that is completely cut off from the world of the immigrant family and young men of immigrant origin and, as in *Samia*, is located outside the *banlieue*, and, indeed, outside France.

Conclusion

Both *Samia* and *La Squale* depict rebellious teenage girls who challenge the imposition of an unjust, violent patriarchal order, questioning the way they are treated within the domestic sphere and asserting their right to a place in the *cité*/city. In each case, the young women seek to free themselves from the excesses of their family backgrounds, be it the oppressive patriarchal Algerian family or the neglectful, black, single-parent family, and the films thus risk conforming to majority French cultural assumptions about inadequate immigrant families whose daughters need to be rescued. What makes them interesting is that they create heroines capable of rescuing themselves (with a little help from other ethnic minority women) and able to negotiate a provisional space of resistance for their emergent subjectivities. Each film ends on shots of them occupying a transitional, liminal space close to the sea, with its connotations of movement and the transgression of moral boundaries. Yet the (white, male) filmmakers' recourse to these transnational spaces also implies a reluctance to envisage and articulate the young women's hybrid subjectivities within a French national framework.

The films reportedly divided *banlieue* youth audiences along gender lines, with boys generally reacting to them less favourably than girls.[8] Arguably, this is because there is more at stake than just the desire to foreground hitherto marginalised feminine spaces and female subjectivities. Both films depict the empowerment of ethnic minority teenage girls through self-assertion, female solidarity and geographical displacement (though *La Squale* does so in a more problematic manner than *Samia*). But the principal obstacles to their protagonists' achievement of freedom and justice are the supposedly aberrant black or *beur banlieue* youths (white youths feature only in secondary roles). *Samia*'s sympathetic, documentary-like study of the immigrant Algerian family takes care to avoid demonising the Maghrebi male, placing all its protagonists within a carefully constructed socio-economic context and recognising the possibility of change from within. In contrast, *La Squale* embroils its heroine in a sensationalised narrative of sex, crime and violence which draws uncritically on all the representational clichés of the *banlieue* and suggests that the endemic violence of its male youth subculture can only be addressed through further violence, including that of the grrrls.

Notes

1   This chapter was first published as 'Grrrls in the *Banlieue:* Philippe Faucon's *Samia* and Fabrice Génestal's *La Squale*, in Mireille Rosello (ed.), *Gleaning Images: Gender in Contemporary French Cinema, Esprit Créateur*, fall 2002, 28-38.

2   The year after *La Squale*, Samira Bellil published a courageous personal account of her experience of gang rape, *Dans l'enfer des tournantes* (Bellil 2002), which was something of a media event.

3   *La Squale* was shown to local dignitaries as a transparent reflection of *banlieue* life, as *La Haine* had been in 1995.

4   Nini's novel was based on her experiences of growing up in the 1970s and Faucon has acknowledged that attitudes today vary greatly, particularly according to the age of the mother and the position of the girl within the family (Faucon 2001). According to Fadela Amara, however, the situation of young women in the *banlieue* has deteriorated significantly since the early 1990s. Thanks to mass unemployment and the loss of authority of the immigrant father and family traditions, young women are now subjected to the even more oppressive authority of *les grands frères*, whose masculine honour depends on their control of the 'tribe of women' (Amara 2003: 37).

5   Since this article was written, groups of young women from the *banlieue*, supported by the Fédération nationale des Maisons des potes and SOS Racisme, have organised a protest movement under the slogan of 'Ni Putes Ni Soumises' ('Neither Slags Nor Slaves') (see introduction). The movement, initiated in 2001, led to a manifesto of demands being sent to all the candidates for the 2002 presidential elections, and to the 'March of Women from the Estates for Equality and against the Ghetto' in February 2003.

6 Interestingly, in the source novel, the reference is not to an Algerian terrorist group but to the KGB.

7 The source novel ends with the protagonist walking out on her family, having found her salvation through education.

8 See Elodie Lepage's article on *La Squale* in *Le Nouvel Observateur* (Lepage 2000) and Faucon's interview with Jean Roy in *L'Humanité* (Faucon 2001).

8

Memories of immigration: *Sous les pieds des femmes* and *Vivre au paradis*[1]

The *beur*-authored films discussed in previous chapters have been associated either with *beur* cinema of the 1980s or *banlieue* cinema of the 1990s, both of which privilege contemporary urban or *banlieue* settings and foreground the dilemmas faced by young, particularly male, working-class youths in their attempts to integrate into French society. However, the work of *beur* film-makers has never been homogeneous – Mehdi Charef and Rachid Bouchareb have both made films about other disadvantaged groups, as has Franco-Tunisian filmmaker Karim Dridi – and the late 1990s saw the appearance of the first *beur* films to turn to the past for their inspiration. These films challenge mainstream French heritage cinema by constructing the histories of the genre's normally marginalised others, particularly first-generation Maghrebi immigrants. The corpus to date includes: *Sous les pieds des femmes* by Rachida Krim (1997) and *Vivre au paradis* by Bourlem Gherdjou (1998), two first feature films set in part during the time of the Franco-Algerian war; *Le Gone du Chaâba* (1998), a feature film by white director Christophe Ruggia, but faithfully adaptated from Azouz Begag's 1986 autobiographical coming-of-age novel, set in a *bidonville* (shanty-town) outside Lyons in the mid-1960s; and Yamina Benguigui's highly acclaimed documentary triptych, *Mémoires d'immigrés: l'héritage maghrébin* (1997–98), based on contemporary testimonies by first-generation immigrants about their hitherto unvoiced, unrecorded experiences of immigration (Durmelat 2000).[2] These films make a significant, if belated, attempt to address some of the 'trous de mémoire' in France's recollection of its chequered colonial and postcolonial past, and in so doing challenge French cinema's conventional construction of history.

I take it as axiomatic that fictionalised cinematic representations of the past are less concerned with historical accuracy than with appropriating aspects of the past to serve the needs of the present. Whether based on memories of lived experiences or on the research and imagination of cultural entrepreneurs, they act as potential 'vectors of memory' (Wood 1999: 6), fashioning popular understandings of history and thereby contributing to a sense of collective identity. The hegemonic heritage film typically functions to produce a eurocentric understanding of French history and national identity, privileging traditional 'French' values and cultural norms. The cluster of films identified here, however, not only propose alternative understandings of Franco-Maghrebi history and culture, they also import and recycle the preoccupations of earlier *beur* films with questions of identity and belonging from a minority perspective. That they can do so is in itself indicative of the *beurs'* integration into French society (and access to media production). However, they are also informed by the dilemma facing minority filmmakers, caught between the desire to confront and inflect eurocentric accounts of the immigrant experience in order to recapture the specificity of their own (and their parents' generation's) histories, and the need to produce a sufficiently consensual version of history to enable both the majority population and French citizens of Maghrebi, and more particularly Algerian, origin, to recognise and accept the part each has played (and continues to play) in the production of today's multicultural French society.

Since the struggle for Algerian independence, relationships between the two groups have been charged with unresolved tensions and antagonisms. The situation has been exacerbated by the fact that experiences of the Algerian War of Independence and of the shameful treatment of Maghrebi immigrants recruited to work in France during the years of postwar prosperity (*les trente glorieuses*) have to date largely been veiled in silence, both by first-generation immigrants themselves and by the dominant majority. Early *beur* films, like *Le Thé au harem d'Archimède* (1985), tended to reproduce this silence in their marginalisation and 'othering' of parental figures, conventionally represented through alienated, impotent fathers and resilient, traditional mothers, none of whom were able or willing to articulate their histories. The focus in these films on the problematic identity of the increasingly estranged second generation highlighted and consolidated the perceived gap between parents and children, who remained divided from each other through their different histories and the ensuing differences in their language, education and culture.

It is significant that, even in the late 1990s, the majority of first films by *beur* filmmakers continued to reproduce this generation gap, as in Djamel Ouahab's *Cour interdite* (1999) and Kamel Saleh and Akhenaton's *Comme un aimant* (2000). Though Zaïda Ghorab-Volta's more personal, woman-centred *banlieue* film, *Souviens-toi de moi* (1997), gives the mother a substantial, sympathetic role, the relationship between mother and daughter remains extremely fraught. Notably, these films still foreground disadvantaged youths struggling to find their way rather than young adults capable of settling down with jobs and families. Despite the *beurs' de facto* integration into an increasingly multicultural France, the way they are represented in *beur* films continues to express a sense of their not belonging, even if this is attributed to the social exclusion they suffer alongside other working-class youths as much as (or rather than) their ethnic difference (a strategy which enables the films to address a wider youth audience). In a context in which their assumption of French citizenship is still periodically experienced as problematic (as exemplified during the 2002 presidential election), films that reconstruct the past and give a voice to their parents' generation potentially offer them a retrospective sense of historical continuity and, as a consequence, an alternative way of envisaging their particular social and collective identity.[3]

This chapter focuses on *Sous les pieds des femmes* and *Vivre au paradis*, the two films that directly address the hitherto virtually taboo topic of the Algerian War of Independence as it was fought out on French soil.[4] These films are interesting not just because their reconstructions of the past tackle potentially divisive material perceived from a Maghrebi immigrant point of view (whereas *Mémoires d'immigrés*, for example, carefully minimises references to contentious wartime experiences), but also because their wartime settings destabilise traditional Islamic gender hierarchies. Directors Rachida Krim and Bourlem Guerdjou,[5] both of whom owe the inspiration for their screenplays to their parents, have made clear in interview that they intend their films to function as vectors of memory. As Guerdjou argues, 'Memory is a factor in integration' ('La mémoire constitue un facteur d'intégration') (Hirschauer 1999). By paying homage to their parents' generation, they aim to provide material to facilitate the temporal and spatial anchoring of the *beur* generation in France. Both films focus on the story of an ordinary, first-generation immigrant family, temporarily torn apart by events relating to the struggle for Algerian independence, and share features that are symptomatic of the present-day need for a consensual understanding of the place of immigrants and their children in France. They are not straightforward male-centred war films, rather they integrate elements of action into more personal, psychological dramas, emphasising the individual circumstances and desires that motivate the main protagonists. In each case, they provoke a critique not just of France and French racism, but also of the FLN (Front de Libération Nationale) and the policies of the newly independent Algeria. They thus leave open the possibility of the protagonists' future reconciliation with their situation in France, as well as that of their children, the future *beur* generation, who are carefully inscribed within the diegesis.

Despite certain similarities, *Vivre au paradis* was a more successful film than *Sous les pieds des femmes*, attracting 80,534 spectators compared with 7,845, and receiving enthusiastic critical reviews. In contrast, *Sous les pieds des femmes* was dismissed as a worthy and ambitious topic whose execution did not do it justice. Clearly, neither film has been as successful as *Le Gone du Chaâba*, which attracted 390,000 spectators, thanks not just to its higher production values but also to its uncontentious, even nostalgic story of a young *beur*'s success in getting out of the ghetto (Begag is, after all, the embodiment of successful integration). Nevertheless, differences in their reception suggest that one way of reconstructing history may be more palatable than another. The rest of this chapter is concerned with comparing their approach to history, memory and identity through their selection of material and mode of narration.[6]

Sous les pieds des femmes/Where Women Tread (1997)

The screenplay of *Sous les pieds des femmes* (co-written with Catherine Labruyère-Colas) is based in part on Rachida Krim's interviews with her mother, a former FLN activist who carried on living in France, and with other women of that same generation who participated in the struggle for independence but later returned to the new state of Algeria. As has been documented by Danièle Djamila Amrane-Minne (1994: 164–77) and Benjamin Stora (1992: 310–13), women played an important, though largely unrecognised (and still under-researched) role within the FLN's French Federation throughout the war, through their liaison work, their collection of party dues, their participation in and organisation of demonstrations and hunger strikes. Like the mother represented in *Sous les pieds des femmes*, many of them were also imprisoned as a result. However, the end of the war returned them to a state of isolation and passivity, a paradox that is fundamental to the dramatic structure of the film.

Shot with an international cast, *Sous les pieds des femmes* has a framing narrative which centres in the present on Aya (played rather problematically by Claudia Cardinale), an apparently westernised married woman in her late fifties living in the south of France with her husband Moncef (Yorgo Voyagis), a retired miner. Aya's memories of the formative events that took place between 1958 and 1962 (the end of the war) constitute the principal dramatic action of the film, but they are triggered by and interwoven with her reactions to an overnight visit from her former lover, Amin (Mohamed Bakri), whom she has not seen since he returned to Algeria 35 years earlier. A series of subjective flashbacks, initiated by Aya's questioning gaze into the mirror and linked by her voice-over, reconstruct her trajectory from illiterate young immigrant wife and mother (played in the past by Fejria Deliba) to competent, independent-minded FLN activist. The first, sensuous flashback shows her learning to write her name, instructed by the young, handsome Amin (played in the past by Hamid Tassili), the leader of the local FLN group, who takes refuge in her flat because he is wanted by the police. Subsequently Aya starts collecting party dues, witnesses a brutal police raid in which her husband is arrested, helps Amin escape from the police and, while her husband is in prison, agrees to abandon her children and take on the identity of a French woman – Rose

Benoît – to transport arms and carry out an assassination in Marseilles, for which she is subsequently tortured, tried and imprisoned (figure 25). Inspired by her unspoken, transgressive love for Amin (and assisted at times by various French women), the young Aya is able to cross cultures and perform unthinkable deeds, and in the process to develop her own sense of what it means to be an independent Algerian woman. However, when Amin then refuses to accept her new identity, Aya rebels against him and, at the end of the war, reduced to silence, opts for exile in France with her unassuming, understanding husband, repressing her fractured identity beneath a heavily made-up westernised mask.

The film's framing narrative device allows her to re-enact her role as the agent of dramatic action, this time with a more positive outcome. The title, *Sous les pieds des femmes*, which references the Arabo-Islamic proverb, 'Sous les pieds des mères, le paradis' ('Where mothers tread lies paradise'), is given its full meaning only as the film draws to a close. Amin, an Algerian journalist whose own life is at risk from religious fundamentalists (and whose own son forces his mother to wear the veil) is now a sadder and wiser man who finally accepts Aya's attempt to convince him that Algeria's future lies in the emancipation of both women and men. He tells her (in voice-over), 'Sous les pieds des femmes, la vérité' ('Where women tread lies truth'). Thus the film uses a contemporary Algerian woman's troubled voice and memory not just to draw attention to and commemorate the unsung heroines of the war years, but also to produce a feminist re-writing of history and an analysis of the failure of the FLN which has implications for the present and future.

The film directly addresses the failure of the Algerian revolution and its ongoing consequences for life in contemporary Algeria. It draws attention to past internal divisions through references to attacks on the FLN by the MNA (Mouvement National Algérien), but primarily it attacks the brutality of the FLN's gender politics. In a key scene, Aya witnesses the cowardly and hypocritical decision taken by Amin's all-male FLN cell, including her husband, to execute a couple of adulterous lovers, based on their belief that the new Algeria must be based on the most puritanical interpretation of Islamic values. (The shot of the cold-blooded execution that follows stands out as the only scene from the past that is not shot from Aya's subjective point of view). Amin's authorisation of this act returns to haunt Aya as she herself embarks on an adulterous relationship, and underpins the pivotal scene where Aya finally realises that Amin's vision of a future independent Algeria is not one she can share. Following Amin's bitter (and justified) tirade against the French colonisation of Algerian culture that has left him able to read French but not Arabic, Aya changes out of her Rose Benoît costume into a beautiful traditional dress (in which she had earlier hidden the guns she was asked to transport), hoping to prove to him that there are still elements of Algerian culture that the French cannot destroy. The camera assumes her point of view, circling around Amin

25 Aya (Fejria Deliba) carries out an assassination in *Sous les pieds des femmes* (1997).

as the object of her desire, and anticipating his pleasure. However, Amin reacts by ordering her to remove the dress, violently rejecting the image she projects of herself as an independent woman who can still claim to be Algerian, and demonstrating the narrowness and limitations of his vision. The moment crystallises Aya's revolt as she vows that she will never lower her eyes to a man again. But she loses both the love of her life (Amin as a young man disappears from the diegesis) and her dream of an Algeria in which women would be emancipated. The stylised, fragmented flashback of the trial scene that follows underlines her split identity, her smart appearance in her Rose Benoît suit belied by the voice-over that stresses her feelings of isolation and despair. However, although she is condemned by the prosecution for her transgressive behaviour as a wife and mother, she is praised by the defence (in what sounds like a very contemporary piece of rhetoric) as a model of an emancipated woman. The film thus makes clear that, whatever the injustices of French colonialism, Aya has more chance of being accepted as a liberated woman in France than in Algeria.

Sous les pieds des femmes, then, does not offer a straightforward alternative history of the struggle for independence. Rather, it criticises it on gender lines because of its investment in the Arabo-Berber-Islamic sex/gender system, making the Algerian victory at the end of the war, which is not visualised, a cause for despair rather than celebration. The film does not seek to redress the *non-lieux de mémoire* of Franco-Algerian history by consecrating new *lieux de mémoire* for the *beur* generation – the locations are lacking in specificity, the events are not claimed as authentic representations of the past, and Aya's modern present-day home bears no obvious traces of what she has lived through (apart from the blue-spotted Rose Benoît dress which Amin had also disapproved of, and which her daughter can now wear with impunity). Instead of reifying the past, *Sous les pieds des femmes* links the problems of the past with hopes for transforming the future, in particular by inscribing its intended spectators within its present-day narrative space. On the one hand it offers Aya's story to spectators of second- and even third-generation Maghrebi descent through the figures of Aya's confident, respectful daughter, Fusilla (Nadia Fares), a stand-in for Krim herself, and, more particularly, her beloved granddaughter, the product of Fusilla's apparently successful mixed marriage, who is constantly at her grandmother's side, asking her questions. On the other, through the incorporation of Aya's former FLN lover and her discussions with him about the past and its effects on the present, it addresses those with the possibility, however limited, of influencing the future course of events in Algeria. In the process it constructs an empowering image of a first-generation Algerian immigrant woman, representing her both as a sexual, desiring subject and as an active historical agent, thus completely revising the way Algerian mothers have conventionally been represented in French cinema.

Vivre au paradis/Living in Paradise (1998)

Whereas the memories evoked in *Sous les pieds des femmes* inform and disrupt the framing narrative present of Aya's painful remembering, *Vivre au paradis* (like *Le Gone du Chaâba*) more obviously consigns its topic to the distant past. The film is a loose adaptation of the autobiographical novel of the same name by Brahim Benaïcha (1992), which chronicles the coming-of-age story of a young *beur* growing up in a *bidonville* in Nanterre, the *bidonville* being a privileged site for the anchoring of the *beurs*' own memories of immigration (as in *Le Gone du Chaâba*). However, it is inspired in part by the imagined lives of Guerdjou's own parents, who migrated to France in the 1950s, and by Guerdjou's desire to commemorate the events of 17 October 1961.[7] The principal roles are played by *beur* actors (even if Roschdy Zem is of Moroccan descent), who were forced to learn to speak Arabic (though the Canal + television version is mainly in French), and the film thus invites second-generation spectators to identify imaginatively with their parents' predicament.

The film differs from the source novel both in its displacement of the voice and point of view of the novel's *beur* narrator and in its handling of time. Its third-person linear narrative omits the preface in which the narrator starts telling his story to his children in the present, and condenses the events of the novel to the period 1960 to 1962. (The novel itself, written as a diary, ranges from 1959 to 1970, the date of the narrator's departure from the *bidonville*, and also prefaces the entries for each year with information about events in the wider world.) This condensation gives the film its dramatic intensity, enabling it to focus on particular determining dates that, underlined by the strategic use of non-diegetic intertitles, provide a commemorative framework for the history of first-generation immigrants. The first, '1960, Nanterre, 3 kilometres from Paris', which occurs at the end of the pre-credit sequence, accompanies images of men in the *bidonville* getting up and preparing to go to work and exposes the irony of the *bidonville*'s juxtaposition to the 'city of light' glimpsed on the horizon; the second, '17 October 1961', mid-way through the film, highlights the date of the fatal FLN-organised demonstration against the curfew imposed on Algerians in Paris, and is followed by text informing the spectator that over 200 Algerians were killed that night; the third, '5 July 1962', near the end of the film, references the end of the war, and is followed by a final statement that the new Algerian government showed as little interest in the fate of the immigrant community as the French, and that the film's protagonists, the Ferouz family, had to wait until the destruction of the *bidonville* on 7 July 1970 to be housed in a *cité de transit* (figure 26). These dates structure the film by interweaving the individual history of the Ferouz family with the collective history of Algerian immigration but, arguably, they also leave the spectator on a note of defeat, representing members of the immigrant community as the victims rather than the agents of history.

Within this externally imposed but symbolic spatial and temporal framework, *Vivre au paradis* foregrounds the fictionalised first-generation immigrant couple formed by Lakhdar (Roschdy Zem) and Nora (Fadila Belkebla) and their attempts to escape their destiny and make something of their lives. The film centres primarily on Lakhdar, a strong-minded, ambitious labourer, whose decision to bring his family to France and obsessive desire to acquire decent housing lead to his moral decline and progressive isolation from the community and family life. His trajectory contrasts with that of his initially timid, illiterate young wife, who discovers within the squalor of the *bidonville* the values of community and political struggle, thanks to her chance witnessing of a brutal police raid and her encounter with Aïcha, an FLN activist, who offers her a different model of female behaviour. The somewhat schematic narrative reaches a climax when Nora's support of the FLN is directly responsible for Lakhdar's failure to realise his dream. Following their participation in the 17 October demonstration, she secretly allows Aïcha and other activists to shelter in the flimsy new shack Lakhdar has built to extort money from a friend; but the illegal shack gets destroyed by the police and Lakhdar, forced to return his ill-gotten gains, reacts to Nora's perceived perfidy by throwing her out. However, after a period of separation in which the disillusioned Lakhdar gambles away all his hard-earned money and Nora attempts to build a role for herself and her family within the community, the couple are apparently reconciled. In the final sequence, after Aïcha has gone back to Algeria, Rachid, a

26 The Ferouz family in their *bidonville* shack in *Vivre au paradis* (1999).

former friend, invites the departing Lakhdar to join Nora at the *bidonville*'s victory celebration party. But the couple are barely able to communicate, and the last brief shot of the film shows them sitting in silence with their children outside a shack in the isolated, enclosed *bidonville*. Arguably, then, Lakhdar's fervent adoption of the values of French individualism and Nora's positive support of the FLN are shown to be equally meaningless, their actions doomed to failure by the historical circumstances in which they are embedded (as the end title suggests).

Although *Vivre au paradis* centres on Lakhdar's physical presence and his ambition, humiliation and defeat, it also challenges conventional representations of Algerian women, re-writing the history of the Algerian struggle to accommodate feminist-influenced rethinking of what constitutes resistance and political action (like *Sous les pieds des femmes*, and in the manner of work done on the period of the Occupation). Nora's major breakthrough lies in her defiance of Lakhdar's injunction to stay indoors as a dutiful wife and mother. As a result of venturing out into the *bidonville*, she meets Aïcha, who encourages her to join in activities with the other women within the community as well as becoming an FLN activist. To Lakhdar's dismay, Aïcha proves to be a good friend as well as an inspirational role model, accompanying the 'brothers' collecting the FLN dues and giving the speech rallying the inhabitants of the *bidonville* to participate in the 17 October demonstration. But the potentially transgressive theme of intimate female friendship between Nora and Aïcha is never developed, and Aïcha's subsequent departure ultimately links her with the shortcomings of the FLN and the failure of the newly independent Algeria to support the immigrants living in France. *Vivre au paradis* thus glosses over the question of the impact of Islamic law on women's roles addressed in *Sous les pieds des femmes*, and fails to problematise either Aïcha's leadership position within the FLN or Nora's identification with Algerian culture and community.

In fact, the construction of the *bidonville* as an imagined community cut off from the rest of the world is absolutely central to *Vivre au paradis*. Even though the *mise-en-scène* is dominated by shots of mud, rain, barbed wire, planks and corrugated iron, the wretchedness of the environment is countered by a visual emphasis on the collective experience, with repeated shots of groups of men crossing the railway lines to and from the city and work. The film does not minimise the hardship of life in the *bidonville*, deliberately including scenes to demonstrate the primitive housing conditions, the problems of getting water, the difficulties of sexual relations, the risks of illness and mental breakdown, the impact of police brutality. But at the same time it invests the inhabitants with dignity, especially through the glow of paraffin lamps lighting up faces in the darkness (including the Ferouz children, the future *beurs*) and the way the camera alights on ordinary people's faces. It also shows their solidarity at times of need (Lakhdar writes a letter for an illiterate friend, Rachid helps Nora block the hole in her roof during a storm) and their shared community culture (the women doing the washing and sewing Algerian flags, the men playing dominos in the cafe, the families celebrating a wedding and holding an impromptu party at the end of the war). Nevertheless, the moments of communal activity also demonstrate the growing rift between Lakhdar and Nora. They are divided over whether or not to participate in the 17 October demonstration, an event that takes them out of the *bidonville* and puts their lives at risk (though it has little impact on the rest of the film). They are also divided over whether or not to attend the wedding, since Lahkdar's obsession with bettering himself means that he is as reluctant to provide a wedding gift as he is to support the FLN, while Nora looks to the community for her sense of identity. However, the choice of an arranged marriage as the occasion for a celebration of community demonstrates how the film fails to address potentially oppressive aspects of traditional Algerian culture, and also prefigures the way in which Nora's bid for independence is (presumably) covered over by a return to traditional values at the end of the war.

Indeed, a comparison of the ending of *Vivre au paradis* and *Sous les pieds des femmes* is telling. The final shot of the reunited family in *Vivre au paradis*, trapped within the confines of the *bidonville* and haunted by Lakhdar's dream of a return 'home', closes over the tensions produced by Lakhdar and Nora's individual desires and recreates the silence, passivity and resignation which have since weighed so heavily on the *beur* generation, and which the film originally set out to deconstruct. In contrast, the final scene of *Sous les pieds des femmes*, which shows Aya standing in the countryside with her daughter and grand-daughter by her side, her features at last relaxed in a smile, provides a positive affirmation of Aya's voice and place in contemporary metropolitan France.

The two films thus address the *trous de mémoire* in France's colonial history in rather different ways, despite their shared concern with recycling questions of identity and belonging more commonly associated with *beur* films set in the present. Each works to dignify and humanise the history of first-generation Algerian immigrants and their families, inviting spectators to recognise and respect their experiences of the Algerian War of Independence as well as their reasons for continuing to live in France. Each condemns the violence and bru-tality of the French forces of law and order as well as criticising the FLN and the newly emergent state of Algeria, if for different reasons (*Sous les pieds des femmes* because of its fundamental failure to address questions of gender and sexuality, *Vivre au paradis* because of its abandoning of first-generation immi-grants left in France). However, whereas *Vivre au paradis*' period reconstruction of the *bidonville* as an imagined community consigns its material to the past and so makes the events it depicts available as the basis for a collective memory, *Sous les pieds des femmes* deconstructs the very notion of community and insists on the divisive repercussions of the past in the present. Unlike the more straightforwardly commemorative *Vivre au paradis*, then, its more fragmented and uncomfortable mode of address presents the spectator with an ongoing challenge both to oppressive Arabo-Islamic values and to the possibility of shared, collective memories and identities.

Notes

1   Earlier versions of this chapter were presented at a research seminar on 'Memory and Immigration' at the University of Sussex in 1999 and (thanks to a British Academy Overseas Conference Grant) at the XXIst Century French Studies conference on 'Recycling' at UC Davis in 2001. It was subsequently published as 'Memories of Immi-gration in Beur Films of the Late 1990s', in Hafid Gafaïti, Anne Mairesse and Michèle Praëger (eds), *Imaginaires interculturels/Intercultural Imaginaries*, Paris: L'Harmattan, 2005, in the series *Etudes Transnationales, Francophones et Comparées/Transnational, Francophone and Comparative Studies*, edited by Hafid Gafaïti.

2   Since this article was written, two more *beur*-authored period dramas have appeared, Benguigui's first feature, *Inch'Allah dimanche* (2001) and Chad Chenouga's first feature, *17 rue Bleue* (2001). Both centre on the dilemmas of Maghrebi women immi-grants in France in the late 1960s/early 1970s (see chapter 11).

3   Kédadouche reports on moves to set up a 'National Museum of the History of Immigration' as a *lieu de memoire* which would enable the French to recognise their past and move on (Kédadouche 2002: 24).

4   This was also the topic of *Les Sacrifiés* (1983) by Algerian filmmaker Okacha Touita.

5   Krim (born in Alès in 1956) has a background in the fine arts, and made a first highly acclaimed short film, *El Fatha* (1992), about the rituals involved in an Algerian

wedding. Guerdjou (born in 1966 and brought up in the *banlieue* of Asnières-sur-Seine) worked first as an actor (including a role in *Le Thé au harem d'Archimède*), then made a couple of short films, including the award-winning *Le Ring* (1996), about boxing.

6 For a comparative study of the representation of the father in *Le Gone du Chaâba* and *Vivre au paradis*, see Hargreaves (2000).

7 A commemorative plaque near the Pont Saint-Michel, dedicated 'To the memory of those Algerians who were victims of the bloody repression of a peaceful demonstration' ('A la mémoire des Algériens, victimes de la répression sanglante d'une manifestation pacifique'), was unveiled by the Socialist Mayor of Paris, Bertrand Delanoë, on 17 October 2001. The first official recognition of the massacre of 17 October 1961 (though the date had been unofficially commemorated ten years earlier), it met with strong protests from the Right. A commemoration of the event at the Forum des Images, Paris, supported by the associations '17 octobre 1961 contre l'oubli' and 'Au Nom de la Mémoire', among others, included a screening of *Vivre au paradis*.

9

Beurs in the provinces: from *L'Honneur de ma famille* to *Drôle de Félix*

An important aspect of the socially aware strand of the *jeune cinéma français* of the mid-1990s was its rejection of Parisian settings typical of a certain type of *intimiste* bourgeois French cinema, in favour of spaces suitable for addressing the experiences and subjectivities of those generally marginalised or excluded from mainstream cinema. In addition to films set in the *banlieues*, there was a significant move towards films set in the provinces as the site of the exploration of class and/or ethnic differences. This chapter focuses on a selection of films located in the North of France.

The North is not the only provincial setting to preoccupy French filmmakers of the 1990s and early 2000s.[1] However, it has proved to be of particular interest, perhaps because the theme of the bleakness of life in post industrial France can be mapped on to the perceived bleakness of the flat landscape. Indeed, René Prédal refers to it as 'the hell of the North' ('*[l]'enfer du Nord*'), while arguing that the 'places, people, time and light' of the area, paradoxically, also confer a universal quality to the narratives set there (Prédal 2002: 117). It has inspired a number of compelling studies of the lives of the homeless, unemployed, working-class or disaffected, including *Nord* (Xavier Beauvois, 1992), *Le Fils du requin* (Agnès Merlet, 1993), *Faut-il aimer Mathilde?* (Edwin Bailly, 1993), *Les Amoureux* (Catherine Corsini, 1994), *Rosine* (Christine Carrière, 1995), the beginning of *En avoir (ou pas)* (Laetitia Masson, 1995), *Je ne sais pas ce qu'on me trouve* (Christian Vincent, 1997), *La Vie rêvée des anges* (Erick Zonca, 1998), *Ça commence aujourd'hui* (Bertrand Tavernier, 1999), *Rien à faire* (Marion Vernoux, 1999), *Qui plume la lune?* (Christine Carrière, 1999) and *Ressources humaines* (Laurent Cantet, 2000).[2] Most of these films do not directly address questions of ethnic difference, though some include apparently well-integrated secondary characters of Maghrebi origin, as in *Ça commence aujourd'hui* (a female social worker), *En avoir (ou pas)* (a hotel manager and his sister) and *Ressources humaines* (a factory worker). However, as indicated in Yamina Benguigi's *Inch'Allah dimanche* (2001), set in the 1970s (see chapter 11), the industrial North was a prime target for immigration from the Maghreb. Indeed, the troubled exile of a lonely, blind first-generation Maghrebi immigrant is at the centre of Robert Kramer's last disturbing, fragmented film, *Cités de la plaine* (2001), shot with local people from Tourcoing, mostly with a handheld digital video camera.

The five films discussed here are all set (at least initially) in the North and structured around the presence of second-generation immigrants of Maghrebi origin. *L'Honneur de ma famille* by Rachid Bouchareb is the only film directed by a *beur* filmmaker and represents the immigrant community and its internal conflicts from a *beur* perspective; *La Vie de Jésus* by Bruno Dumont and *Karnaval* by Thomas Vincent both focus on the dramatic impact of the presence of an attractive young male *beur* on the dominant white community; *Sauve-moi* by Christian Vincent engages with a multi-ethnic group of marginalised men and women; and *Drôle de Félix* by Olivier Ducastel and Jacques Martineau introduces a different perspective on ethnicity by centring on a young mixed-race, gay man with AIDS.

The representation of immigrants of Maghrebi origin in places other than the more conventional cinematic spaces of the city centre or rundown working-class *banlieues* raises the question as to whether alternative spaces allow for new ways of approaching issues of difference and identity. For Prédal, the representation of the North displaces the emphasis on language characteristic of bourgeois Paris-based films with an emphasis on behaviour and the body. He argues that the provincial setting encourages a less intellectual approach to character, enabling filmmakers to capture the 'essence' (*sic*) of the characters through the observation of their silences and the emptiness of their daily lives, an approach which is prevented by the continuous bustle of life in Paris (Prédal 2002: 118). Elsewhere, however, he acknowledges that films centred on a *beur* character challenge conventional narrative and psychological conventions because *beurs* have to create a place for themselves on screen (Prédal 2002: 138). While his first statement seems to deny the shifting nature of identity and the constructedness of all filmic characters, the second allows characters of immigrant origin the potential for movement and change. By displacing the *beurs* from the cinematic spaces of the *banlieue* and inner-city ghettos, spaces in which the way they are represented is in constant dialogue with the stereotypical imagery produced by the dominant media, to more open, less heavily mediated spaces, films set in the North may allow the *beurs* (and others) to occupy space in more constructive and imaginative ways. Certainly Manuel Poirier's road movie *Western* (1997), set in Brittany,[3] offers a sense of both fluidity and belonging for its marginalised protagonists (though they are notably of white European rather than Maghrebi or African-Caribbean origin). As the following analyses demonstrate, however, the presence of second-generation immigrants of Maghrebi origin in the North generates a diversity of approach, some films placing more emphasis on difference and 'otherness', others more anxious to represent the possibility of integration.

L'Honneur de ma famille/My Family's Honour (1997)

Bouchareb's *L'Honneur de ma famille* contrasts strongly both with the *banlieue* films of the mid-1990s and with his own earlier films, which are mostly set outside France. An underrated film, which was actually made for television and has had a very limited distribution, it offers not only a different deployment of space but also an imaginative use of comedy, fantasy and colour. Set on the outskirts of Roubaix near the Belgian border,[4] it centres on the friendship between Nora (Seloua Hamse) and Carole (Karole Rocher), two trendy but impoverished young women, who work in a bar some twenty-five miles away in Belgium, and dream of escaping from their boring home environment by travelling to Goa. The film's *mise-en-scène* returns repeatedly to the realist setting of the dreary cul-de-sac of terraced houses where Nora and her immigrant Maghrebi family live, and where the neighbours congregate when Nora's behaviour puts the honour of her family at stake, in their eyes if not in hers. The gloomy street scenes contrast with the life and colour that Nora and Carole seek in their lives: their drug-taking and nightclubbing result in a number of surreal, hallucinatory scenes, while their devotion to all things Indian is expressed in the colourful décor of Carole's flat, including posters of Krishna and Ganesh, and by an early scene in which they both get their shoulders tattooed with a tantric motif. Their border crossings between France and Belgium, usually in Carole's blue and yellow camper van, structure the narrative, emphasising both their mobility and its limitations (the need to return home) (figure 27).

The narrative is triggered by Nora's discovery that she is pregnant, a fact which not only upsets her plans to go to Goa but also brings her into conflict with her family. Unwilling to get an abortion and unable to rely on the (white, French) father, Nora eventually confesses to her mother, who is already shocked by the discovery that her daughter does not work in the emergency ward of the local hospital, as she had claimed. The mother's reaction is one of horror at the shame her daughter risks bringing on the family and determination to force her into an arranged marriage in order to save the family honour. Negotiations are set in motion to wed Nora to Hamid (Roschdy Zem), a naïve, overly serious young man, who lives with his suspicious mother and owns the biggest draper's shop in the area. The film contrasts Nora's defiant attempts to live a free, independent life with the hypocrisy and narrow-mindedness of the older generation (her mother lies through her teeth to secure the marriage), highlighting generational differences within the immigrant family (which are also the topic of Ghorab-Volta's *Souviens-toi de moi*, discussed in chapter 5).

27 Nora (Seloua Hamse) and Carole (Karole Rocher) on the road in *L'Honneur de ma famille* (1997).

In fact, Nora goes along with her mother's plans whilst secretly planning to get divorced as soon as she has had the child, and live out her dream with Carole. However, her plans are thrown into jeopardy: first when Carole falls for a beautiful black conman (played by Alex Descas), who claims to be an illegal immigrant in need of false papers and a hiding-place, and persuades her into giving him the money the women have saved for their trip to India; second when her mother, anxious because Hamid's mother wants a certificate of virginity, phones in her troubles to a radio programme and so alerts the whole community to her situation. The resulting crises lead each of the young women to the local hospital, Nora to have an abortion after calling off the marriage, Carole to be treated for an overdose after realising that she has put her friendship at risk. However, when the two women see each other, they flee the hospital together, Carole still carrying her drip. Their escape is witnessed by Hamid, who arrives at the hospital at the same time, accompanying his mother who had collapsed after he had locked her up to stop her opposing the marriage. Hamid, who has become besotted with Nora, to the extent of espousing her interest in Indian culture, still wants to marry her, and follows the young women out of the hospital, leaving his mother behind. He sees Nora take his car and use his keys to enter the draper's shop where she steals the wedding jewellery; then Carole, in her excitement, accidentally drops a cigarette end which sends the multi-coloured drapes up in flames. As the two women drive off, however, the boot lid flies up to reveal Hamid, a big smile on his face.

The film then cuts to a whimsical sequence parodying Bollywood melodrama, in which a romantic lover shoots down the balloons which are transporting his beloved across the countryside. If this sequence is read as Hamid's fantasy, as opposed to a dream that he shares with Nora, then the ending, however light-hearted, suggests that Nora may not be able to abandon her ethnic heritage or the weight of masculine expectations as easily as she had hoped.

L'Honneur de ma famille is critical of first-generation immigrants who derive their identity from clinging to traditional values rather than attempting to recognise the different aspirations of the younger generation who have grown up in France. If the father figures play little part in the drama, the larger-than-life mother figures are represented as unable to see further than the need to save face, regardless of how this affects their children. In her roof terrace conferences with her black friend (Firmine Richard), Nora's mother demonstrates that she has no horizon beyond the street community below where the neighbours gather to observe the honour of the family being stained. Hamid's mother's treatment of her adult son is equally perverse in that she has turned him into a wimpish man who enjoys arranging wedding dresses.[5] In contrast, Nora represents the younger generation who are potentially well integrated and desire to live their own lives, even if it means rebelling against the values of their culture of origin. Indeed, even the black youth who talks about the nefarious effects of the Pasqua law, and the need to recuperate black history, is shown to be adept at manipulating the system to his advantage (though his role may inadvertently feed into stereotypical constructions of the feckless sponger). The film evacuates questions of racism by making Carole the only significant white character and, like the banlieue films, emphasising what she and Nora have in common. Ultimately, then, it focuses on the shared problems of two young women who do not have a secure economic future and who are desperately searching for a more rewarding life, even if it means leaving their families behind. To a certain extent it ends where Baton Rouge (1985) begins, with young people of diverse ethnic origins setting out to live out their dream of a more pleasurable existence in an exotic elsewhere. In Baton Rouge, the dream of life in the United States ends with a return to the banlieue. The fact that L'Honneur de ma famille ends on a fantasy of escape testifies to the ongoing difficulty of representing young people of Maghrebi descent as happily settled in France. Nevertheless, the choice of young female protagonists combined with the setting in the North enables Bouchareb to avoid the violence of the male-oriented banlieue films and represent a more fluid vision of a multicultural France.

La Vie de Jésus/The Life of Jesus (1997) and Karnaval (1999)

L'Honneur de ma famille foregrounds the presence of immigrant families in the North and takes for granted inter-racial friendships between black-blanc-beur young people (a trope typical of *beur*-authored films). In contrast, both *La Vie de Jésus* and *Karnaval* are primarily concerned with the representation of a traditional self-contained white community, already threatened or devastated by the effects of postindustrial economic change, and exploring the impact on it of another figure of change and difference, an attractive young male *beur*, isolated from his marginalised immigrant family. The presence of the *beur* at a period marked as out of the ordinary, a heat wave in the first instance, the Dunkerque carnival in the second, is thus a narrative strategy which activates the desires and fears of the white community rather than a vehicle for the exploration of *beur* subjectivities.

In *La Vie de Jésus* and *Karnaval*, the *beur* youth who becomes an object of desire and fear is first shown to be alienated from his parents and culture of origin. In *Karnaval*, Larbi (Amar Ben Abdallah) reacts angrily to the harsh treatment meted out to him by his father, who runs a garage on the outskirts of Dunkerque, and decides to leave home for Marseilles. Finding that he has missed the last train, and ignoring the carnival celebrations taking place in the town, he takes shelter from the driving rain in the hallway of a block of flats, and so enters the space of working-class carnival reveller Béa (Sylvie Testud) and her husband Christian (Clovis Cornillac), who is so drunk that he requires Larbi's help in negotiating the stairs. In *La Vie de Jésus*, Kader (Kader Chaatouf) is first seen sitting with his family in the local café run by the mother of Fredy (David Douche), and exchanging a quick glance with Marie (Marjorie Cottreel), Fredy's girlfriend. The immigrant family, whose 'otherness' is apparent from their language and dress, are subsequently driven from the café by the racist comments of Fredy's gang and members of the town band; but Kader's angry reaction marks him out as different from his parents and, like Larbi, he is subsequently shot in isolation from his family. In each case, then, the *beur* character is set up, sympathetically, as a lonely, vulnerable outsider attracted by a young woman representative of the majority population. Unlike *beur*-authored films which emphasise the sexual inadequacies rather than the sexual potency of young *beur* men, and unlike *banlieue* films in which the *beurs* seek integration by forging alliances with other marginalised youths, these two films set up triangular plotlines in which the *beur*'s relationship with a white woman leads him into conflict with a white man, thus conventionally mapping racial difference on to sexual jealousy.

The pleasures of both *La Vie de Jésus* and *Karnaval* lie to a large extent in their imaginative construction of place and in the depiction of traditional working-class popular culture through their observation of behaviour and the body (as noted by Prédal). The first is set in Bailleul, Bruno Dumont's home town, and focuses on the grim, empty, rural and small-town landscape which reflects the grim, empty reality of the lives of its inarticulate, unemployed youth, represented primarily by dysfunctional, epileptic Fredy and his gang (figure 28). The monotony of the environment is artfully mirrored in the film's elliptical

28 Fredy (David Douche) and his gang in the empty streets of Bailleul in *La Vie de Jésus* (1997).

editing and use of long takes, which make place and time seem to stand still. The second is set in dismal, rain-soaked Dunkerque at the time of the local carnival, scenes from which evoke a transgressive space which contrasts with the mundane everyday lives of the alienated working-class men and women who find solace and solidarity in its rituals. Both settings imply the need for individuals caught up in unrewarding, unproductive lives to find ways of (temporarily) blocking out social and economic realities. The colourful Dunkerque carnival, introduced in *Karnaval*'s magnificent opening scene with muted shots of chanting revellers appearing out of the dunes in their monstrous costumes and blacked-up faces, licenses liberation from normal social and domestic constraints. Shot in part with documentary-style footage, the film depicts the revellers' celebration of pleasure and excess in dress, drink and sex, evident in particular in the men's cross-dressing, bawdy songs and brandishing of an effigy of a (pink) phallus. In *La Vie de Jésus*, the gang of youths (played by local non-actors) counter their alienation and impotence by driving aggressively through the country lanes and town streets on their scooters, while Fredy, who is subject to uncontrollable fits, is also graphically shot having brutal sexual intercourse with Marie and kicking against the walls of the hospital in frustration. The film's oscillation between movement and stasis is brilliantly illustrated in a scene where Fredy's gang play their drums in the town band outside a bar aptly named Le Coin Perdu (The Middle of Nowhere), their bodies vibrating in intensity, but their movement leading nowhere.

However, if Fredy and his gang, and the carnival revellers, seek to obliterate themselves in order to relieve their economic and existential anguish, the women characters are also looking for more rewarding human relationships. Marie, a supermarket cashier, who finds sex with Fredy painful, breaks off her relationship with him when she learns of the gang's sexual assault on a dumpy young majorette. Béa, a young wife and mother, is momentarily alienated from Christian when he shows signs of unwarranted and unreasonable jealousy. Each of the films thus sets up a situation in which the *beur* outsider offers a desirable alternative to the unsatisfactory, insensitive white male. In *La Vie de Jésus*, Kader is better looking, better dressed, more articulate and tender than Fredy (and is shocked by the crudeness of Marie's language and attitude to sex). In *Karnaval*, whereas Christian is large, moody and potentially violent, Larbi woos Béa with his humour, looks and soft words, but also by his decision to drop his prejudices, wear a wig, have a drink and enter into the world of carnival. In each case, the *beur* figure holds out the possibility of a more egalitarian relationship than is possible with a white macho working-class male, as well as appealing to the woman's desire for the exotic other. And in each case, the relationship is consummated, the elliptical shot of Kader and Marie kissing in the ruined church in *La Vie de Jésus* mirrored in *Karnaval* by an extended sequence in which Béa and Larbi make love amid the utopian frenzy of carnival.

However, the films do not allow the inter-racial couple to develop further. In *La Vie de Jésus*, Fredy's racism, fuelled by his jealousy of Kader's relationship with Marie, leads directly to murder: the gang force Kader off the road on his scooter and Fredy kicks him to death. Though the final scene of the film may suggest that Fredy feels some remorse for what he has done (a ray of sun appears through the clouds, a slight whimper is heard on the soundtrack), Kader (and Kader's family) is nonetheless effectively dismissed from the film's image and soundtrack, the narrative structure thus reflecting the elimination of the racial other which is criticised within the diegesis. In *Karnaval*, Christian's instinctive reactions to Béa's perceived interest in Larbi are channelled into self-defeating acts of violence, linked to the intrusion of the real world. Having been forced by an uncaring boss to return to work during carnival (as a watchman at the port), he abandons his post, gets into competitive drinking with Larbi and dances with Béa; but when, still wearing his uniform, he is discovered by his boss and fired, he drives out to the port where he douses the gates and the guard dog with petrol and sets them on fire. The crisis leads Béa to recognise that her place lies with her vulnerable, immature young husband, who wraps her in a bear hug when she appears in the bathroom doorway. The film then ends with a shot of Larbi walking down the steps from the station in Marseilles, the city displayed in front of him. In this instance, then, carnival is over, order is restored and the *beur* youth is forced to recognise that he has to find a life elsewhere.

In *La Vie de Jésus*, the *beur* youth is structurally marginalised since the film is mainly preoccupied with the behaviour of Fredy. The spectator has only a limited access to Kader's subjectivity and is encouraged to view him primarily as a victim. Yet towards the end of the film there are shots of Kader and friends occupying spaces in the centre of the town which suggest that, were it not for Fredy's hostility, Kader would be as integrated into the life of Bailleul as his aggressors. In *Karnaval*, the *beur* youth has a far more central role, and initially appears to be the main subject of the narrative. Yet as the film progresses, it becomes clear that he functions rather as a device to illuminate the marriage of Christian and Béa, and can ultimately be dispensed with. Whereas Béa (like her girl-friend) is aware that carnival is an inversion of the normal experience of everyday life which momentarily licenses disruptive desires and transgressive behaviour, Larbi deludes himself into thinking that he can not only penetrate the white community, but also persuade Béa to abandon her husband and child and accompany him to Marseilles. The return to order makes it clear that the *beur* has no lasting space in the town, either with his family or without. Both these films, then, seem ultimately to express white male fears about the sexuality and desirability of the Maghrebi other and differ only in the ways in which they expel the *beur* outsider from the white heart of the provinces.

Sauve-moi/Save Me (2000)

For his fifth film, after working on regional news programmes for France 3, Christian Vincent opted for a radical change in his working methods, deciding to develop a film out of his involvement in a particular place and the people living there.[6] In collaboration with Ricardo Montserrat, he set up a writing workshop in Roubaix for the unemployed, which first gave rise to a novel, *Ne crie pas*, published in Gallimard's *Série noire* in 2000. Inspired in part by Ken Loach's *Raining Stones* (1993), the film *Sauve-moi* was 'the echo of stories and situations that were told, heard and lived during that adventure' (Vincent 2003).[7]

Set in Roubaix, *Sauve-moi* opens with a sequence in which Medhi (Roschdy Zem) is driving his car around the city to a rap accompaniment, looking (illegally) for lifts. The panning camera espouses his point of view, particularly on the groups of unemployed men hanging about in the streets. Medhi's precarious situation is matched by that of his friends, who are of various ethnic (if majority white) backgrounds: Willy works in a warehouse, Marc is a security guard, Sergio works in a supermarket and Marc's girl-friend, Cécile (Karole Rocher), who is also the mother of Mehdi's dead brother's child and is having a secret affair with Mehdi, works as a chamber-maid. Hélène Louvart's handheld camerawork emphasises Vincent's interest in character and situation rather than in any standard plot development. The plot, such as it is, is occasioned by the impact on their lives of Agatha (Rona Hartner[8]), a quirky but impecunious young Romanian woman (of mixed origins), whom Mehdi picks up at the station and helps find the lover she met in the summer at a medical conference in Romania. Amusingly, Agatha is at first impressed by Roubaix, thinking that a revamped factory is actually a château. However, she quickly discovers that her lover, a doctor who had promised to make her 'Queen of Roubaix', had not expected to see her, and it is Mehdi and his friends who help her find food and a primitive shelter (in the unfinished house that Sergio is building for himself). In return uninhibited, free-spirited Agatha (a somewhat romanticised embod-iment of the displaced 'other') shows them how to get more pleasure out of life (figure 29).[9]

The film oscillates between moments when daily life appears bleak and hopeless (particularly when Mehdi takes on a job assisting a debt collector), and moments of conviviality when the friends meet to work on Sergio's house or share a meal. It also traces their individual stories. During the course of a picnic excursion, Marc goes crazy with frustration and jealousy and Cécile breaks off her relationship with him. Mehdi and Agatha make love and plan to go away together. Willy unsuccessfully attempts to persuade Marc's violent boss to pay Marc his dues but, when the boss is accidentally killed in a fall, decides not to run away, even though Mehdi wants to help him escape. Agatha gets money from her former lover and decides to leave alone, both because of the difficulties of life as an undocumented alien in France and because she senses that, without her, Mehdi and Cécile would have a future together. After finding Agatha a lift with a long-distance lorry-driver heading for Holland, Mehdi makes his way, alone, to Cécile's house, opening up the possibility of future happiness. The final sequence takes place back at the site of Sergio's house, where a potentially threatening visit from the police turns out to be just a question of sorting out a dispute with a neighbour. The film ends on a freeze frame of the group of friends laughing together, a sign of hope and comradeship amid adversity.

29 Medhi (Roschdy Zem) with Agatha (Rona Hartner) in *Sauve-moi* (2000).

Sauve-moi provides a sympathetic portrait of a group of people living on the margins, emphasising the precariousness of their position by its focus on places of transit and traffic (also a feature of the soundtrack), yet also centring on their potential settlement, through the metaphor of the house that they are building together. It offers a strong protest against the ways in which the poor and vulnerable are exploited, particularly in the scenes in which Mehdi visits the wretched rundown flats and terraced housing where the debt collector's victims live (including an immigrant Maghrebi family). But it also offers images of revolt and solidarity, as when Mehdi ruins the paintwork of the debt collector's car after seeing him go into a woman's flat for sex in payment of her debts, and eventually throws in the job by advising another 'client' not to let the debt collector into the house. Although one brief scene indicates that Mehdi is still living at home with his immigrant family, the film takes for granted his acceptance both within his peer group and within French society. Though he may have difficulty establishing his place (even his taxi is illegal), he is not expelled from the narrative or from French territory; instead he ends up with the possibility of a loving relationship with Cécile and the security of a group of friends with a place of their own, Sergio's house built with their shared labour. The film thus emphasises that, unlike Agatha, the illegal immigrant who is just in transit, Mehdi, the *beur*, like Sergio, who is of Italian immigrant origin, has the right to settle in France.

Drôle de Félix/The Adventures of Felix (2000)

Ducastel and Martineau are politically concerned filmmakers who attempt to arouse spectator awareness of social and political issues by appropriating and subverting popular cinematic forms. Their first film, *Jeanne et le garçon formidable* (1998) was a musical comedy that addressed the question of AIDS. In *Drôle de Félix* they have created a road movie which addresses questions of ethnicity and sexuality as well as AIDS.

Drôle de Félix begins with a very long take of the appropriately named Félix (Sami Bouajila), humming to himself as he cycles along the deserted road bordering the beach at Dieppe, accompanied on the soundtrack by a nostalgic song celebrating the pleasures of life ('La vie c'est épatant'/'Life is wonderful') (figure 30). As he cycles by the port, his conversation with the ferry workers reveals their unease about the future, and it transpires that Félix himself has lost his job as a steward on the ferry. If the scene appears to be setting up a similar socio-economic context to that of the preceding films, however, this is dispelled by the cut to Félix's upwardly mobile home life. In the bright, art-filled flat he shares with his teacher lover, Xo (Pierre-Loup Rajot), Félix looks set to spend his unemployment happily making love and watching television (particularly the morning soap), even if he still has to sign on at the ANPE (the employment exchange) and go to the hospital for his AIDS treatment. His routine is disturbed, however, when he decides to clear out his mother's flat and discovers traces of his past. In an old box is a wad of banknotes, a photograph of his mother and himself as a baby (his mother is white), and letters to his mother from Youssef, the man whom he presumes must be his father. Inspired by the sight of a mixed-race couple and their young son by the seaside, Félix makes the decision to visit his father in Marseilles, buys himself a kite, and arranges to meet his lover in Marseilles in five days' time.

Félix's journey is clearly an invitation to engage with questions of identity, particularly what it means for someone brought up in France to have a (missing) father of Maghrebi origin. Since Félix is of mixed race rather than a *beur* and, having had no contact with his Maghrebi relatives, thinks of himself primarily as *un Norman* (someone from Normandy), the quest for the father opens up the prospect of discovering a completely different aspect to his identity. (As in the representations of Bailleul and Dunkerque, there appear to be no other characters of Maghrebi origin in Dieppe.) Yet Xo and other people he encounters on his journey to Marseilles repeatedly call into question the purpose of his journey, insisting that there is no point in getting in touch with a father who has abandoned his child. No one, not even Félix himself, suggests that contact with the father's culture could be an enriching experience in itself – Félix, who is not even motivated by feelings of anger, simply wants to meet his father. Undoubtedly (and no doubt unintentionally), the film confirms that

30 Félix (Sami Bouajila) celebrates life in *Drôle de Félix* (2000).

the most loveable ethnic 'other' is the one who is least culturally different, and that, if Félix wants to be integrated, he should accept that his family is to be found elsewhere.

Indeed, Félix's journey through France, apart from the experiences of his first night in Rouen, is structured through his meetings with members of a surrogate family. It is loosely divided into five episodes, each labelled by the relationship to be explored, namely, 'mon petit frère', 'ma grand'mère', 'mon cousin', 'ma soeur' and 'mon père' ('my little brother', 'my grandmother', 'my cousin', 'my sister', 'my father'). In each case, Félix proves himself to be the perfect companion and/or lover. In Chartres, he helps a young lad sitting outside the cathedral sketch a detail of one of the sculptures and (later) come to terms with his sexuality; they (chastely) spend the night together and, the following day, steal a car to drive out to Le Puy-du-Dôme for the day, before separating when Jules gets thrown out of a nightclub for being under age. In the Auvergne, he gets picked up as he is resting on a bench by Mathilde (Patachou), an elderly woman who makes him carry her shopping bag and move her furniture, shares her stories with him, lets him stay the night, and ends up sharing her breakfast TV soap and pill-taking ritual with him. Further south, he gets a lift with a railway worker, with whom he flies his kite in a mountain meadow full of flowers and then makes love, the normality of the situation indicated by the emphasis on Félix's nettle stings and the problems of disposing of a used condom. Close to Avignon, he offers to help a woman struggling to change a tyre in a lay-by, and spends the rest of the day and night (again chastely) with her. The woman, Isabelle (Ariane Ascaride), proves to be a sympathetic, unconventional policewoman, who is transporting her three children to their three different fathers for the weekend; Félix helps her with the children, and she later talks to him about his troubles. Finally, close to Marseilles, he encounters an older man, who could be of Algerian origin, fishing in the river.[10] They exchange stories and the man dissuades Félix from troubling his biological father. Instead of rushing to Marseilles, Félix shows him how to fly his kite and they end up giving each other a big hug. It only remains for Félix to appear at St-Charles station where his lover is waiting for him.

What has been left out of this account is Félix's experiences in Rouen, which open up the possibility of a completely different, more conventional kind of narrative, in which the mixed-race youth falls victim to racism. In Rouen, Félix witnesses a racist attack, gets pursued and violently beaten up by one of the attackers, and makes his way to the police station, only to retreat at the sight of a youth in custody. The scene evokes the difficult relationship between ethnic minorities and the law, since Félix clearly fears being judged by the police on his appearance. The repercussions of this incident reverberate periodically throughout the film, as Félix learns from the television that he actually witnessed a murder and has a nightmare when, coincidentally, he sees one of the murderers being arrested when he is with Isabelle. It also affects his journey in that he determines not to use main roads or travel through major cities (particularly Vitrolles, a town newly under the control of the Front National). Although he plans to come forward as a witness, it is not clear whether he will have the courage to do so, and the film thus retains a salutary ambivalence about his place in France. At the same time, through the role of the unconventional, non-judgmental Isabelle, it demonstrates the possibility of a different relationship between the police and ethnic minority others.

If the film mostly works to dismantle and downplay the significance of Félix's ethnic body, his gay and AIDS-affected body is clearly on display, making the point that sexuality and AIDS are also to be deplored as grounds for discrimination. Each episode of the narrative contains sequences where Bouajila's beautiful, apparently healthy star body is discreetly exhibited as the object of a desiring gaze, be it making love, dancing, on the road, or simply lying asleep. That this body is also an object of desire for women is evident in the sequence where Mathilde is shown in the bedroom doorway gazing admiringly at Félix's naked body reflected in a mirror as he prepares for bed. Such a plurality of desiring gazes at the body of a youth of Maghrebi descent is extremely unusual in French cinema. Although a desiring homosexual or homosocial gaze is to be found in films such as Gaël Morel's *A toute vitesse* (1996) and Jean-Pierre Sinapi's *Vivre me tue* (2003), the ethnic minority bodies which are the objects of desire in such narratives are often subsequently contained or destroyed.[11] In this case, however, Félix is not just the object of the gaze, but also an active, optimistic, desiring subject in his own right. The film deliberately subverts tragic, negative stereotypes of gay men and the AIDS-affected body, and offers a more positive representation of it than Cyril Collard's *Les Nuits fauves* (Tarr 1999), or, indeed, than *La Vie de Jésus*, which exhibits the diseased body of Fredy's friend Cloclo dying of AIDS. The delightful, sunny Félix deals with his illness in a practical, matter-of-fact way (each episode includes a shot of him taking his pills) and his desirability, sexuality and illness do not preclude him from being actively involved in a committed, loving relationship.

The film ends with the happy reunion between Félix and his lover at the top of the steps leading down from St-Charles (the site of Larbi's arrival in Marseilles in *Karnaval*), and their immediate departure on the ferry on holiday, even though Félix has not found his biological father (and Xo has not acquired a new 'father-in-law', as he jokingly remarks). Shots of them kissing on the boat are accompanied by a panorama of Marseilles disappearing from view and the words of the song, 'Plus je t'embrasse, plus je t'aime embrasser' ('The more I kiss you, the more I love kissing you'). The film constructs Félix as a subject on the move, untroubled by his bicultural ethnic origins, but happy because he is loved, and because he can create an alternative family for himself wherever he goes – at least, as long as he keeps to the byways. It thus sets him up as a model of successful assimilation, whilst demonstrating the limits of Ducastel and Martineau's vision of a multicultural France. Not only is Félix not allowed to reclaim his Maghrebi heritage but, as a mixed-race gay man, he is not in a position to establish his own place and his own lineage and, even if Isabelle's children start calling him 'papa Félix', significantly, the surrogate family he acquires on the road does not present him with the opportunity to meet 'Mon enfant' ('My child').

Conclusion

The five films considered here explore the dynamics of the relationships available to young people of Maghrebi descent in spaces which allow their characters to develop without reference to *banlieue* stereotypes. They construct images of second-generation Maghrebis who are caught between adherence to their families and the desire for integration, but who, unlike *banlieue* youths, are not necessarily associated with delinquency and are able to find (temporary, provisional) places for themselves within the wider society.

In particular, they explore the possibility of intimate sexual relationships which are absent from most *beur* and *banlieue* films. *L'Honneur de ma famille* is a typical *beur* film in that Hamid is represented as a gauche, ungainly and impotent figure, and Nora's primary relationship lies in her cross-racial friendship. In contrast, in the four white-authored films, *beur* males are represented as both sexy and sexually active. In *Karnaval* and *La Vie de Jésus*, the *beurs* enjoy momentarily successful relationships with white women until their behaviour results in them being expelled from the white community. In *Sauve-moi*, Mehdi's relationship with Cécile is actually given the possibility of future development. As for *Drôle de Félix*, the film's eponymous hero is attractive to both men and women, and develops a series of relationships in addition to his primary relationship with Xo which open up spaces of class, generational, sexual and racial tolerance.

These films also offer a more nuanced portrayal of relationships between ethnic minorities and the law. The police are absent from *Karnaval* and only appear in *L'Honneur de ma famille* on the occasion of a road check when, ironically, the black youth who claims to be an illegal immigrant proves to have papers which are in order! In *Sauve-moi*, despite the accidental death of a white man, the police turn out to be equally non-threatening. They are more directly implicated in *La Vie de Jésus* and *Drôle de Félix*, both of which involve the racist murder of a *beur*. *La Vie de Jésus* ends with a disturbing lack of closure, since Fredy is allowed to run away from the police station and hence suffers no legal punishment for his crime within the diegesis. In *Drôle de Félix*, however, the police are seen closing in on the criminals and, as discussed above, the role of the policewoman suggests the possibility of new relationships between the police and ethnic minority others. Unusually, then, the construction of the police in these films offers little evidence of police aggression and hostility towards ethnic minorities.

However, the acceptability of the *beurs* seems to be directly related to their degree of commitment to their Maghrebi origins. The films' depictions of the immigrant Maghrebi family maintain the view that the values and attitudes of first-generation immigrants are the primary obstacle to the *beurs'* desire for integration and settlement in France, and suggest that integration is possible only for those who choose to isolate themselves from their family and culture of origin. In *L'Honneur de ma famille*, Nora's life is rendered intolerable, not by the ambient racism (which is barely evident) but by the pressures caused by having to lie to her immigrant parents, the only resolution to which lies in fleeing the family. The starting-point for *Karnaval* is Larbi's inability to communicate with his parents, a trope also hinted at in *La Vie de Jésus*, while in *Drôle de Félix*, the protagonist eventually rejects the possibility of finding his Maghrebi family connections. Even in *Sauve-moi*, which contains a brief, silent scene in which Mehdi returns to his family home, the Maghrebi family is not integrated into the narrative. None of these films, then, is able to imagine a truly multicultural French society, in which the majority culture would be able to accommodate and incorporate difference (not evacuate or assimilate it) and in which difference would be an asset rather than a disadvantage. Not surprisingly, three of these films end with the ethnic other displaced to the borders of

France, while in one (*La Vie de Jésus*), he is simply killed off. Thus, French films set in the North of France seem to suggest that young people of Maghrebi descent can only hope to achieve a place in the provinces if they operate within the strict limitations on cultural integration expected and imposed by the dominant white majority.

Notes

1 The other most privileged provincial setting is Marseilles, as in *Les Innocents* (Téchiné, 1987), *Bye-Bye* (Dridi, 1995), *Nénette et Boni* (Denis, 1997), *Comme un aimant* (Akhenaton and Saleh, 2000), *Samia* (Faucon, 2001), and the corpus of films directed by Robert Guédiguian.

2 See Wayne (2002: 64–70) for an analysis of *Ça commence aujourd'hui* and *Ressources humaines*, and Tarr with Rollet (2001) for an analysis of the films by women.

3 The credits for *Western* stress the multi-ethnic nature of Frenchness by humorously acknowledging the ethnic origins of the cast and crew.

4 The opening scene of Bouchareb's earlier film *Cheb* (1991) is set in Roubaix, prior to the young *beur*'s deportation to Algeria. Roubaix was also the setting for Gérard Blain's tragic *Pierre et Djemila* (1986).

5 A critique of the excessive influence exercised by the immigrant mother over her son is also a feature of *Inch'Allah dimanche*.

6 Vincent's previous films include the award-winning *La Discrète* (1990), *Beau fixe* (1992) and *La Séparation* (1994).

7 Paul Vecchiali's *Zone franche* (1996), set in Mulhouse with a cast of amateur actors, also derives from collaboration with local people. It has a simplistic fantasy narrative in which solidarity among members of the multi-ethnic *banlieue* community overcomes both racism and police corruption.

8 Hartner made her name as the co-star of Tony Gatlif's *Gadjo dilo* (1998), where she plays a similarly exuberant young Roma woman.

9 The temporary sojourn of an East European immigrant in France also structures the multi-stranded narrative of Claire Denis' *J'ai pas sommeil* (1994) (see Beugnet 2000b: 231–72).

10 Actor Maurice Bénichou was born in Algeria.

11 *Vivre me tue* also contains a sequence set in Lens in the North of France, where the *beur* protagonist realises that he has no place among the settled traditional white working-class community there.

10

Heroines of cross-cultural social protest: *Marie-Line* and *Chaos*[1]

In 1996, under the rightwing government of Alain Juppé, a significant number of filmmakers associated with the *jeune cinéma français* became involved in protests against the state's treatment of the *sans-papiers* ('undocumented' immigrants). The *sans-papiers*' occupation of the church of St-Bernard in Paris to protest at the effects of the Pasqua laws on their status in France (after earlier occupations of St-Ambroise and other public spaces), and their brutal expulsion in August by the CRS, was followed by a large demonstration featuring actress Emmanuelle Béart, among others. In April the following year, filmmakers spearheaded a petition protesting at the law designed to prevent French nationals from offering hospitality to the *sans-papiers*, and a short manifesto film, *Nous sans-papiers de France*, was made by a group of about fifteen filmmakers brought together by Nicolas Philibert (including Catherine Corsini, Claire Devers, Philippe Faucon, Serge Le Péron, Claire Simon and Marie Vermillard, all of whom have made films addressing questions of ethnicity and difference). *Nous sans-papiers de France* was signed by 175 filmmaking professionals and shown at the Cannes Film Festival in 1997. It consists of a three-minute close-up of Madjiguène Cissé, the articulate, intelligent spokeswoman for the *sans-papiers* of St-Bernard, herself of Senegalese origin, addressing the spectator directly with a moving text explaining their absurd and unjust situation, published in *Libération* on 25 February 1997. However, as Sylvie Agard points out, media coverage of the occupation of St-Bernard did not generally allow the *sans-papiers* to articulate their own perspectives on events (Agard 2004). Although a number of documentary films were authorised to bear witness to their struggle, only *D'une brousse à l'autre* (Jacques Kebadian, 1998) received a cinematic release (others were screened on the festival circuit). Whilst *Nous sans-papiers de France* undoubtedly aimed to 'bring people closer together in ways which are difficult in the real world, and allow the idea of a possible community of action and destiny to emerge' (Saussier 2001: 326, cited in Agard 2004), it also raises the question as to the conditions in which ethnic minority others are able to articulate their own voices.[2]

This chapter analyses two feature films, made since the *sans-papiers* protest began, which are critically concerned with the place of undocumented immigrant women in the French and, indeed, the wider economy. Mehdi Charef's *Marie-Line* (2000) focuses on a multi-ethnic team of women night cleaners working for a company ('Euro-Nettoyage') run by members of the Front National, while Coline Serreau's *Chaos* (2001) features a young *beur* woman prostitute working for a vice ring run by men of indeterminate central European origin. Neither film uses a self-reflexive style to draw attention to the politics of the image in the manner of post-1968 avant-garde political cinema. Their interest lies in the fact that they address their audience through, and draw their social protest and political commitment from, a narrative structured by the productive encounter between ethnic majority and minority women. Films focusing on relationships between women are relatively rare in French cinema (see Tarr with Rollet 2001), and even feminist filmmakers generally take care to address a mixed audience by privileging women's relationships with men.[3] These two films thus demonstrate a courageous commitment to both feminism and anti-racism through the unusual tropes of feminist heroines and cross-cultural inter-ethnic sisterhood.[4] Yet neither film was made by a woman of immigrant origin, and their representations of ethnic minority women need to be seen in this context.

The foregrounding of women's concerns will come as no surprise to spectators familiar with the works of Charef and Serreau (which pre-date the appearance of the *jeune cinéma français*). Charef focuses on women's marginality and exclusion in *Au pays des Juliet* (1992), a drama centring on three women prisoners on parole.[5] Serreau is well known for her 1970s feminist documentaries – *Mais qu'est-ce qu'elles veulent!* (1978) and *Grand-mères de l'Islam* (1978) – and although her best-known comedies centre primarily on dysfunctional white middle-class men, they nevertheless include significant roles for ethnic minority women, such as Juliette in *Romuald et Juliette* (1989) and Djamila in *La Crise* (1992). Furthermore, the emergence of *Marie-Line* and *Chaos* at the turn of the millennium can be located in relation to other narrative films of the 1990s and early 2000s which address social issues affecting white women (for example, Laetitia Masson's *En avoir (ou pas)* (1995) and *A vendre* (1988), Christine Carrière's *Rosine* (1995), Erick Zonca's *La Vie rêvée des anges* (1998), Marion Vernoux's *Rien à faire* (1999), Dominique Cabrera's *Nadia et les hippopotames* (2000)) or the problematic identity of women of Maghrebi or mixed-race origin (for example, *Les Histoires d'amour finissent mal en général, Souviens-toi de moi, L'Honneur de ma famille, Les Soeurs Hamlet, Sous les pieds des femmes, Samia* and *Inch'allah dimanche*). Indeed, as Vincent Amiel notes in his analysis of Arte's 1999 TV drama series entitled *Gauche/Droite* ('Left/

Right'), which includes Cabrera's *Retiens la nuit* and Claire Devers' *La Voleuse de St Lubin*, contemporary films centred on women seem to be more able to envisage the possibilities of action and change than those centred on men (Amiel 2000).[6]

The possibilities of action and change in relation to prejudices and inequalities in contemporary multicultural France are articulated in *Marie-Line* and *Chaos* through the establishment of common ground between white women and ethnic minority women. Cross-racial friendship among young men is a recurring trope of male-centred *beur* films as a sign of (partial) integration into French society. However, female solidarity across and despite ethnic difference is more unusual. It is a feature of *Souviens-toi de moi* (discussed in chapter 5), *La Squale* (discussed in chapter 7) and *L'Honneur de ma famille* (discussed in chapter 9), as well as *Baise-moi* (2000), the controversial revenge road movie by Virginie Despentes and Coralie Trinh Thi;[7] it is also a secondary theme of a number of women's films, including Corsini's *La Nouvelle Eve* (1999) and Benguigui's *Inch'Allah dimanche* (2001). In *Marie-Line* and *Chaos*, however, female solidarity results in a significant joint challenge to the cross-racial patriarchal abuse of power. No doubt, any forging of links between women across differences of race and ethnicity can be seen as politically progressive at a time when the Front National continues to attract French voters and policies on immigration are becoming increasingly illiberal. The films' focus on women also challenges more conventional (male) mainstream understandings of what might constitute political filmmaking (and political action). However, their progressive construction of cross-racial sisterhood is potentially undermined by the different cinematic strategies deployed to represent the different women. The chapter examines first what the films have in common, then analyses the problematic construction in each film of its 'heroines'.

Despite differences of genre – *Marie-Line* is a social/poetic realist film, *Chaos* is a postmodern hybrid of comedy, melodrama and action movie (which did extremely well at the French box office) – the films have as their common terrain the investigation of difference, juxtaposing the otherness of ethnic minority women, vulnerable to exploitation as clandestine workers because of their precarious citizenship (supermarket cleaners in *Marie-Line*, prostitutes in *Chaos*), with that of white women, be it the working-class woman exploited by her boss and family, as in *Marie-Line*, or the professional middle-class woman exploited by her family, as in *Chaos*. In each case the encounter between the two follows a similar structural pattern.

The narratives begin with a demonstration of the hierarchical difference and apparent lack of sympathy between the two sets of women. The eponymous Marie-Line is in charge of a team of cleaners in a hypermarket, only two of whom have proper jobs, the rest being an assortment of *sans-papiers* whom she treats with a mix of aggression and indifference; Hélène in *Chaos* is a privileged if alienated bourgeois wife and mother who, with her husband Paul, witnesses from the safety of her car the brutal beating up of Noémie/ Malika, a prostitute of Maghrebi descent. In each case the film is initially focalised from the point of view of the white woman, who is the one to learn most from her encounter with the other. Marie-Line gradually and grudgingly becomes involved in the lives of her co-workers (protecting a black child when his parents get detained, for example), realises the poverty of the alternative sets of values available to her (her joyless marriage, her subjection to the Front National, her failed attempt to begin a new life in *la France profonde*), recognises what she has in common with her co-workers (their exploitation), and takes action to demonstrate her solidarity with them, even if it means breaking the law (stealing goods for the children) and risking her job. In *Chaos*, Hélène, already guilty about her failure to come to the aid of the young woman, realises the poverty of her family and professional life (her uncaring husband, equally indifferent son, meaningless job), gets involved in Noémie's life by nursing her back to health and rescuing her from her pimp, recognises what they have in common (exploitation by men) and takes action to show her solidarity with Noémie, again, by breaking the law when need be, and putting her marriage at risk. In each film, then, the white woman finds meaning in life by learning compassion for and co-operation with others, throws into question the future of her privileged position (as cleaning inspector, as bourgeois wife and mother), and enables the film to end on images of female solidarity. As Michel Cadé points out, 1990s films about members of the working classes do not have a clear political programme and, to withstand the chaos of contemporary social and economic forces, fall back on individual protests and the solidarity of 'the couple, the nuclear or extended family, and friends' (Cadé 2000: 67). What is interesting about both *Marie-Line* and *Chaos* is that they refuse to fall back on the couple or the family, replacing them with a new form of solidarity, however precarious and provisional, that of a community of women (a theme reminiscent of second-wave feminism of the 1970s).

Both films were criticised for the number of targets they attack.[8] *Marie-Line* foregrounds sexual harassment at work, the economic exploitation of female working-class and immigrant labour, the Front National's abuse of managerial power, the survival problems of the *sans-papiers*, and the domestic problems of working-class women. *Chaos* denounces everyday sexism and machismo within the bourgeois family, the patriarchal values of the immigrant Algerian family, and international prostitution networks. In each case, however, the films foreground the violence done to women by men, making explicit the effects of economic, mental and physical violence on women's bodies and showing how they can be more severe for ethnic minority women. In *Marie-Line*, the fear of unemployment, arrest or expulsion leads to Marie-Line suffering forced sexual relations with the boss, an Algerian woman attempting suicide and an Albanian woman giving birth at work trapped in the lift-cage; in *Chaos*, the daily disparagement or indifference suffered by Hélène is juxtaposed with the fear of an arranged marriage and the rape, torture and enforced prostitution suffered by Noémie. The films stress how ethnic minority women can be exploited in the black economy because of their need for an income to support their families and their insecurity as citizens: in *Marie-Line* a black woman worker and her husband are deported; in *Chaos* the vulnerability of the *sans-papiers* is echoed in Noémie's desperate need to regain possession of her passport. They also make the link between the patriarchal organisation of work (the cleaning company, the vice ring) and the patriarchal organisation of the family, where women are also objects of exchange and exploitation by men, whether in the white working-class family of *Marie-Line* or the bourgeois and Algerian immigrant families of *Chaos*. Furthermore, in each case, problematic relations with men and male authority are contrasted with moments of pleasure when the women have time alone together, be it the outing to the beach in *Marie-Line* or the escape to the sea in *Chaos*.

These films, then, draw critical attention to unpalatable issues in ways which are potentially empowering for women, whether or not one agrees with their often rather unsubtle analyses of the wrongs of the world. (Serreau's somewhat Manichaean attribution of the source of all evil to men is less manifest in *Marie-Line*, which includes women among the police force and the Front National cadres, and represents ethnic minority men as either absent or helpless.) At the same time, any representation of women of Maghrebi descent as victims is problematic within both Western and non-Western feminisms.[9] On the one hand, Western feminists have long argued for a recognition of the double exclusion suffered by minority women, and fought for women's rights across a range of varying socio-cultural conditions. On the other, eurocentric representations of minority women as the victims of a non-Western patriarchal culture, however well intentioned, run the threefold risk of denying minority women their own subjectivities and agencies, salving liberal Western consciences, and playing into a reactionary agenda through the vilification of ethnic minority men.

The issue raises the question as to whether ethnic minority women's protest at their exclusion in France can be adequately articulated by others. *Marie-Line* and *Chaos* both offer textual analogies between the situation of majority white and ethnic minority women, a device which allows ethnic minority women an apparently equal voice. Yet inequalities in the way they are represented suggest that these analogies function as a catalyst for and intensification of white women's discovery of their alienation in a 'chaotic' eurocentric patriarchal world rather than as a way of understanding the specificity of the double exclusion suffered by ethnic minority women. I would argue that both these films foreground white women as 'heroines' and in the process reduce ethnic minority women to secondary roles in *Marie-Line* and stereotypical roles in *Chaos*. If this is the case, the films' messages of solidarity and multicultural understanding between women may well be muted, if not counter-productive. The rest of the chapter focuses first on the effects of Muriel Robin's star role as the eponymous *Marie-Line*, then on the differences in style and point-of-view between the two heroines of *Chaos*.

Marie-Line (2000)

The title of *Marie-Line* clearly foregrounds the role of an individual rather than a community, and the casting and marketing of the film highlighted the fact that the role was embodied by well-known comic star Muriel Robin, playing against type (for which she was nominated for a César). The film is given its coherence by being focalised primarily from the perspective of its white heroine, tracing the shifts in her attitudes and behaviour from her subjection to her Front National bosses to her defiant assertion of her place among a marginalised, multi-ethnic community of women. This device no doubt enables the film to address a majority audience, but Robin's role and performance risks relegating the other disadvantaged women to the sidelines.

Marie-Line enjoys a controlling vision of the feminised spaces of the hypermarket at night from the vantage point of her motorised cleaning vehicle.[10] She watches the women at work, checks on their every action, and, initially at least, rules them with a rod of iron. (She is determined to keep her job and win the company's prize for the best cleaning team.) The power of her gaze is periodically challenged by those in authority (Léonard the boss, who transfixes Marie-Line from his panoptically designed office, the company inspectors, the police searching for illegal immigrants); but her reaction shots enable even these episodes to be mostly focalised from her point of view. Multiple close-ups of her grim, impassive face thus generate a critical, female perspective on the unwarranted surveillance the women are forced to endure, their insecurity and their lack of a space to call their own, a perspective which by the end of the film is translated into action on their behalf. The diegesis thus works to show how solidarity with ethnic-minority women enables the white working-class woman to gain new self-respect. Nevertheless, apart from Meriem (Fejria Deliba, later the star of *Inch'Allah dimanche*), the ethnic minority women themselves are given little interiority, their life outside work is rarely glimpsed, and they are important mainly as they impact on Marie-Line's life and are validated by her interest in them.

Marie-Line is set up not just as the subject of the gaze, but also as the object of the gaze of the other women. And whereas they first regard her with fear and loathing, they grow to relish her strength, her craziness and her moments of vulnerability. In fact, they constitute a diegetic audience for Robin's star performance, stopping work to watch her as she demonstrates, for example, her strength in lifting a display cabinet, her joy in dancing in one of the shop's wedding dresses, or her folly in walking along a cross-beam in anticipation of winning the cleaning award. Though the spectator has the first privileged view of Marie-Line performing a number by Joe Dassin in costume in the privacy of her home (where she runs a Joe Dassin fan club from her cellar), elsewhere a shot of Meriem coming to fetch a child from her flat serves as a way of catching her unawares in another Dassin impersonation. Robin is thus set up as star in ways which construct ethnic minority women as onlookers.

This is not to deny that *Marie-Line* opens up a certain amount of space for the other women to tell their stories or express their opinions. For instance, the spectator learns that Marnia's family in Algeria was slaughtered while she herself was raped, had her throat cut, and was then left for dead; pregnant Maïna escaped from Albania, but was forced to leave behind her husband who could not cross the Italian border; Bergère (Valérie Stroh) has a daughter who has chosen to wear the Islamic headscarf and live with her father. Early in the film, various women voice their unease with Marie-Line's management style and her relationship to the bosses, directly accusing her of racism. And throughout the film, the camera lingers longer than necessary on Meriem's reproachful, silent gaze, inviting both Marie-Line and the spectator to speculate about her critical reactions to Marie-Line's behaviour. Thus, the film gives the women moments of resistance and enables the spectator to attribute Marie-Line's change in attitude to the ways in which the other women make her aware, not just of their individual problems, but also of the inequities of the company's abuse of power and its collusion with the state's exploitative treatment of illegal immigrants (a situation which is particularly ironic given that the company's slogan is 'for a clean Europe'). This is particularly true of the scenes involving the police, when Marie-Line is supported by Meriem and Bergère as they confront the intruders, and the collaboration between the cleaning women is contrasted with the alienation of the white, deaf and dumb police inspector, a female boss in her own world as Marie-Line is in hers, but a woman who is apparently unable to feel compassion for others (figure 31).

It is also true that Meriem, the most reliable member of her team, comes to occupy an increasingly prominent role in the diegesis. Meriem may be the daughter of a *harki*[11] who lives in fear of her husband's disapproval (though the husband is never seen), but as Marie-Line's neighbour, she colludes with Marie-Line in helping the black *sans-papiers* family and sympathises with her dreams of escape. Though the hierarchy of power relations between them is never quite eroded, Marie-Line comes to recognise the value of her assistance, visiting her when she is held in custody for sheltering the destitute black family, sharing with her the attempt to free Maïna from the lift (Meriem insists on being the one to cut the baby's cord), stealing clothes and toys with her for the

31 Marie-Line (Muriel Robin) and co-workers confront intruders in *Marie-Line* (2000).

black children (including Zidane football shirts), and so on. What the spectator does not have access to, however, is Meriem's private life and thoughts.

Arguably, the film could have developed the relationship between the two
women in ways that gave Meriem more of a voice and allowed her more interiority. Instead the effect of their cross-cultural dialogue becomes clear in the
action taken by Marie-Line in the film's final sequence. After the ceremony at
which she is presented with her award and promoted to the inspectorate, she
refuses to do her Dassin impersonation, as requested by the management, and
instead begins to play Arabic music over the loudspeaker. By so doing, she
demonstrates that she has begun to listen to the music that Meriem loves so
much. She thus openly challenges the values of the Front National management team and demonstrates her solidarity with her colleagues, to whom she
dedicates her trophy. The moment recalls earlier scenes in which, by playing
their music of origin, two *sans-papiers* women, now absent from the diegesis,
had revealed their presence to the police. But it also suggests that cross-cultural
dialogue can generate cultural exchanges which enhance the majority culture
without the minority culture being sacrificed.

Marie-Line's act of defiance is supported by reaction shots to the smiles of
her daughter, Meriem and Bergère, while the men who have made her life mis-
erable (including the husband who has left her for a Front National activist)
quickly leave the room. The scene emphasises Marie-Line's interdependency
with the other women, but it also confirms her in her role as heroine, ending
on a medium close-up of her tearful, smiling face as the music switches to a

Dassin song, 'A toi – à ta façon d'être belle' ('To you – to your way of being beautiful'). If she appears to be providing a voice for other, even more disempowered women than herself, her action does not prepare the ground for any future, shared industrial (or other) action at work which would make the women's lives more bearable. Though the smiling women are left occupying the company's meeting-place, they have been isolated as a group, their voices silent and their future job prospects uncertain. Meanwhile, the privileging of Robin's role continues to emphasise the importance of the white woman rather than the ethnic minority women as the significant agent of history and change. Marie-Line is a channel through which a white audience can learn about, understand, and sympathise with ethnic minority others and their problematic economic and political situations; but there is still a danger of ethnic minority women themselves remaining marginalised.

Chaos (2001)

In *Chaos*, Serreau resorts to the fairy-tale narrative structure of her earlier comedies, 'bringing together two people from different and potentially antagonistic class and ethnic backgrounds and producing social awareness, humour and romance' (Tarr with Rollet 2001: 181). Unlike any of her other feature films, however, the romance of *Chaos* lies in the relationship between two women, making this her most openly feminist feature film to date. However, the film raises a number of problems in its construction of the ethnic minority woman, not just through its structure, which seems to bring together heroines from two different films and, arguably, still privileges the white woman's perspective, but also through its use of stereotypes and its message of assimilation.

The confusion of *Chaos*' postmodern play with genres – at once a bourgeois comedy of manners, a social problem film, an at times comic action thriller, and a moral and political fable – is compounded by its shifts in narrative focalisation. The film seems deliberately to deny the majority spectator the comfort of a coherent, Eurocentric point of view from which the interconnectedness of its themes can be made apparent, and this can be attributed in part to its desire to give the ethnic minority woman her own agency and voice. The film's more multi-vocal texture is evident to some extent in its casting. The bourgeois couple, Hélène and Paul, whose lives are changed by their encounter with a Maghrebi prostitute, are played by white stars, Catherine Frot and Vincent Lindon; the prostitute/victim herself, Noémie/Malika, is played by a stage actress of Maghrebi descent, Rachida Brakni, who subsequently won the 2002 César for Most Promising Actress.[12] The film also provides a key role for Line Renaud as Paul's unhappy, unloved mother, Mamie. However, the actress playing her counterpart, Noémie's younger sister Zora, does not get a parallel mention in the film's publicity (and has a much briefer role). The casting thus suggests once again that the film will privilege a white perspective.

Indeed, despite its fragmented narrative strands, the first (long) section of the film definitely privileges the point of view of Hélène, whose discovery of the callous indifference of her husband and son leads her to abandon her affectless domestic and professional life in order to devote herself to the recovery of the unknown but hospitalised and helpless young *beur* woman. Noémie spends the first section of the film in a coma, voiceless and motionless, the object of Hélène's gaze and dependent on Hélène for her safety, whereas Hélène becomes an active (if comic) heroine, rejecting the sexism and selfishness of the male members of her family and experiencing a sense of commitment and adventure which gives her life new intensity and meaning (as when she knocks out the pimp pursuing Noémie with a plank and later transports Noémie to the seaside with Mamie).

In contrast, the second (middle) section of the film is a long cartoonlike flashback to Noémie's past, narrated in voice-over by Noémie herself when she recovers her ability to walk and talk. The flashback establishes her both as a victim (first of patriarchal Algerian traditions, then of an international vice ring), and as a rebel determined to live her own life. It traces key moments of her life from her childhood in Algeria (where she witnesses her mother being punished for adultery) via her schooldays in France (where her father sells her into marriage in Algeria), to her escape and capture by a pimp (as a result of which she is drugged, raped and turned into a prostitute). It then shows her attempts to escape and save her sister from a similar fate. She uses her position to acquire financial skills, persuades a terminally ill Swiss banker client to leave her his fortune, and secretes all but the jewels away in her own name. Her story reaches a climax when her bosses discover what she has done and want her to sign over the money, leading to the moment when she stumbles headlong into Hélène and Paul's car in her attempt to get away (the moment which initiates the encounter between the two women). The condensation of such a dramatic life in flashback form is decidedly over-ambitious, resulting in a series of brief visualisations (including scenes at which Noémie could not have been present, like her mother's suicide and the banker's despair) which allow the character very little interiority. Rather, the flashback breaks up the narrative continuity and disrupts Hélène's established point of view. At the same time, it provides material for Brakni to demonstrate her star potential both as the subject of the action and as the object of the gaze.

Although the spectator is required to read the flashback images in the light of Noémie's explanatory voice-over, Brakni's flawless body is persistently set up as the object of the spectator's look as she is transformed from innocent, studious young *beurette* to streetwise prostitute and then intelligent high-class tart.[13] The film challenges stereotypical imagery of the young Maghrebi woman as both prostitute and victim by showing Noémie reading the financial pages and becoming a financial genius. Indeed, it also establishes Noémie as the active subject of the look, sizing up her victims, and knowingly trading on the stereotype of the young Maghrebi woman as victim to seduce them, before stripping them of their assets. However, by transforming the sexy *beurette* into a *femme fatale*, who is calculating and untrustworthy (she is clearly playing a role) but all-powerful (everyone succumbs to her), Serreau seems simply to be replacing one stereotype with another.[14]

The first two sections of the film set up a parallel between Hélène and Noémie, despite differences of ethnicity and treatment, which anticipates their coming together in the final section of the film, as indeed, to an extent, they do. With Hélène's help, Noémie sets out both to set her own life to rights, by claiming her money, shopping the bosses of the prostitution racket to the police, and saving her sister from her unpleasant family, and to teach Hélène's husband and son a lesson by seducing and abandoning them, thus putting them back in touch with their feelings (though such an unconvincing project only confirms her status as the 'sexy *beurette*'). At various key moments the two women are shot together, as when towards the end of the film they gaze down through their binoculars from the windows of the Hotel Lutetia to watch the police operation Noémie has masterminded (unknown to the police). As the dying pimp looks back up at them, his emasculated gaze takes in both the woman he has tortured and prostituted and the woman who snatched her away from him. The importance of their joint action is further underlined when Hélène assists Noémie in rescuing her sister just as her vicious Algerian father is about to take her to Algeria (figure 32).

However, the narrative is not consistently focalised from either Noémie's or Hélène's point of view, and it is Hélène's changing consciousness which still provides the main point of identification for a majority audience (as when she watches Noémie start seducing Paul, for example). Furthermore, the difference between the genres to which the two heroines belong becomes more invidious. Hélène's bourgeois family comedy drama allows its characters a certain amount of cinematic space, interiority and hope of redemption; even Paul is able to shed a tear when, thanks to Noémie (who eventually identifies herself as the prostitute he had failed to help, and reunites him with his mother), he finally realises what is wrong with his life (a narrative development which conveniently lets the white European male off the hook). In contrast, Noémie's cartoonlike action-movie/police-thriller depends on two-dimensional stereotypes, be it Zora, the dutiful daughter–victim destined for an arranged marriage, the evil pimps and the equally evil Algerian immigrant family for whom women's bodies are nothing but objects of exchange, or, arguably, Noémie herself, who despite some long, angry, demonstrative speeches is more convincing as a larger-than-life action heroine capable of

32 Zora (Hajar Nouma) is rescued by Noémie (Rachida Brakni) and Hélène (Catherine Frot) in *Chaos* (2001).

playing the evil capitalists and exploiters of women at their own game than as a complex, rounded individual.

Chaos ends with a brief scene beside the sea focusing on images of cross-race and intergenerational female solidarity and friendship.[15] Hélène and Noémie share a bench with Zora and Mamie, each having escaped from families characterised by ungrateful sons and unfeeling patriarchs. However, Hélène's solidarity with Noémie is also made possible by the film's tacit message that Noémie needs to reject her Algerian background and culture in order to be free. (The point is underlined by a scene in which Noémie seeks help from SOS Racisme and gets abused by a man of Maghrebi origin.) Noémie's enterprise, education and wealth enable her buy a villa by the sea and thus potentially to assimilate into Hélène's bourgeois lifestyle. Unlike *Marie-Line*, then, the film's cross-cultural dialogue does not fundamentally challenge the white female protagonist's attitude to ethnic others, since Noémie (as the assumed name suggests) is already completely assimilated into Western bourgeois culture.

At the same time, the desirability of the ending is also ambiguous. After a long shot of the group from the rear, the camera pans from face to face, framing each woman individually looking out to sea, their facial expressions unreadable. Does the scene just mark a pause for introspection before they resume their lives? Or is Serreau suggesting that their alliance, with its accompanying withdrawal from the chaos of the patriarchal world, is not necessarily the most desirable happy ending? And if so, is she in fact, in good Brechtian tradition, inviting spectators to speculate themselves as to the best (and necessarily feminist) alternative solutions? The ending is suitably open.

Conclusion

Both these films are concerned with the exploitation of women at work and in the home, both invite compassion for and action on behalf of ethnic minority women in France, and both draw on cross-race female solidarity as a way of countering oppression. At the same time, their construction of ethnic difference is problematic. The social realist approach of *Marie-Line* brings into representation a range of portraits of immigrant (and other) workers who are normally invisible in film, and addresses recognisable issues and relationships deriving from their subordinate and marginalised positions. However, the film does not fundamentally challenge their position within the social hierarchy, maintaining them in secondary narrative roles, and it is the white woman's awakening to social consciousness which structures the narrative for the predominantly white spectator. In contrast, *Chaos*' *mélange* of genres and points of view enables the ethnic minority protagonist to emerge from a role as passive victim and object of the look to that of active action heroine. Yet its fantasy of female revenge does not fundamentally challenge the racism of French society (Noémie's Algerian and East European enemies are more terrifying than Hélène's heartless French husband) and, arguably, Serreau does not so much deconstruct stereotypes of young women of Maghrebi descent as create a new westernised fantasy figure to represent the white woman's *alter ego*. While these films articulate social protest and provide a welcome representation of female solidarity, their unequal deployment of heroines does not necessarily represent the hopes and aspirations of a pro-feminist multicultural France in the most politically effective way.

Notes

1 An earlier version of this chapter was presented at a conference on 'Contours of Commitment in French cinema' at Nottingham Trent University in September 2002.
2 Many of the French filmmakers involved in the *sans-papiers* protest were criticised for not incorporating such issues in their own (feature) filmmaking. Fictionalised accounts of the actions taken by the *sans-papiers* are now to be found in *Paris selon Moussa* (Cheik Dutouré, 2003) and the Tunisian film *Bedwin Hacker* (Nadia El Fani, 2003). Other films addressing the plight of individual *sans-papiers* include *Nos vies heureuses* (Jacques Maillot, 1999), *L'Afrance* (Alain Gomis, 2002) and *Wesh wesh, qu'est-ce qui se passe?* (Rabah Ameur-Zaïmèche, 2002).
3 In the latter half of the 1990s and early 2000s, there has been a renewal of feminist activity in France with regard to parity, job titles and combating sexism in the

media, campaigns which are not necessarily of primary interest to working-class or immigrant women.

4   Filmmakers have come together to make compilation films on a variety of social issues, including AIDS and racism, both of which include short films by and about women. However, there has been no such film specifically devoted to women's issues.

5   The position of women in Algeria is a central theme of Charef's later film, *La Fille de Keltoum* (2002), discussed in chapter 12.

6   It is notable, in contrast, that in Hervé Le Roux's *Reprise* (1997), the woman worker at the centre of the 1968 film footage concerning the failure of the strike at the Wonder batteries factory is never found; her voice remains silent.

7   *Baise-moi* focuses on a non-hierarchical relationship between a sexy young white woman and a sexy young woman of Maghrebi descent. Though the *beurette* is initially represented as a victim of her ethnic background, the narrative emphasises the women's shared desires and agency as rampaging murderers on the run. True to the road movie format, however, their anarchic protest at exclusion leads to death and destruction, rather than to a more politically acceptable form of feminism.

8   See, for example, the review of *Marie-Line* in *Cahiers du Cinéma* (Larcher 2000: 88) and the review of *Chaos* in *Libération* (Lançon 2001).

9   Conventional Eurocentric representations of women of Maghrebi descent as exotic, sexualised or criminalised others and/or as victims of the Arabo-Berber-Islamic sex/gender system are still to be found in, for example, *Clubbed to Death*, *Raï* and *La Squale*.

10   The most immediately significant element of *Marie-Line* is its use of space, which centres on the image of the hypermarket at night. To quote Saskia Sassen's description of the timetabling of public spaces, 'the fact that at night a whole other, mostly immigrant workforce installs itself in these spaces … and inscribes the space with a different culture (manual labour, often music, lunch breaks at midnight) is an invisible event' (Sassen 1991: 101, cited in Morley 2001: 163). *Marie-Line* draws attention to women normally evacuated from film, and focuses on the tensions and pleasures to be found in a woman-centred space, which nevertheless remains precarious, subject to control and risk.

11   Charef has also written a novel about the *harkis* in France, entitled the *Le Harki de Meriem* (1989).

12   The film received five nominations for the French Césars, the other four being Best Film, Best Screenplay, Best Actress (Catherine Frot) and Best Supporting Actress (Line Renaud). (In 2001, Brakni also had a role in Téchine's *Loin*.)

13   Mark McKinney has identified the 'studious *beurette*' and the 'sexy *beurette*' as key comic-book character types (McKinney 2000).

14   Serreau's play with stereotypes has often been controversial, as Mireille Rosello has discussed in relation to *La Crise* (1992) (Rosello 1998: 101–27).

15   *Samia* and *La Squale*, discussed in chapter 7, also end with shots of the female characters by the sea.

11

Beur filmmaking in the new millennium: from *Le Raïd* to *Jeunesse dorée*[1]

The first years of the new millennium provide an opportunity for assessing how *beur* filmmaking has developed since the flourishing of the *banlieue* film in 1995 and the surprise success of Djamel Bensalah's *Le Ciel, les oiseaux . . . et ta mère* in 1999. Since 2000, there has been an increase in the number of *beur* filmmakers – Kamel Saleh, Karim Abbou (born in 1968 in Puteaux), Kader Ayd (born in 1976 in Nanterre), Rabah Ameur-Zaïmèche, Yamina Benguigui (born in 1957 in Lille), Zakia Bouchaala, Lyèce Boukhitine and Chad Chenouga have all made their first feature films – and their films offer a wider range of styles and representations. Whilst some filmmakers aspire to enter the mainstream, others continue to produce personal, low-budget, often semi-autobiographical films. This chapter focuses on the *beur*-authored films of 2001 and 2002, grouped into, first, potentially mainstream action films and comedies, including *Le Raïd* (Bensalah, 2002) and *Origine contrôlée* (Ahmed and Zakia Bouchaala, 2001), then period dramas exemplified by *17 rue Bleue* (Chenouga, 2001) and *Inch'Allah dimanche* (Benguigui, 2001), and, finally, reworkings of the *banlieue* film in *Wesh wesh, qu'est-ce qui se passe?* (Ameur-Zaïmèche, 2002), *La Maîtresse en maillot de bain* (Boukhitine, 2002) and *Jeunesse dorée* (Ghorab-Volta, 2002).[2]

Arguably the turn of the millennium was a crucial period for competing representations of the *banlieue*, race relations and national identity. One of the key factors contributing to Jean-Marie Le Pen's success in the first round of the 2002 presidential elections was the feeling of insecurity generated by persistent negative media images of so-called illegal immigrants and disorder in the *banlieue*. Following their support of the *sans-papiers* in the late 1990s, a number of filmmakers tried to combat such discourses, as in the portemanteau anti-racist film *Pas d'histoire! Douze films sur le racisme au quotidien* (2001), Charef's *Marie-Line* (2000), and films such as Bernard Dumont's *Ligne 208* (2001) and Gilles de Maistre's *Féroce* (2002), which address critically the fascination of the extreme Right.[3] However, although Le Pen was defeated by

Jacques Chirac in the second round of the presidential elections, policies introduced by interior minister Nicolas Sarkozy under the rightwing government
led by Jean-Pierre Raffarin look set to apply heavy-handed police measures to
the *banlieue* rather than addressing the many underlying socio-economic
causes of unrest (not the least of which is the continuing disproportionately
high rate of unemployment). In this context, the question is whether, and
in what ways, *beur*-authored films are able to challenge dominant discourses
on ethnicity and citizenship and construct alternative spaces of cross-cultural
understanding and awareness.

Comedies and action films

Comedy has been the genre most frequently used to address ethnic difference
for a popular mainstream French audience, particularly in the construction of
ethnic communities in Paris, as in Thomas Gilou's *Black micmac* (1986), *La
Vérité si je mens!* (1997) and *La Vérité si je mens! 2* (2001).[4] Though these films
can be criticised for drawing on dominant stereotypes of ethnic minority
others, they also allow ethnic minority others (and the actors who embody
them) a measure of agency and subjectivity. However, there is no white-
authored ensemble comedy representing *beurs* and Maghrebis as a community, perhaps because the notion is still too disturbing for majority French
audiences.[5] Rather, *beurs* and Maghrebis have generally been incorporated into
mainstream comedy either by way of the *black-blanc-beur banlieue* mix or as
isolated individuals.

Yet comedy is also a genre which has allowed comedians of Maghrebi
descent to flourish. Stand-up comedians such as Smaïn and Jamel (Debbouze)
are more familiar to audiences than actors with a more serious repertoire such
as Roschdy Zem, Sami Bouajila or Zinedine Soualem. Indeed, for a long time
Smaïn was the only *beur* actor with a substantial reputation. As well as influencing the scenario of *L'Oeil au beur(re) noir* (Serge Meynard, 1987), he wrote
and co-directed (with Longwal) *Les Deux Papas et la maman* (1996), an
intriguing story of a buddy relationship between two professionals, white
(Antoine de Caunes) and *beur* (Smaïn), which attracted over a million spectators.[6] The plot centres on impotent de Caunes who persuades his accident-
prone *beur* friend to donate sperm to impregnate his wife. The two friends
become estranged when Smaïn gets proprietorial over the baby-to-be, especially after an unfortunate accident leaves him equally impotent. But a happy
end is achieved when Smaïn discovers that his former (white) girlfriend is also
pregnant! The final scene shows the two fathers nursing their babies together,
both of whom are actually (unseen) mixed-race babies fathered by a *beur*, a
potentially subversive theme which plays into fears about the potency of the
ethnic other (a topic also addressed in Kassovitz' *Métisse*, discussed in chapter

3). The film provides a nice antidote to Lauzier's *Le Plus Beau Métier du monde* of the same year, an uneasy comedy starring Gérard Depardieu as a beleaguered white schoolteacher coping with a range of deprived multi-ethnic *banlieue* kids, which also achieved over a million spectators.

The most popular comedies of the 1990s to star *beur* actors, however, were *Taxi* (Gérard Pirès, 1998) – and later *Taxi 2* (Gérard Krawczyk, 2000) – and Bensalah's *Le Ciel, les oiseaux . . . et ta mère*, discussed in chapter 9. These films were star vehicles for Samy Naceri and Jamel[7] respectively, and set the pattern for a number of films to come, including Bensalah's subsequent action comedy, *Le Raïd*. Naceri, who first received critical attention in Olivier Dahan's *Frères* (1994) and Gilou's *Raï*, has now built up a considerable filmography in both comic and dramatic roles, including *Féroce*, in which he plays a would-be *beur* assassin, and Manuel Boursinhac's *La Mentale* (2002), co-written by his brother, Bibi, in which he plays a mob leader of mixed-race origins. However, the *Taxi* films provide his best-known character, that of Marseillais former-pizza deliverer Daniel, who drives an imaginatively souped-up taxi. Based on a fraught buddy relationship between Daniel and an incompetent young white policeman who is completely unable to drive (Frédéric Diefenthal, co-star of Chibane's *Douce France*), and aided by a series of spectacular stunts, the film's comedy derives in part from the way Daniel is mobilised in spite of himself in support of the police and helps them catch German bank robbers in *Taxi* and Japanese terrorists in *Taxi 2* (a backward-looking twist on the ethnic enemy). Ironically, at the end of *Taxi*, Daniel's dream of becoming a racing-driver becomes true – but only because he is sponsored by the CRS. And at the end of *Taxi 2* – assisted by some judicious digital image-tampering and his (white) girlfriend's father, a mad General in the French army – he finds himself driving his taxi past the President on the 14 July parade in Paris. Arguably these images represent a major step forward in the incorporation of a *beur* actor into the mainstream film industry, especially as Daniel/Naceri is, if reluctantly, located on the side of the law and at the heart of the Republic. But the films downplay the actor's potential otherness and identify Daniel as a *banlieue* outsider who effectively penetrates and dynamises the centre, rather than locating him within a *beur* or Maghrebi family or community. Their refusal of ethnic typecasting could be considered progressive, but it is disappointing that they do not attempt to integrate a more obviously hybrid *beur* character.

The formulae which provided the success of *Le Ciel* and the *Taxi* films have not always been easy to emulate. For example, Eric Rochant's attempt to import the *black-blanc-beur banlieue* group into a gangster film with a rural setting met with only a limited success. *Total Western* (2000) pitches Samuel Le Bihan against a gang of vicious (mainly white) organised criminals against the background of an isolated farmhouse in *la France profonde*, used to rehabilitate *banlieue* youths. The ethnically mixed *banlieue* teenagers (including a *beurette*) show some resourcefulness in coming to his aid, but their aptitude for violence and criminality is shown to be small beer in comparison with the 'real thing', and the film, like *Le Plus Beau Métier du monde*, revolves principally around the performance of its white star. *Old School* (2000), a tongue-in-cheek but self-indulgent gangster comedy written and directed by first-time directors Kader Ayd and Karim Abbou, also imports the *black-blanc-beur banlieue* group into a potentially more popular format. Old School is the name of a multi-ethnic gang of comic bank robbers and killers, who are the object of a TV documentary being made by reporter Fabienne Babe. Two of the gangsters are played by members of the cast of *Le Ciel*, and the spoof documentary also draws on *Le Ciel*'s self-reflexive filming techniques (and pays homage to the 1992 Belgian black comedy *C'est arrivé près de chez vous/Man Bites Dog*, by Rémy Belvaux, André Bonzel and Benoît Poelvoorde, the topic of which is a documentary team filming a murderer). However, despite being advertised as 'le premier polar rap' and numerous cameo appearances by the likes of Joey Starr, Elie Semoun, Ramzy, Bernie Bonvoisin and Smaïn, the film basically has just two gags: inept *banlieue* youths playing deluded, violent gangsters indulging every sadistic whim; and the media's quest for a scoop regardless of the moral issues involved. Unfortunately, the characters are simply-drawn caricatures, the costumes (especially the wigs) are ludicrous, the jokes repetitive and misogynistic, the violence excessive and, above all, there is no sense of satire or comment on social integration.

Le Raïd/The Race (2002)

Le Raïd, Bensalah's second film, co-written with Gilles Laurent, also testifies to the attempt to emulate the success of *Le Ciel* and imports two of its actors, Lorant Deutsch and Julien Courbey, but replaces Jamel and black actor Stéphane Soo Mongo with Atmen Kelif and older, more serious *beur* actor Roschdy Zem. In this instance, Bensalah projects the comic multi-ethnic *banlieue* group into the unfamiliar world of an American-style action-adventure-comedy film. Shot in CinemaScope on a budget of about £12 million, *Le Raïd* was produced by Gaumont and, like *Le Ciel* (and perhaps thanks to Gaumont's handling of distribution), attracted over a million spectators. The plot sets the youths up first as unsuccessful burglars out of their depth in central Paris, then, improbably, thanks to a series of mistaken identities, as would-be assassins of a Canadian heiress. Their mission requires them to travel to South America as members of her team to participate in a televised adventure gameshow called 'Le Raïd', as a result of which they are transported to a variety of other exotic but demanding locations. Action and spectacle are combined with an element of self-reflexivity based on a parody of the techniques and (im)morality of reality TV shows and their apparent indifference to the fate of their participants. However, the making of the spoof TV programme, like the spoof documentary in *Old School*, does not lie in the hands of the *banlieue* youths, unlike the use of the film-within-the-film in *Le Ciel*.

Le Raïd departs from the successful formula of *Le Ciel* in a number of other ways. First, though the characters' *banlieue* origins in *le neuf-trois* (93), north of Paris, inform the film throughout, through their use of *banlieue* speech and their appearance, gestures and attitudes (especially their self-assertive and misogynistic, but impotent, masculinity), there is no visual or narrative link to the *banlieue*. The locations and events of the film belong entirely to a world of fantasy, which ends with the *banlieue* characters (and their prey) as the unlikely winners of 'Le Raïd', clutching a huge cheque. The ludicrous, misogynist plot, involving comic cameos by Gérard Jugnot as their gangster boss and Josiane Balasko as their evil rival, depends as much on (not very impressive) visual gags and special effects, a surreal plotline involving UN troops (determined literally to wipe out any troublemakers), and obsessive toilet humour, as it does on the protagonists' reactions to and comments on events. The *banlieue* youths are stereotyped as aggressive, materialistic and inadequate, particularly in their relationships with women, and lack any depth of characterisation to make them sympathetic (making the hint of romance between the gutsy heiress and the Roschdy Zem character completely unconvincing). Bensalah's exotic locations do not show *banlieue* youths able to adapt to alternative spaces and become active subjects in the world (their survival is entirely due to chance and the skills of the heroine); rather *Le Raïd* reduces them to stock comic characters completely divorced from any social or political comment on life in the *banlieue*.

Origine contrôlée/Made in France (2001)
A rather more interesting foray into popular filmmaking is to be found in *Origine contrôlée*, a comedy by Ahmed Bouchaala (director of *Krim*, 1995, discussed in chapter 5) and his wife, Zakia, with a soundtrack by Khaled. *Origine contrôlée* is an ostensibly light-hearted, even farcical comedy of mistaken identity, but it consistently raises pertinent questions relating to people's prejudices about appearances, and in so doing provides an eloquent critique of the relationship between individuals, the police and the state. As a statement from the film's trailer says, 'In France we're very attached to labels: tranny/whore/Arab'. The film proceeds to demonstrate that the three principal characters to whom these labels appear to apply are not in fact what they seem, undermining both the audience's preconceptions and those of the characters themselves.

The film focuses on the nightmare experiences of Patrick (Patrick Ligardes), an unemployed middle-class white man dressed in drag for a fancy-dress party who, after a series of misunderstandings, gets mistaken for an illegal Algerian immigrant transsexual (also later wanted for murder), finds himself thrown in jail overnight with Youssef (Atmen Kelif), a *beur*, and Sophia (Ronit Elkabetz), an Algerian prostitute (who later reveals that she is a male transvestite and would-be transsexual). He is condemned to be deported 'back' to Algeria, reluctantly escapes from the police with his fellow prisoners (he is handcuffed to Youssef), and so finds himself on the run. The comedy of mistaken identity then turns into a road movie as the ill-assorted trio find themselves hiding in the environs of Lyons and obliged to overcome a series of obstacles to their friendship, before deciding to return to Paris so that Patrick, who still clings to a belief in the law, can prove his innocence (figure 33). Despite being led to believe otherwise by the police, Sophia and Youssef are once more condemned to deportation, but are rescued at the last moment by the now liberated Patrick, who uses the police guards' prejudices to persuade them that the travellers in the airport who look like 'Arabs' are in fact members of the terrorist GIA about to assassinate them if they do not set their prisoners free. The film thus ends with the trio escaping to freedom on Patrick's former girlfriend's purloined scooter, Patrick having learnt at last how to understand and manipulate prejudices based on appearances instead of being the victim of them.

The film inflects concerns about ethnic difference and identity with an interest in 'deviant' sexualities which recalls other successful French comedies such as *Gazon maudit* (Balasko, 1994) and the more reactionary *Pédale douce* (Aghion, 1996), as well as dramas such as Liria Begeja's *Change-moi ma vie* (2001), which focuses in a more melodramatic style on alienated immigrant transvestite prostitutes (improbably embodied by Roschy Zem and Sami Bouajila alongside 'real life' transvestites and prostitutes).[8] It centres on Ligardes' performance as the bewildered, straight, white guy who is mistaken for an Arab transsexual because of the way he looks and because he has not got the right papers, and so invites the majority white spectator to share what it feels like to enter into the world of abused and excluded sexual and ethnic minorities, and experience the prejudices of fellow Frenchmen and the law. Dressed in high heels, a pink bolero and a dress with fitted bosoms, Patrick, already in a state of disarray because he has discovered that his girlfriend, Marie, is having an affair, finds that no one believes a word he says and that his legal rights can be waived. In the course of the film, then, he undergoes a transformation, learning that appearances can be deceptive, that justice and the law are fallible, and that neither race nor gender nor sexual orientation is an impediment to love, since he develops feelings for Sophia irrespective of her 'race' and biological sex. Sophia is not the hard, grasping whore she is initially perceived to be, but a doubly oppressed caring woman in a man's body. And Youssef is not just a loud-mouthed, self-deluded *beur* who is always putting his foot in it, but another lost soul, an 'Arab' who has never set foot in Algeria, has lost his family, and is condemned in advance by the way others see him. (He is also the most violent of the threesome, but his willingness to use violence is shown here to be sometimes necessary and effective.)

33 Patrick (Patrick Ligardes), Sophia (Ronit Elkabetz) and Youssef (Atmen Kelif) on the road in *Origine contrôlée* (2001).

The basis of their solidarity, then, which compares favourably with the intolerance of those around them, is the freedom from prejudice that they learn, a freedom which is translated into their joyful escape from the confines of the labels attached to them by others, and shown visually by their unorthodox, somewhat surreal journey back to Paris in a luxury yacht transported on a trailer and by their final getaway on a scooter. At the same time, the film leaves open the question of their destination, though both Algeria and Geneva are mooted: Algeria so that Youssef can connect with his roots, Geneva because Sophia wants to get a sex-change operation there. Despite the feelgood feeling the film engenders in relation to both ethnic and sexual differences, it is unable to envisage a place in France where such differences would be accepted and where origins would no longer be the yardstick of identity.

Period dramas

As chapter 8 demonstrated, in the late 1990s *beur* filmmakers began to take stock of their past, specifically by excavating and reworking their parents' painful experiences of immigration during and immediately following the Algerian War of Independence. In 2001 two more *beur*-authored period dramas were released, based this time on women's patterns of immigration in the 1960s and the 1970s, the latter being the period during which family immigration was promoted and consolidated. Both focus on the immigrant family home rather than the *bidonville* familiar from *Vivre au paradis* and *Le Gone du chaâba*: that is, on family dramas rather than public history. However, both highlight the figure of the young immigrant mother and her attempts to come to terms with her displacement, torn between her emotional ties with her culture of origin and the demands of her new life in France.

Chenouga's first feature, *17 rue Bleue*, set in Paris, is autobiographical in inspiration and has an end dedication to the director's younger brother.[9] It centres on the young mother's physical and mental breakdown and the coming of age of her elder son, Chad (named after the director). Benguigui's *Inch'Allah dimanche*, set in the town of St-Quentin in the North of France (where Benguigui grew up), is also loosely inspired by her mother (and offers a more complex representation of Maghrebi families in the provinces than the films discussed in chapter 9). After interviewing various Maghrebi women for the second part of her documentary tryptich, *Mémoires d'immigrés* (1998), Benguigui, who had been ashamed of her mother as a child, realised how little she knew about her mother's life at the time of her arrival in France. The film's opening statement maps out the historical background to Maghrebi women's immigration in France in the 1970s, suggesting that its story is to be seen as one among many rather than as clearly autobiographical. Compared with *17 rue Bleue*, the children (the future *beur* generation) are comparatively young and the narrative is more clearly focused from the woman's point of view. Though the films share a common concern with the troubled identity of first generation Maghrebi immigrants, *17 rue Bleue* charts a woman's decline, whereas *Inch'Allah dimanche* ends with at least a glimmer of hope at the possibility of change.

17 rue Bleue (2001)

Actor Chad Chenouga developed *17 rue Bleue* (co-written with Philipe Donzelot) from an earlier César-nominated short film called simply *Rue Bleue* (2000). The film opens with a striking pre-credit sequence of stamped addressed envelopes floating in water, signalling the links between Algeria and France which underpin the narrative. At first its central protagonist, Adda (Lysianne Meis), seems to conform to the image of a fully integrated, westernised woman who is confident about her future in France since her (white, French, married) lover, also her boss and the father of her second son, Samir, is determined to provide for her. Though she speaks Arabic with her sister, Leila, she wears smart western clothes with a flick-up hairstyle and false eyelashes, watches French TV with her family and gets everyone to dance the cha-cha-cha. Her happiness (and her ability to integrate) comes to an end with the news that her lover has died of a heart attack without leaving her his house and laboratory as he had promised. She embarks on an obsessive but lonely, fruitless quest to claim her inheritance through the courts and has still not achieved a settlement when, some years later, her mother (Chafia Boudraa)[10] comes to visit from Algeria, giving her an amulet as a gift. The visit proves to be a disaster when, on a family picnic, the mother suddenly starts calling her a whore, plunges her head under water (revealing her hairstyle to be a wig), insults her about her children's fathers, and blames her for the fact that Leila is pregnant (father unknown). After the mother returns to Algeria, taking Leila with her, Adda starts to disintegrate. Claiming to be unable to work because of her ongoing lawsuit, she becomes addicted to Valium, takes to her bed, her pills and the bottle, neglects to look after her sons or her flat, refuses to be parted from her mother's amulet, and becomes obsessed with finding a treasure (once predicted by a fortune teller because of a birthmark on Chad's hand). On one occasion Chad returns home to find her hacking up a wardrobe, on another she is knocking down the wall into the empty flat next door (at which point the film cuts to a nightmare vision of a skeleton in a coffin draped in jewels and Adda's voice telling Chad as a little boy that he must not touch). Adda's mental and physical deterioration is further expressed through the increasingly disgusting condition of the flat, which she refuses to relinquish, even though she cannot pay the bills. When Chad eventually finds her dead on the bed, the police comment on the stench.

Adda's inability to take her life into her own hands and her regression to a state of childlike dependency on her son may be due in part to the particular circumstances of her isolation as a single parent immigrant in Paris in the 1970s. But the identity crisis she experiences on the occasion of her mother's visit compounds her burden of shame and guilt (symbolised by the amulet). Her decline is observed by her young sons who are in turn solicitous, angry and repelled. During her first stay in hospital they start to quarrel and play truant; later they race cockroaches, experiment with alcohol and cigarettes, and make obscene phone calls. Subsequently, however, their quarrels lead to Adda sending Samir away to a foster home, forcing the favoured (more Algerian) son Chad into an increasingly unhealthy, almost incestuous relationship with his frail mother. Chad's life is, symbolically, split between the outside world, where he tries to behave like a normal youth, and the inner darkness and squalour of 17 rue Bleue, which he is eventually obliged to enter through the window. The camera registers the infestation of cockroaches, Chad's shame at the sight of his mother's chamber pot, his disgust at having to clean her up and his anger as he burns her amulet in a vain attempt to rouse her to activity. But his attachment becomes clear when at the end he grabs and hides one of her dresses as a keepsake, before being driven off in the police van in the opposite direction to the ambulance bearing Adda's corpse.

The film provides an ambiguous portrait of the damaged Algerian immigrant woman and her misplaced determination to cling to what she knows rather than forge a new identity. It is also an expressive representation of the trials and tribulations of a disturbed *beur* adolescent, caught between the demands of life in France and those of his immigrant mother who, significantly, will not reveal the identity of his unknown Algerian father. Chad secretly searches for clues to his father's identity in his grandmother's photograph album, but he cannot communicate with her directly as he only speaks French. His unsatisfied quest for origins can be linked both with the broader historical canvas of separated families after the Algerian War of Independence and with the *beur* generation's search for roots in the 1990s. The film indulges in an element of mourning and nostalgia, both through Adda's memories of her beloved, dead younger brother in Algeria, and through evocative panning shots of the empty walls of the reconstructed 17 rue Bleue. But above all *17 rue Bleue* constructs a fantasy space, both a womb and a prison, where the young *beur* is forced to work out his troubled relationship with his Algerian roots, represented here rather negatively by the figure of the neurotic, superstitious mother, from whom he continues to have difficulty separating himself.

Inch' Allah dimanche/Inch' Allah Sunday (2001)

Like *17 rue Bleue*, *Inch'Allah dimanche* begins with a setting which references the link between Algeria and France, in this case a harrowing scene at the port of Algiers, where a young woman, Zouina (Fejria Deliba), is being implacably wrenched away from her mother on to the ferry taking her and her children to France by an old woman who turns out to be her mother-in-law Aïcha (Rabia Mokedem) (figure 34). The film cuts to Zouina's arrival in St-Quentin to join her husband Ahmed (Zinedane Soualem), and emphasises the coldness and unfamiliarity of the setting seen through her eyes. Her husband is a virtual stranger, a domestic despot with whom she has no communication and who expects her to be confined to the home; her mother-in-law exercises her authority to maintain her in a state of cowed submission and isolation; and there are no other Algerian women to provide sisterhood and solidarity. But strong-minded Zouina gradually comes into contact with the French, both negatively, in the shape of her caricatural racist neighbours, and positively, through a friendly neighbour (Mathilde Seigner) and through the radio advice programme of Ménie Grégoire, thanks to which she begins to learn not just French but also a way of conceptualising her desires and fears. She dreams of finding a friend with whom to share the celebration of Eid el-Kebir, and for three Sundays running, when her husband and mother-in-law go out to make preparations for Eid, Zouina and the children secretly escape the claustrophobia of the home in search of such a friend (hence the film's title). But when she does eventually track down another Algerian immigrant family, helped by an eccentric widow (Marie-France Pisier) whose husband was an army officer in Algeria, she discovers that her counterpart, Malika (Amina Annabi), is a fearful woman driven by traditional Algerian values, who has closed herself and her daughter off from any attempt to adapt to living in France. Malika's

34 Zouina (Fejria Deliba) is wrenched from her homeland in *Inch' Allah dimanche* (2001).

disapproval of Zouina's independent behaviour leads to a violent confronta-tion (Zouina breaks a window and cuts her arm) and leaves Zouina with no option but to rely on her own instincts and resources. The film ends with a fan-tasy sequence in which a charming bus driver (Jalil Lespert), who regularly drives past her window, empties his bus for her and drives her home, where her family and neighbours are waiting for her, and where her husband finally takes her side instead of agreeing with his mother.

Benguigui's film traces the strained relationships between the members of an immigrant Algerian family as they are forced to re-evaluate their tradi-tional customs and values in relation to life in France. In particular it focuses on the state of mind and body of its central character, Zouina, the concrete banality of her everyday life and the lack of outlet she has for her emotions. Her world is initially grey, lacking in sunshine and dominated by closed doors and locked cupboards. Her husband is a dour, contradictory character, coping with his own status as a paria in France, who can only communicate with her through violence. Her next-door neighbours live in a world of colour, their impeccable flower garden populated with garden gnomes; but they are repre-sented humorously as repressed, narrow-minded bigots whose obsessive neatness contrasts unfavourably with the wild but child-friendly space nego-tiated by Zouina. Nevertheless Zouina's gradual exposure to the French world she sees through her window or hears on the radio makes it clear that it is only through her willingness and ability to embrace aspects of French culture that she will be able her make a life for herself and her children. In her final stand against her husband, she asserts that in future she will be the one to take the children to school (the principal agent of integration), and she unexpectedly gains his assent.

Both films use the figure of the mother as a way of working through zones of tension within the immigrant community, rather than exploring lines of difference between Maghrebi immigrants and the majority French. Both set up the problematic of women's place within Maghrebi culture, constructing an older generation of mothers (Adda's mother from Algeria, Zouina's mother-in-law) as the embodiment of otherness, superstition and cruelty. At the same time, Adda's despair at being rejected by her mother and Zouina's loss of her loving relationship with her own mother signify both the immigrant women's attachment to their homeland and the ties of affection between Algerian women which are ruptured by their displacement in France. However, whereas Adda, the single mother, ends up unable to forge a new identity in her adopted homeland, Zouina's inner strength and determination enable her to negotiate a place for herself within her marriage which also opens up the possibility of integration. *Inch'Allah dimanche* has had a considerable success on the film festival circuit, and has been well received by immigrant women. Like *Sous les pieds des femmes* and *Vivre au paradis*, these films counter the silence of dominant French culture with regard to the family memories of a community in exile, at the same time as they argue for the necessity of integration.

Banlieue films

Despite the trend to incorporate *banlieue* youths into mainstream popular genres, a number of *beur* filmmakers are still preoccupied with realist depictions of life in the *banlieue*, as the three *banlieue* films considered here demonstrate. Ameur-Zaïmèche's *Wesh wesh, qu'est-ce qui se passe?* is an instantly recognisable reworking of the genre which incorporates a critique of the *double peine*, the ruling by which young men of Maghrebi descent can be deported once they have completed a prison sentence, regardless of the fact that they may have never set foot in North Africa (the topic of Bouchareb's *Cheb*, 1991, discussed in chapter 1). Boukhitine's *La Maîtresse en maillot de bain* expands the genre to take in a different type of setting (outside Lyons) and the problems of a slightly older group of men. And Ghorab-Volta's *Jeunesse dorée* provides an innovative woman-centred inflection of the genre, which turns into a road movie. These films need to be seen in the context of other films by non-*beur* filmmakers which address issues relevant to *banlieue* youth, such as *La Squale* and *Samia*, discussed in chapter 7. Bertrand Tavernier's documentary *Histoires de vies brisées* (2001) is another protest film against the inhumanity of the 'double penalty', as is *On n'est pas des marques de vélo* (Jean-Pierre Thorn,

2003), while Eric Pittard's imaginative 'documentary-opera', *Le Bruit, l'odeur et quelques étoiles* (2002) is (like *La Haine*) a protest about police *bavures* and the fact that they go unpunished (over 300 cases between 1981 and 2000).

It is worth dwelling briefly on Pittard's film, which reconstructs events following a *fait divers* which took place in Toulouse in December 1998, when a policeman shot dead a seventeen-year-old youth, Habib, known as Pipo, tried to cover up the incident, then claimed the gun went off accidentally. Pittard tries to introduce a self-reflexive format to his film by intercutting interviews with those who knew Pipo and the policeman with musical protest numbers by Zebda, a successful multi-ethnic rap group from Toulouse, whose hit 'Le Bruit et L'Odeur' ('The Sound and Smell') refers back, like the film's title, to Jacques Chirac's infamous statement in 1991 about the noise and smell caused by immigrants. In contrast, the *étoiles* ('stars') refer both to the young people on the estate who, after days of urban guerilla warfare with the police, tried to find other ways of making their voices heard (setting up the association '9bis', issuing pamphlets, organising a peaceful march to the Town Hall, and so on) and to Zebda themselves, whose success demonstrates that people need not be trapped by the *banlieue*.[11] The film lays bare what Pittard calls 'the contempt' of the ruling classes, exemplified in the role of the mayor, Dominique Baudis, who refused to receive the protesters, and the state of French justice, which resulted in 2001 with the policeman being given a three-year suspended sentence! As Annie Copfermann comments, it provides 'a useful testimony on the climate of the *banlieues*' (Copferman 2002), particularly as during the year it came out there were riots in the Hautespierre district of Strasbourg which echoed those in Toulouse. It certainly leaves the spectator with images of the *banlieue* as a place of state-sanctioned injustice and highlights how *banlieue* youths are deprived of *le droit de cité* (citizenship).

Wesh wesh, qu'est-ce qui se passe?/Wesh Wesh, What's Up? (2002)

Wesh wesh is a low-budget film by first-time filmmaker Rabah Ameur-Zaïmèche, co-written with Madjid Benaroudj, which took many years to make (as was the case with the first films of Malik Chibane and Zaïda Ghorab-Volta), but was rewarded with the Louis-Delluc Award for Best First Film in 2002. It was shot on video in the Cité des Bosquets in Seine Saint-Denis, with an amateur cast headed by the filmmaker himself, along with other members of his family, which gives the film its feeling of 'authenticity'. Dedicated 'To all the victims of the double penalty', it is a protest film at the ongoing exclusion of young men of Maghrebi descent from mainstream French society. In a manner typical of the *banlieue* film, imagery of the *banlieue* dominates its *mise-en-scène* from beginning to end. Repeated long shots of the blocks of flats emphasise the immensity, sameness and lack of horizons of the *banlieue* space. Individual scenes set in the places where the (male) youths congregate focus on steps and hallways, graffiti, broken windows and dark interiors (figure 35). The police are shown regularly patrolling the area and harassing the youths, their faces and number-plates pixillated in an ironic parody of television techniques which normally single out the faces of supposed criminals for such treatment.

The film opens with shots of Kamel (Ameur-Zaïmèche) trying to hitch his way home after a period of deportation, intercut with shots of his younger brother Mouss and friends playing football in the green spaces on the housing estate. The opening rap music accompaniment articulates Kamel's sense of disorientation and loss as he realises what has happened to the estate during his absence. The double narrative focuses on the one hand on Kamel's hopeless attempts to regularise his position, get a job and reintegrate himself, and on the other on his brother Mouss's increasing involvement with dodgy drugs-dealing. When Mouss gets shopped to the police, and a violent armed police raid on the family home results in their mother being hospitalised due to the effects of tear gas, Kamel's suppressed rage and frustration finds an outlet. He test drives a Harley Davidson from a motor showroom, follows and assaults the police officer responsible for the attack on his mother, and then finds himself the target of the policeman's revenge.

The film offers two alternatives to conventional imagery of the *banlieue*. On the one hand, it explores the *banlieue* as a place of intercultural exchange and solidarity through the role of Irène, a white schoolteacher with a strong sense of justice, who puts a stop to the unjustified police harassment of two young *beurs*. When Kamel gives her the flowers the lads have bought for her and arranges a date, the night lighting, the glowing reddish hues of the buildings and the soul music soundtrack transform the *banlieue* into a place of potential romance. However, Kamel almost immediately feels oppressed by the relationship, and when Irène visits his home, she is received by his mother with unrestrained hostility, even though the mother's insulting remarks – in Arabic – are mistranslated by Kamel's westernised lawyer sister into polite nothings. The *banlieue* as the site of cross-cultural relationships for the *beur* male, then, is opened up only to be closed down, in contrast with the destiny of the sister. *Wesh wesh* thus draws attention to gender difference in the expectations of young people of North African descent.

On the other hand, the film also sets up an alternative space, which is not a space of belonging or of intercultural exchange, but rather of retreat from the 'real' world. Thanks to his affectionate relationship with *les petits frères*, the young lads living on the estate, Kamel gets shown how to get into a park with a lake where he can go fishing. However, this idyllic 'natural' space, free from *banlieue* constraints, proves to be a lure. At the end, after defying the policemen lying in wait for him outside the *banlieue* flats (to the cheers of his *banlieue* peer group), Kamel attempts to use it as an escape route. But the policemen follow him, and the film ends on the sounds of two gunshots

35 Kamel (Rabah Ameur-Zaïmèche) feels the weight of exclusion in *Wesh wesh, qu'est-ce qui se passe?* (2002)

which, presumably, indicate his death, followed by a coda which returns the spectator to the relentless imagery of the housing estate and finally pans up to the grey, cloudy sky, consigning the violence to the realm of the 'natural'. The film thus underlines both the institutionalised racism of the police/state and the lack of space or place for male *banlieue* youths, particularly those of North African origin, in France. Interestingly, it fails to incorporate a reflection on Ameur-Zaïmèche's own way of taking charge of his life through filmmaking.

La Maîtresse en maillot de bain/Teacher in a Bikini (2002)

La Maîtresse en maillot de bain is another first film, written and directed by Lyèce Boukhitine, who also co-stars in the film alongside Eric Savin and Franck Gourlat. In this film Boukhitine plays Karim, a *beur* in his late twenties/early thirties, who has a DEA from University but lives at home with his traditional Maghrebi family and has not done anything else with his life. His home is a *pavillon* in a small working-class town outside Lyons rather than an estate typical of most *banlieue* films, and the spaces constructed in this film (like those in the films discussed in chapter 9) are not subject to the same surveillance as cinematic city spaces.

Karim spends his time meeting up with Eric (Savin) and Jean (Gourlat), two (white) former schoolfriends leading equally dead-end jobless lives, one separated from his wife and daughter, the other desperate for a job and sex. Like the young men of *Comme un aimant*, discussed in chapter 6, the threesome are depicted as having not quite grown up. Lacking money, they spend their time in the local café making a cup of coffee last as long as possible (while Jean can only afford a few francs-worth of petrol at a time for his ancient red BMW), and wax nostalgic about their youth, regularly preventing the local street-cleaner, played by Zinedine Soualem, from removing the graffiti on the wall opposite the café, which commemorates a moment when they saw their teacher in her bathing costume (hence the film's oblique title). They are periodically involved in a series of pranks and scrapes which horrify Karim's father. However, matters become potentially serious when Eric's chance theft of an unattended mobile TV camera, which they unsuccessfully try to sell in Lyons, leads them to witness and record a murder (also the result of Jean's car running out of petrol), after which they become caught up in misunderstandings with the mob. (Interestingly the theft of the camera, a potentially self-reflexive cinematic device, initiates the action but ultimately leads to false dreams and entrapment rather than empowerment.)

Whereas in *Comme un aimant* the encounter with the mob ends in tragedy, *La Maîtresse* maintains a comic tone, through caricatural representations of the gangsters and an emphasis on how the three friends, who think they are about to make their fortune, are persistently unable to understand the realities of the situation they have got themselves into. However, the threesome are finally forced to make a decision as to which side of the law they wish to be on, a decision which brings out the differences between them (symbolised finally by their acceptance of the obliteration of their graffiti). Eric joins the mob (but is last seen as a bouncer outside a casino, ignored by the high-ups he used to frequent); Jean acquires a girlfriend and a cleaning job in the local printing-works (and is last seen with new house, wife and baby). But Karim, who has distanced himself throughout from the delinquent and sexual excesses of his peers, is last seen in an ambiguous sequence which takes place in a local community centre. He first appears in a position of authority, mediating a dispute between two young boys. But in the subsequent scene, he appears as the only adult pupil in a class of children learning Arabic. His exchange of glances with the teacher hints at the potential for romance, but the setting continues to foreground his difficulty in growing up and finding a place. Meanwhile, the cycle continues as another generation of schoolboys attempt to inscribe new graffiti on the wall opposite the café.

In the provincial setting of *La Maîtresse*, then, the inter-racial male friendship characteristic of *beur* and *banlieue* films is put under pressure by the process of ageing and the involvement of the *beur*'s white peers in either organised crime or work and domesticity. But, unlike *Comme un aimant* and *Wesh wesh*, where the ageing *beur* protagonists are driven to crime and end up either dead or in despair, the future of Boukhitine's better-educated and potentially upwardly mobile *beur* character remains open.

Jeunesse dorée/Golden Youth (2002)
The ironically titled *Jeunesse dorée*, Ghorab-Volta's third film after *Souviens-toi de moi* and *Laisse un peu d'amour*, is another low-budget film (though shot in

35mm) which, like *Wesh wesh*, relies on an amateur cast – the two central leads came from the unemployment agency (ANPE) in Colombes where the film is set, and where Ghorab-Volta herself grew up. More unusually, however, it focuses on underprivileged young women. It begins, like *Wesh wesh*, with a panning shot of the *banlieue*, in this case a 360° shot which emphasises the immensity of the conurbation and the distance of the horizon, but which is accompanied by modern classical music rather than rap. The shot is located as the point of view of sullen, introverted seventeen-year-old Gwenaëlle (Alexandre Jeudon), looking out from her window in a block of flats, who, with her more extrovert friend Angéla (Alexandre Laflandre), is looking for a way to escape her constricted existence. Both young women suffer from frustrating home lives: Gwenaëlle's harassed mother expects her to look after her younger sisters and do the housework while she is at work, and her father is in a psychiatric ward in hospital; Angéla's parents are always quarrelling. Nevertheless, Angéla is also a backing singer in a local rock group, while Gwenaëlle has a modelling job for a local artist. The two young women put together a winning project for a competition organised by a local association on the estate, namely photographing housing estates throughout the French countryside for an exhibition. They thus earn themselves a journey away from the *banlieue*.

In Ghorab-Volta's representation of the *banlieue*, the topic of the first part of the film, stereotypical expectations are repeatedly frustrated. Male youths, drugs and violence exist *en filigraine* rather than being foregrounded (Ghorab-Volta 2002), there is no police presence (though Angéla's boyfriend is seen leaving prison), people do not talk in *banlieue* slang, and young men and women communicate as equals, though the film privileges relationships between women (the two young women visit Maghrebi-French girlfriends before their departure, while the crowd celebrating the results of the competition are both male and female, black, white and *beur*). The poverty of the young women's family life contrasts with their determination and intellectual curiosity, encouraged in intercultural spaces such as the library (not often featured in *banlieue* films). Furthermore, the self-reflexive use of the camera empowers them to take control of their environment. While preparing their project, they photograph various inhabitants of the *banlieue* against the background of their homes, asking them to look happy, sad or crazy in turn, and so provide a diversity of characters, moods and spaces which testify to the multi-layered realities of the *banlieue*. This strategy not only humanises the objects of the camera's gaze and constructs the *banlieue* as a social space, it makes the young women the subject of the gaze, invites the spectator to view the world through their eyes, and suggests that such representations can be undertaken by anyone with sufficient desire and determination.

In the (longer) second part of the film, Gwenaëlle and Angéla take to the road in their borrowed car and travel through France, ending up in the Pyrenees. A series of shots documents them photographing (and hence commemorating) various blocks of flats in odd places in the countryside, demonstrating what Michel Mélinard calls 'a France built against nature' and what Ghorab-Volta claims are 'places where highrise flats are the least legitimate, where there is really the place to construct something else' (Mélinard 2001). It also documents their uniformly sympathetic encounters with people en route, often improvised as the result of the film crew's actual encounters on the road (figure 36). Its images of *la France profonde* demonstrate the nationwide implantation of *banlieue*-type housing and refuse any normative postcard-type representations of France for tourists. At the same time its narrative subverts dominant expectations of both road movie and *banlieue* film: people are hospitable; the car never breaks down; groups of potentially threatening black-*beur* youths turn out to be friendly and nice; and former inhabitants of the tower blocks being demolished in the *banlieue* of Saint-Etienne express a sense of loss for their community.

Subsequently, the film moves into a different space, when the two young women are invited to stay with a trio of self-sufficient, ecologically conscious white youths in their idyllic mountain retreat, and there ensues a moment of respite, folkloric activities and, potentially, romance. Again, however, Ghorab-Volta foils expectations as the young women decide to move on again, and the film ends as they take a train ride together up into the mountains. Though the ending is inconclusive, their journey functions to demystify the *banlieue* and break down perceived divisions between the *banlieue* and the rest of the country.[12] This is an unusual, potentially subversive inflection of the *banlieue* film. But it is no doubt telling that Ghorab-Volta has chosen white women as her nomadic subjects, and that the possibility of black or *beur* women accomplishing similar feats is less easy to imagine.[13]

Conclusion

At the beginning of the new millennium, it is clear that a new generation of male and female filmmakers of Maghrebi descent are making films alongside those who began in the 1980s, and that their films are broadening out into new directions, be it through action films, comedies, period dramas or reworkings of the *banlieue* film (or various combinations of these). A number of their films focus on the problems of other disadvantaged populations. But the majority still address issues of place and identity in France and, to varying degrees, highlight the specificity of the *beurs'* experiences, particularly through the development of family dramas set in the past.

Bensalah's successes demonstrate that *beur* filmmakers can now contemplate making films which are popular at the French box office. The question is whether commercial success can only be achieved at a cost. The significance of *banlieue* filmmaking has been its implicit or explicit social criticism, linked to

36 Gwenaëlle (Alexandre Jeudon) and Angéla (Alexandre Laflandre) in *Jeunesse dorée* (2002).

the construction of the *banlieue* as a place of exclusion and injustice for young males, whatever their ethnic origins. *Le Raïd* draws only on the misogynistic inter-racial male camaraderie of the *banlieue* film, and parachutes its characters into a genre and a place which deprives them of their perceived authenticity and ability to articulate social protest.[14] In contrast, *Wesh wesh* suggests that the realities of life in the *banlieue* are even harsher than they were in the 1980s. Even if *Jeunesse dorée* provides a salutary reminder that, for women at least, the *banlieue* can be represented in alternative (and equally authentic) ways, it remains the case that most *beur* filmmakers are still unable or unwilling to imagine young men from the *banlieue* either successfully investing the spaces they inhabit or negotiating alternative spaces. This panoply of films can thus be read as an ongoing sign of the failure of political will in France to tackle social deprivation and exclusion, as well as, paradoxically, of the ability of individual *beur* filmmakers to continue bringing *banlieue* characters to life on screen.[15]

Notes

1 An earlier version of part of this chapter was presented at the ECRF conference on 'Re-viewing Space: Space and Place in European Cinema' at Bath University in April 2003, under the title 'Transmutations of the *Banlieue* in French Films of 2002'.

2 Other *beur* films of 2001–2 include Bouchareb's *Little Senegal* (2001), Kechiche's *La Faute à Voltaire* (2001) and Charef's *La Fille de Keltoum* (2002). The latter two films are discussed in chapter 12.

3 In *Ligne 208*, a white bus driver, happily married to a young *beur* woman, gets assaulted by a youth of Maghrebi descent, starts to sympathise with the extreme Right, but eventually saves his proposed victim from his tormentors. In *Féroce*, a *beur* infiltrates the headquarters of an extreme Right party in order to assassinate its leader, but becomes corrupted and meets his match.

4 Other less successful examples include *Le Fils du Mékong* (François Leterrier, 1991) and *Antilles-sur-Seine* (Pascal Legitimus, 2000).

5 The community constructed in Zemmouri's musical comedy, *100% Arabica*, is discussed in chapter 12.

6 Smaïn seems to have remodelled himself on classic comic actor Fernandel, exemplified by his role in the remake of *Le Schpountz* (Gérard Oury, 1998).

7 Jamel first appeared on screen in the prison drama, Zonzon (Laurent Bouhnik, 1998). His success in *Le Ciel* was followed by the even less threatening role of the appealing young grocer's assistant, Lucien, in *Le Fabuleux Destin d'Amélie Poulain* (Jeunet, 2001), and led to his consecration among the heavyweights of French comedy in the blockbuster *Astérix et Obélix: Mission Cléopâtre* (Chabat, 2002).

8 See also Amal Bedjaoui's *Un fils* (2003).

9 Chenouga's brother, who was present at a screening of the film in Paris, declared that the director had a strong imagination!

10 The casting of Chafia Boudraa recalls Bahloul's *Le Thé à la menthe* (1985), in which she plays a traditional but far more loving mother.

11 Zebda stood at the municipal elections in Toulouse in March 2001 with the political list 'Motivé-e-s' ('Motivated'), and got 12.3 per cent of the vote.

12 The journey also strengthens the women's friendship and allows Gwenaëlle in particular to confront her fears of commitment in a relationship.

13 A road movie precedent can be found in *Drôle de Félix*, discussed in chapter 9, but in that instance the single gay male *beur* protagonist is not a character from the *banlieue*.

14 Dridi's *Fureur* (2003), set in the 13th *arrondissement* of Paris, is an equally disappointing foray into genre filmmaking.

15 Abdellatif Kechiche's second film, *L'Esquive* (2004), has provided another, subtly subversive take on the *banlieue* film. Working directly with young people from the *banlieue*, Kechiche uses the device of the school play to bring together the delicate emotions and language of Marivaux's *Jeu de l'amour et du hasard* and those, apparently more robust but actually equally fragile, of the *banlieue* adolescents.

12

Voices from the Maghreb: from *Le Thé à la menthe* to *La Fille de Keltoum*[1]

The *beur* and *banlieue* films discussed in previous chapters have been the work of either *beur* or white French filmmakers. However, the book would not be complete without a consideration of how difference has been reframed by Algerian filmmakers working in France.[2] The transnational status of such film-makers makes their work particularly difficult to categorise. The 2003 film season 'Hommage aux cinéastes algériens', held at the Institut du Monde Arabe under the auspices of Djazaïr, the Year of Algeria in France, actually brought together films by Algerian filmmakers working in Algeria, émigré Algerian filmmakers working in France, and *beur* filmmakers, also working in France.[3] An implicit distinction was made between films ascribed to 'Algeria' and those ascribed to 'France-Algeria' (though most of the latter were funded and set in France). However 'France-Algeria' as a category effectively blurs differences between émigré filmmakers and the *beurs*, and recalls the collapsing of differ-ence in majority French usage of the category 'Arab'. The ongoing cultural asso-ciation of *beur* filmmakers with Algerians and/or Arabs means that their films are often discussed as Algerian films rather than as films which have a signifi-cant place within contemporary French national cinema.

Such a blurring of difference is also to be found, surprisingly, in Hamid Naficy's influential study of exilic and diasporic cinema, *An Accented Cinema* (2001). Naficy argues that accented cinema varies according to the filmmakers' relationship to place. For Naficy,

> exilic cinema is dominated by its focus on there and then in the homeland, diasporic cinema by its vertical relationship to the homeland and by its lateral relationship to the diaspora communities and experiences, and postcolonial ethnic and identity cinema by the exigencies of life here and now in the country in which the filmmakers reside. (Naficy 2001: 15)

One might thus expect films by second- and third-generation *beur* directors to come primarily into the category of postcolonial ethnic and identity cinema and the work of émigré Algerian filmmakers to be more typical of exilic cinema, because of their closer lateral relationship to the homeland. However, Naficy stresses the commonalities and continuities to be found in *beur* cinema, *banlieue* cinema and films by Algerian filmmakers in exile in France. For Naficy, *banlieue* cinema demonstrates 'an expansion of *beur* cinema aesthetics', *beur* and *banlieue* films evoke 'the shared experiences of unemployment and cohabitation by disadvantaged populations of *beurs* and poor whites and the concomitant shared anomie, alienation, and anger' (2001: 99), and films by émigré Algerian filmmakers are open 'to exilic tensions and to hybridized identities – central themes in *beur* cinema' (2001: 97). If *beur-* and white-authored *banlieue* films share common themes and settings, however, there are nevertheless important differences between them, as the preceding chapters have demonstrated. In particular, *beur* films place greater emphasis on the problematic identity of the *beurs* themselves, their troubled relationship with their culture of origin and, in the case of male youths, their difficulty in assuming their masculinity. They also seek to confound dominant media representations of immigrant and underclass youths in France by downplaying representations of violence and confrontations with the police. There are likely to be similar differences of emphasis between *beur* and émigré films, even if both, to a greater or lesser extent, address the long-term after-effects of French colonialism in the Maghreb on deterritorialised individuals in France. One of the aims of this chapter, then, is to assess the extent to which the inscription of displacement and identity in films by émigré Algerian filmmakers overlaps with or differentiates itself from that found in *beur* cinema.

The films to be discussed here include films of the 1980s and 1990s by four displaced Algerian filmmakers – Merzak Allouache (borne in 1944 in Algiers), Mahmoud Zemmouri (born in 1946 in Boufarik, Algeria), Abdelkrim Bahloul (born in 1950 in Rebahia, Algeria) and Nadir Moknèche (born in 1965 in Paris).[4] Bahloul has lived and worked in France since the early 1970s but has retained his Algerian nationality, Zemmouri has worked between France and Algeria since the Algerian Ministry of Culture turned down his first script for *Prends dix mille balles et tire-toi* (1980) and currently lives in France, Allouache – who has enjoyed an international reputation since the success of *Omar Gatlato* (1977) – moved to France after *Bab El Oued City* (1994) was refused distribution in Algeria because of its criticism of the rise of Islamic fundamentalism, and Moknèche, who was brought up in Algeria, left to study abroad and has worked in various capacities in a number of countries. Zemmouri's experiences demonstrate some of the difficulties facing Algerian filmmakers, since he received death threats during the shooting of *De Hollywood à Tamanrasset* (1990) and, whilst filming *L'Honneur du tribu* (1993) in exile in Paris, his team were accused of being 'puppets of the West'. Unlike most *beur* filmmakers, Bahloul, Zemmouri and Allouache all received a professional training, either in France or in Algeria (or both). Their films tend to draw on the conventions of popular genres (comedy, musical comedy, crime fiction, melodrama, road movie, period drama), thus differentiating themselves stylistically from those *beur* films which depend on more loosely constructed, episodic 'realist' narratives.[5]

Before addressing this body of films in detail, it might be useful to consider briefly how the representation of Algeria, the presumed 'homeland', has shifted since the *beur* films of the early 1980s. Farida Belghoul's *Le Départ du père* was an early representation of Algeria as the desired homeland to which first-generation immigrants, the parent(s) of the *beur* generation, aspired to return. A short, fragmented film, it illuminated the contradictory aspirations of different generations of immigrants by juxtaposing the father's pleasure in the return to his native soil with its ambivalent effects on his grown-up daughter, who is more problematically caught between two cultures. The visual representation of Algeria in subsequent *beur* films is rare, not only because of the difficulties of filming in Algeria, but also because the *beurs'* interests lie in the 'here and now' of their internal exile in France. Traces of their culture of origin are represented through the ways in which first-generation immigrants strive to perpetuate traditions by means of items of décor, clothing, food, prayers, rituals, language and music, and so on. However, the parents' continuing adherence to Islamic Maghrebi culture is juxtaposed problematically with the meanings of that culture for the *beurs* themselves. As noted elsewhere, their refusal of aspects of their parents' culture combined with the exclusion and racism they face outside the family home mean quite literally that they do not belong anywhere, a situation represented through their constant displacement in and from public spaces. But even if the establishment of their identity in France continues to be problematic, the prospect of crossing the border to Algeria or other countries of the Maghreb represents a threat to the *beurs'* westernised identity, exemplified by the refusal of the kid brother to go 'home' in Dridi's *Bye-Bye*, and the determination of the protagonists of Bouchareb's *Cheb* and Ameur-Zaïmèche's *Wesh wesh, qu'est-ce qui se passe?* to return to France after being deported.[6]

In the late 1990s and early 2000s (as discussed in chapters 8 and 11) a number of *beur* filmmakers began to investigate their roots, representing Algeria through the filter of the imagined and remembered experiences of their parents as first-generation immigrants. Two of the films represent brief moments of nostalgia relating to the mother's ruptured past: Guerdjou's *Vivre au paradis* includes a scene set in a timeless, fetishised oasis; Benguigui's *Inch'Allah dimanche* begins with the port of Algiers and the separation of the heroine from her mother. But both films go on to demonstrate how Algerian immigrants and their families ultimately settled for exile in France. Elsewhere, as in Krim's *Sous les pieds des femmes* and Chenouga's *17 rue Bleue*, the visits to France of

Algerian characters from the parents' past represent negative values which are best left behind. These films account for the parents' generation's emigration from the Maghreb and their ensuing silence about their past; but they work primarily to validate the *beurs'* presence in France, inscribing the *beurs* themselves within the diegesis as children. They thus offer *beur* spectators a critical, distanced relationship with their country of origin.

In comparison with *beur* cinema, films by émigré Algerian filmmakers are more heterogeneous in style and less directly autobiographical in inspiration. However, their films set in France all centre on the interactions between Algerian immigrants and *beur* and/or white or black protagonists. They are thus, as Naficy suggests, concerned with questions of belonging and identity in multi-ethnic postcolonial France, like most *beur* films. However, they are also more concerned with, and represent with more despair and longing, the situation of the homeland. Their films are grouped here in three sections: the place of the immigrant/visitor in France, the representation of Islam, and the representation of Algeria. In each case, their inscription of displacement and identity demonstrates what Naficy describes as an 'accented style', involving transitional border spaces, the construction of lonely outsiders, the critical juxtaposition of characters and narratives to compare different cultures, and an emphasis on music and multilingualism.

The immigrant/visitor

As one might expect, films by Algerian filmmakers working in France more frequently foreground the border crossings and subjectivities of contemporary immigrants than do *beur*-authored films, and do so in slightly different ways. For example, two films by *beur* director Mehdi Charef, *Miss Mona* and *Marie-Line,* construct the illegal Maghrebi immigrant as victim, as does Ahmed and Zakia Bouchaala's *Origine contrôlée* (though the film's transvestite immigrant prostitute eventually emerges as a survivor). In contrast, the émigré filmmakers take a more light-hearted approach, constructing Maghrebi immigrants/visitors as likeable, streetwise young people, from Bahloul's *Le Thé à la menthe* and Allouache's *Un amour à Paris* in the 1980s to Allouache's *Salut cousin!* in the 1990s, a film which can be compared with *La Faute à Voltaire* by Abdel Kechiche, a *beur* filmmaker of Tunisian origin.[7] Their protagonists, like the *beur* protagonists of *beur* films, are designed to convince majority audiences both of their ordinary humanity and their ability to integrate into life in France; but they do so from a different position, as isolated, nomadic individuals, free from the oppressive family context, *banlieue* settings and internal identity conflicts of the *beurs*.[8]

Le Thé à la menthe/Mint Tea (1985) and Un amour à Paris/ A Love in Paris (1988)

Bahloul's first feature film, *Le Thé à la menthe*, starring Abdel Kechiche, traces the trials and tribulations of a young immigrant, trying to make ends meet in Paris but ultimately forced to relocate. Hamou (Kechiche) is a loveable streetwise youth, who has been living away from his family for six years. The film opens with a sequence in which he gets a tourist to take a photograph of him standing by an expensive car and then sends it to his mother, pretending that the car is his own. In fact he lives off his wits, like his friends (one a black immigrant, the other a white Frenchman), and dreams only of making the white French girl he spies on down the hallway fall in love with him. His gullibility is exposed when he consults and pays a *marabout* for a spell to charm her, which succeeds only in covering his room and himself in black ash. The surprise visit of his larger-than-life, loving mother (Chafia Boudraa) forces him first to try and hide all the lies he has told her (he goes shoplifting to get her all the things she wants to buy and stays with a friend to cover up the fact that he has no work), then to try to persuade her to leave (he gets his white friend, a security guard, to pretend to be a policeman telling her she has to go). However, the mother, who has already demonstrated her refusal to be cowed by Western customs by taking a glass of mint tea to a policeman on duty who had helped her cross the road, realises her son is trying to get rid of her. She is brought back from her flight across the city by 'real' policemen, who discover a quantity of stolen chequebooks in Hamou's possession (he has got in with more serious crooks) and take him away. When Hamou returns, he is shocked to find his mother making a spectacle of herself in the streets of Barbès by dancing to Algerian music. After a tender hug, he finally succumbs to the pressure she exerts on him to return to Algeria, where she has lined up a young woman for him to marry (figure 37). He is last seen reluctantly accompanying her to the airport, a place of transit signifying the transitory (and transnational) nature of his identity, and a topos typical of accented cinema.

Arguably, Hamou was the first sympathetic film representation of a streetwise but vulnerable young immigrant looking to survive in Paris without being seen as a victim.[9] The film shares some key themes with *beur* cinema, such as the difficulty of finding work, the easy slippage into minor acts of delinquency, and the conflict between the generations; it also demonstrates a similar episodic type of narration. Its difference lies in its more fluid inner-city setting, marked by the presence of immigrants as individuals rather than families, the absence of a *banlieue* peer group, and the stress on the positive values of Algerian culture embodied in the visiting mother. As suggested in chapter 1, however, its solution to Hamou's predicament, the return to Algeria, fitted awkwardly with rightwing policies for repatriating immigrants.

Allouache's first film to be set in France, *Un amour à Paris*, also addresses the
issue of race, immigration and belonging from the point of view of young
people in transit. It centres on an inter-racial love affair, narrated in retrospect
by Marie (Catherine Wilkening), a young Jewish Algerian woman visiting Paris
in the hope of launching a career as a fashion model. Her periodic voice-over
provides the spectator with an outsider's perspective on Ali (Karim Allaoui),
the gentle, handsome *beur* she falls in love with in the supermarket where she
has found a temporary job. Ali, who is fresh out of prison, is waiting to recover
his share of the money from the robbery he committed, and dreams of travelling to the United States to become an astronaut. Marie, who has been staying
with a friend of her father (played by Dany Cohn-Bendit), moves in to Ali's
customised room in a hotel run by an old Vietnamese man, set in a forbidding,
noirish cul-de-sac. However, their romance becomes embedded within a
comic cartoon-like crime narrative, which denies the couple a happy ending:
Ali gets shot dead by the police and Marie finds herself stranded at the airport
where the film began (figure 38).

Thematically and stylistically the film differs from the *beur* films of 1985.
Crucially, like *Le Thé à la menthe*, it is not set in the *banlieue*, nor does it focus
on inter-ethnic male friendships, its hero being more of a loner/dreamer. In
addition, the film is more visually stylised, borrowing its designer sets from the
cinéma du look (together with a cameo performance from Juliet Berto as a fashion photographer), and its plotlines from the romance and thriller genres
(with a nod to political cinema through the presence of Cohn-Bendit). Its
exilic dimension is evident in Marie's sensitivity to the cold, her nostalgic

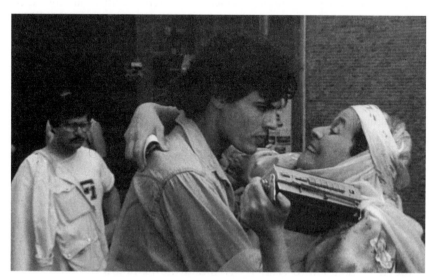

37 Hamou (Abdel Kechiche) hugs his mother (Chafia Boudraa) in *Le Thé à la menthe* (1985).

38 The doomed inter-racial love affair of *Un amour à Paris* (1986).

reminiscences about her life and family in Algiers, and her failure to make headway in the closed world of Parisian fashion. For Ali, however, whose city is Paris, not Algiers, internal exile proves even more destructive. The film shares with *Le Thé à la menthe* a pessimism about the possibility of the immigrant finding a place in France, and with Bouchareb's *Baton Rouge* the impossible dream of finding an alternative place in the USA.[10]

Salut cousin!/Hey Cousin! (1996) and La Faute à Voltaire/ Blame it on Voltaire (2001)

Allouache's next film to be set in Paris was *Salut cousin!*,[11] a French, Belgian, Algerian and Luxembourgeois co-production, co-written with Caroline Thievel, and shot by Pierre Aïm, the cinematographer who worked on *La Haine*. Featuring two main protagonists, Algerian visitor Alilo (Gad Elmaleh, a successful actor and stand-up comedian of Moroccan Jewish descent) and his *beur* cousin, Mok (Mess Hattou), it demonstrates Allouache's return to the comic style of *Omar Gatlato* (the study of a frustrated young man in Algiers in the 1970s). The plot revolves around Alilo's protracted stay in Paris to collect a suitcase of designer clothes from a trader whose address he has lost, and the ensuing clash of subcultures between the country bumpkin and the city slicker.

Alilou is at first portrayed as overly naive. He does not wear trendy clothes, he speaks with a heavy Algiers accent and cannot understand Mok's Parisian argot, he gets ill on his first night after eating too many bananas, and he prefers watching *Perdus de vue* on television to going out clubbing. He blithely accepts Mok's description of the crumbling Moskova district in the 18th *arrondisse-ment* as a fashionable up-and-coming area, and shows his lack of sophistication in his prejudiced attitudes towards black people. However, Alilou quickly adapts to life in Paris, where he proves to be more at home than Mok. In Barbès, he encounters Rachid, a former Algerian cop, now living clandestinely in Paris selling watches on the black market; and in the Sentier, he meets M. Maurice, a Jewish *pied noir* who still laments life in pre-Independence Algeria. These scenes, along with Alilo's constant telephone calls to his boss in Algiers, demonstrate both the proximity and the distance between France and Algeria, combining exilic nostalgia for the past with anxiety about the violence and lawlessness of the present.

However, Alilou also visits the *banlieue* to pay his respects to the family Mok has abandoned, expecting to find his uncle unemployed, his male cousins in prison, his female cousin a prostitute, and his aunt mad. Allouache here allows Mok to set up stereotypical expectations of the immigrant *banlieue* family only for Alilou to overturn them. Alilou discovers that his uncle and aunt are respectable, socially integrated citizens, that his male cousins have high-powered jobs in New York, and that his female cousin is a self-employed taxi driver. The *banlieue* as seen through Alilou's (and the spectator's) eyes is transformed into a meaningful cosmopolitan social space, where people know their way around and the cellars, once given over to drugs and violence, have been transformed into the local mosque (even if Alilou identifies the imam as a thief from Algiers!).

As the narrative progresses, then, Alilo (and the spectator) comes to realise that Mok is a sad fantasist rather than a rap singer on the edge of success as he had initially presented himself. He also receives a lesson in racial tolerance when he falls for Fatoumata (Magaly Berdy), a young black woman from Guinea. (His sexual naivety is revealed when he visits a peep show but can only see Fatoumata – fully clothed – in the place of the woman stripping.) Their diffident romance blossoms on his last, chaste night in Paris, when she takes him to see the Eiffel Tower (the only moment when the spectator is offered a recognisably romantic tourist vision of the city), and leads to a farewell kiss at the station the following day. As a result, Alilou loses sight of his precious suitcase and is last seen phoning Mok to tell him that it has been blown up by the police, that he cannot face his boss in Algeria, and that he is going to stay on with Fatoumata, presumably as an illegal immigrant. His trajectory demonstrates both that France is a land of tolerance and sexual freedom compared with Algeria, and that it is no easy place for the Algerian outsider.

As Alilou becomes more Parisian and self-confident, so Mok becomes more desperate and fragile, a strategy which indicates the deceptiveness of appearances and the fluidity and precariousness of identity. Initially the *beur* cousin appears extremely sophisticated in his aspirations and lifestyle. Insisting on the fact that he was born in France, he refuses to have anything to do with his family in the *banlieue* or his country and culture of origin. However, Mok is actually unable to get a proper job in the music business, has amassed large gambling debts, and has not got his papers in order – significantly his pet gold-fish is named 'Personne' ('No one').[12] Despised and manipulated by others, he lives from hand to mouth (using false papers, agreeing to a *mariage blanc* with an Algerian girl who needs papers), often snivelling pathetically about his situation. He has a relationship with Laurence (Ann-Gisel Glass), the blonde girlfriend of the boxing entrepreneur to whom he owes money, and she eventually reveals that Mok has never fully recovered from a botched robbery in which their friend Roger got burnt. At the end, the police converge on Mok in order to arrest and deport him, preventing him from answering Alilou's phone call because, as they say, 'You aren't here any more'. The film thus, like *beur* films, offers a criticism of French injustice (since Mok has never set foot in Algeria) and illuminates the continuing precariousness of the *beurs* in France (figure 39).

The comic interactions between the two cousins lead to the breakdown of difference and a certain *métissage*, or hybridity, expressed in particular through the use of music. At a key moment, the cousins take flight in fantasy over the streets of Paris, as Mok's scooter turns into a flying motorbike, to the accompaniment of the Skater's Waltz combined with the music of Cheb Rabah. Similarly, Mok's rapping to fables by La Fontaine, though initially mocked, is more successful when he is accompanied by Laurence, and demonstrates the potential of music as a vehicle for hybrid cultures. The film also repackages the spaces of Paris to demonstrate the co-existence of many divergent worlds within the city. At the same time, its representations of Paris are constantly informed by comments and reflections on Algeria. Arguably, then, as Leslie Camhi has claimed, 'the film's heart is elsewhere, in the ravaged country that his hero has momentarily left behind' (Camhi 1997: 70).

The narrative of Kechiche's *La Faute à Voltaire* (winner of the Golden Lion for best first film at the Venice Film Festival) is also concerned with the divergent spaces of the city. It is organised around the arrival, precarious existence and departure of a 27-year-old Tunisian immigrant, Jallel (Sami Bouajila). The difference between Tunisians and Algerians is comically acknowledged in the opening sequence when fellow immigrants seeking their papers advise Jallel that he stands a better chance if he pretends to be Algerian, given the burden of repressed guilt in France at the horrifying events taking place in Algeria. In making the case for the acceptance of immigrants in France, Kechiche himself has argued that 'There's no such thing as a clandestine immigrant. There are men, women and human beings who aspire to a better life and who simply use their fundamental right to freedom of movement to achieve it ... What is really at stake is our humanity' (Kechiche 2000: 132). Inviting the spectator to

39 An altercation between Alilo (Gad Elmaleh) and Mok (Mess Hattou) in *Salut cousin!* (1996).

identify with his clandestine immigrant protagonist, he sets out to establish Jallel's humanity by juxtaposing his situation with that of other marginals in French society and demonstrating their shared material and emotional needs. As a result, the immigrant's risk of being arrested and deported is experienced as an unnecessary affront to humanity.[13]

Unlike *Salut cousin!*, *La Faute à Voltaire* is primarily concerned with the 'here and now' in France, using Jallel (like Alilou) as a naive Candide-like figure whose trajectory in this instance reveals both the miseries and pleasures of life in the parallel universe occupied by France's marginalised others. Jallel's initial alienation is highlighted in an early scene in a Tunisian café, where the language, music and dancing make him feel at home (but leave him penniless). Subsequently, however, he remains silent about life in Tunisia, and the film insists rather on his desire to stay in France, even if it means living from hand to mouth in the black economy, selling fruit or roses in the metro.[14] Indeed, idealistic Jallel (who speaks perfect French) tries to create a new home in France, first by marrying Nassera (Aure Atika), a *beur* waitress in the Tunisian café and a neurotic unmarried mother who lets him down on the day of the ceremony, making off with her child and his hard-earned money; then through his friendship with unstable, childlike Lucie (Elodie Bouchez), who clings to him after they meet in the psychiatric hospital where he is sent to recuperate. However, in a trope common to other *beur* films, Jallel's most satisfactory relationships are to be found in the multi-ethnic friendships he makes among the down-and-outs in the hostel for the homeless, in particular with Franck (Bruno Lochet). The film ends, just as he is starting to recognise his attachment to Lucie, and following a fête celebrating the solidarity of the hostel community, when he is caught in a random police check as he is setting off to sell his roses. It is implied that he will be severed from any 'home' he has created in France and brutally deported (an ending which echoes that of Charef's *Miss Mona*) (figure 40).

If Jallel's period of transit in France is structured through his attempts to make money and his fragile relationships with women, the hostel community constitutes a key background location, characterised by its *métissage*, the mixing of men of different ethnic origins, including white French. These men turn out to be more intelligent and better at keeping themselves together than media images of the *sans-papiers* and the homeless (the 'SDF' or *sans domicile fixe*) would imply, though the film also represents their inner pain. Kechiche here refuses a miserabilist or stereotypical portrayal of the homeless, attempting to create characters who are agents not victims. They give Jallel advice on making money, demonstrate their comradeship by providing him with false papers, and Franck lends him a room where he can at last make love to Lucie. The film thus provides an optimistic vision of their survival skills and continuing humanity and solidarity. It also makes the spectator aware of the existence of a section of the population living in France whose lives are even more precarious than those of many *banlieue* youths.[15] As its title indicates, however, *La Faute à Voltaire*'s critique of French universalism finally draws attention back to the particular problems of citizenship and identity for France's nomadic postcolonial others, crystallised in the ironic setting of the metro station Nation as the site of the illegal immigrant's arrest.

These films map Paris through immigrant eyes, focusing on areas where immigration has been concentrated, such as Barbès, Belleville and (to a lesser extent) the *banlieue*, and identifying ways in which Algeria (or Tunisia) has been recreated through spaces where immigrants feel at 'home' – streets, cafés, markets – and through sounds reminiscent of the homeland (language and music). At the same time, they test out the immigrant/visitor's ability to settle in France. Like *beur* films, they juxtapose their protagonists with peer group characters of different origins in order to demonstrate their shared humanity. Unlike most *beur* films, they also use the inter-racial couple as an important trope for their potential integration. However, despite the immigrants' increasingly hybrid, transnational identity, demonstrated by their adaptation to life in France (albeit on the margins), the films show that their stay can be brutally curtailed at any moment. Their place in Paris is confined to certain delimited areas, their provisional accommodation in seedy hotels, hostels or flats indicates their lack of permanence, and the films' endings depict their demise or their departure (or in the case of *Un amour à Paris* and *Salut cousin!*, the demise or departure of the *beur*, a narrative twist which enables Allouache to warn that

40 Jallel (Sami Bouajila) and Lucie (Elodie Bouchez) sell roses in *La Faute à Voltaire* (2001).

the situation of the *beurs* in France is precarious, too). These films do not offer a political programme in favour of immigration, but invite the spectator to view the world from the point of view of an immigrant, and hence to adopt a compassionate attitude towards the immigrant other.

Islam

The topic of Islam has not been directly tackled by many *beur* filmmakers, no doubt because of the desire to foreground integration rather than difference. The exceptions include Malik Chibane's *Douce France*, where the problems raised by an arranged marriage lead a young *beur* woman to renounce the veil, and Rachida Krim's *Sous les pieds des femmes*, which attacks the FLN's failure to reform Islamic laws pertaining to the sex/gender system. However, in most instances, *beur* films refer to Islam only through scenes of local colour provided by religious celebrations such as Eid and Ramadan. Given the demonisation of Islam in the press and in mainstream cinema (as in Alexandre Arcady's *L'Union sacrée*, 1989), it is perhaps not surprising that Zemmouri's *100% Arabica* and

Bahloul's *La Nuit du destin* address the topic head on. Their different but com-
plementary strategies aim to defuse hostility to Islam on the part of a majority
audience and distance the Islamic community in France from terrorism in Algeria. Whereas the set of films discussed above were organised through narratives
of displacement and deterritorialisation, these two films both focus on a more
settled multi-ethnic/immigrant community.

100% Arabica (1997) and La Nuit du destin/The Night of Destiny (1999)

100% Arabica, a musical farce and a transnational French–Belgian–Swiss co-
production, was Zemmouri's first film to be set in France, and is more light-
hearted in tone than other films addressed in this chapter. Nevertheless its
satirising of Islamic fundamentalism and its positive attitude towards *raï*
music earned the director and lead actor/singer Khaled a fatwa issued by the
Young Muslim League in Lyons. As a result, a number of cinemas, also under
threat, decided to stop showing it or not to show it at all. According to the film's
press notes, 'Raï lyrics have traditionally been bold and often racy, lacing socio-
political commentary and a sassy streak of anti-authority backtalk' (cited in
Berardinelli 2000).[16] The centrality of displaced Algerian *raï* stars, Cheb Mami
and Khaled, together with a plot which mocks and defies Islamic fundamentalism and its manipulation by political parties, make it an allegorical film
indirectly addressing current events in Algeria. At the same time, the fact that
the film (co-written with Marie-Laurence Attias) was shot in Montreuil and
features several generations of a multi-ethnic (if mostly Maghrebi) community, played by a local amateur cast, means that the film also addresses issues of
ethnicity and identity for a *black-blanc-beur* France.

The film's spectacular opening credit sequence follows a mixed-race group
of youths roller-skating down the middle of the Champs-Elysées amid the
Christmas decorations and on out into the suburbs, where they dodge the
police (jumping over a car) and join the crowd enjoying a free open air *raï* and
rap concert given by local musician Rachid (Khaled) and his group Raporient.
The opening invites spectators to displace their gaze from central Paris to the
periphery and take pleasure in the colour and energy of the inhabitants of a
poverty-stricken *banlieue* area, known as '100% Arabica' because of an old
neon advertising sign, where the police are afraid to patrol (source of a number
of comic scenes). The audience, mostly of Maghrebi or African origin, are both
young and old, and male and female, and include youths dressed in gandouras
for attending the nearby mosque as well as the white family of the band's manager (Bernard Lemercier). Their apparent harmony is intercut with shots of a
grotesque, hypocritical imam, Slimane (Mouss), telling the faithful that Islam
is the enemy of rap.

The film's rather tenuous plot is structured by Slimane's malevolent
attempts to destroy the influence of Raporient in order to maintain both his

congregation and his subsidies (he is supported by the local rightwing mayor who is standing for re-election and wants Slimane to re-establish law and order in the neighbourhood by imposing the fear of Allah). Assisted by violent, reactionary ex-con Madjid (Najim Laouriga), Slimane deploys various underhand tactics to bring down the band – the manager's car is burnt out and the illegal immigrant family of one of the black musicians (who all share his identity card) is terrorised to make him opt for the mosque rather than the music. If that were not enough proof of Slimane's disposition to crime and violence, he is also seen beating up an imam from Barbès who is in favour of the music, and enforcing dues from the corrupt local butchers (one of whom is played by Zemmouri himself). In contrast, the Raporient musicians not only produce great music but – as former drug dealers, pickpockets and thieves trying (not always successfully) to go straight – they also constitute positive role models for the young. Faced with the machinations of the fundamentalists, Rachid eventually joins forces with his rival, newly arrived immigrant Algerian *raï* musician Cheb Krimo (Cheb Mami), their solidarity allowing the band to get back into business. The film culminates with a triumphant concert, posters for which are pasted over Slimane's posters for karate classes in the mosque. Enraged by the sight of his sister happily dancing with the band's manager, Madjid leads his sidekicks, wielding baseball bats, in a vicious attack, which is foiled by the musicians and the crowd. The film ends as cowardly Slimane makes an undignified escape in a pork butcher's van!

Zemmouri's implication of political leaders in the promotion of Islamic fundamentalism constitutes an indirect attack on events in Algeria as well as questioning their religious basis. Thus *100% Arabica* expresses both a longing for and the impossibility of life in contemporary Algeria. However, it is first and foremost a comedy, showcasing the music, good humour and tolerance of charismatic Algerian *raï* singers Khaled and Cheb Mami. The band's music (which the enterprising local kids secretly record to sell as bootlegged cassettes) is a mix of *raï* with elements of Western rock, funk and rap, thus constituting a celebration of hybridity. Though the words are not translated, making the film less immediately accessible to those speaking only French, music, song and dance work to bring the community together in rebellion against a misplaced authority, as exemplified in montage sequences which link different characters listening to the music (the older women wearing earpieces hidden under their veils). Zemmouri thus produces an optimistic image of a settled, multi-ethnic community of immigrant origin in France, which (like *Salut cousin!*) overturns the usual clichéd views of the *banlieue* as a place of violence, misery and exclusion whilst constructing it, nevertheless, as a place apart from the city.

Whereas Zemmouri sets out to satirise Islamic fundamentalism, Bahloul's *La Nuit du destin* aims to overturn prejudices about Islam by showing the

Islamic community in France in a more realistic, even positive light. The film thus focuses on the 'here and now' of life in France and is less concerned with coded references to events in Algeria. Set in the north of Paris, its study of contemporary multi-ethnic France, co-written with Pascal Bonitzer and Neila Chekkat, takes the form of an unusual, if rather conventionally filmed, crime drama. It centres on the identity of a devout elderly Muslim, M. Slimani (Gamil Ratib), who becomes an unwitting witness to a murder on his way to the mosque.[17] M. Slimani is only saved from the killers himself by the fact that, when they burst into the mosque, they are unable to identify him from all the other men praying in their white robes! The question is whether he should tell the police what he has seen (he recognises the murderer on the TV news as the company director and assumed friend of the deceased businessman) or mind his own business. When another witness is killed, his wife (Marie-Josée Nat[18]) persuades him to flee to Algeria (after thirty years in France). But when his son puts his life at risk in an attempt to expose the murderer, he returns to shoulder his responsibilities as murder witness and French citizen.

The police investigation, which is led by a sympathetic white detective, inspector Leclerc (Philippe Volter), and is driven by Leclerc's respect for and interest in Arabic culture, represents the local mosque as a site of prayer and reflection, the imam as an intelligent, reasonable and helpful man, and his followers as a community of ordinary people. At the same time, the film foregrounds differences between first-generation Algerian immigrants (with their traditional values) and the more integrated *beurs* (who drink alcohol and do not read Arabic or pray) through the roles of M. Slimani's son, Alilou (Boris Terral), a trainee journalist at a local radio station, and a young *beur* woman student, Noria (Sonia Mankaï), both of whom get drawn into a relationship with Leclerc. Leclerc and Alilou independently discover that M. Slimani is the missing witness, but Alilou refuses to give away his father's whereabouts and instead broadcasts the news that the witness has come forward, getting himself gunned down as a result. As Leclerc holds his wounded body, Alilou sees the light (actually an approaching helicopter) which grants the pure of heart three wishes on the 'Night of Destiny' (a commemoration of the prophet Mohammed's revelation of the Koran). He wishes for life and for his father to return, but whispers only 'Secret, mon capitaine' for the third. The first two come true as Alilou, alive in his hospital bed, is reunited with his father (who is then seen as witness for the prosecution in court). The third wish is revealed in an epilogue sequence shot when he is back at work at the radio station: as he renames a Cheb Mami song 'Secret, mon capitaine', the inter-racial couple formed by Leclerc and Noria are seen walking together in the park, scene of the original crime.

La Nuit du destin reverses the conventions of the traditional French *policier* by representing a law-abiding, middle-class Algerian immigrant family and an equally law-abiding Islamic community (who assist the police in their enquiries) and by making the criminal a corrupt white corporate businessman, whose terrifying henchmen invade the mosque, threaten the faithful with guns, and do not hesitate to kill. The spectator is invited to witness the serious discussions which take place in the mosque as to whether or not the witness should come forward, and to acknowledge the discrepancy between media representations of the Maghrebi community and 'reality'. The film even reverses the cross-border traffic between France and Algeria, allowing M. Slimani to seek temporary refuge in Algeria from violence in France. The resolution of the plot depends on increasing cross-cultural awareness and mutual tolerance on the part of both the majority French and the Maghrebi community: M. Slimani's fear and distrust give way to an acceptance of his role in a wider community; Leclerc learns to read a prayer timetable and write in Arabic, and so merits his relationships with Alilou and Noria; Alilou realises that he does not have to deny his culture of origin, and learns to quote sayings of the prophet to his father; Noria learns to cast aside her distrust of the police.

Even more than *100% Arabica*, then, *La Nuit du destin* insists optimistically on the possibility of a multi-ethnic space of 'belonging' in France, this time within the city, and inclusive of the faithful Islamic community. It even includes a scene of Cheb Mami singing in a bar during Ramadan to a multi-ethnic clientele. Unfortunately the film has not found a large audience, probably because of its low-key TV aesthetics, its lack of stars, and that fact that the cogency and plausibility of the thriller plot are sacrificed to its somewhat didactic investigation of ethnicity and identity.

Algeria

The third major theme of recent émigré Algerian cinema in France is the representation of Algeria itself, to be found in Allouache's *L'Autre Monde*, Charef's *La Fille de Keltoum*, Moknèche's *Le Harem de Mme Osmane* and Bahloul's *Le Soleil assassiné*. Though Charef is considered a *beur* filmmaker, the fact that he lived in Algeria till the age of ten suggests a closer relationship with the lost homeland than that of younger filmmakers of Maghrebi origin. *L'Autre Monde* and *La Fille de Keltoum* each constructs a westernised *beur* woman outsider as their central protagonist, a strategy which establishes the spaces they traverse as sites of struggle for female freedom and means that, despite elements of nostalgia, Algeria cannot be comfortably configured as 'home'. Indeed, the *beur* outsiders end up either dead or departed.[19] In contrast, *Le Harem de Mme Osmane* and *Le Soleil assassiné* are more obviously exilic films which reconstruct the past 'then and there' in order to critique the development of the régime in Algeria and its suppression of individual liberties.

L' Autre Monde/The Other World (2001) and La Fille de Keltoum/ Bint Keltoum/The Daughter of Keltoum (2002)

L'Autre Monde and *La Fille de Keltoum* each offers a critical view of contemporary Algeria through the eyes of a young *beur* woman traveller. The choice of protagonist – and hence of a distanced, outsider's view on events – suggests that the filmmakers' own identities may have been challenged and reconfigured by the experience of exile in France; it also invites *beur* audiences to read the films as potential roots narratives. Each foregrounds the effects on ordinary Algerians of the archaic Arabo-Berber-Islamic sex/gender system compounded by the rise of fundamentalist terrorism. By making these links, they chart the failure of post-independence Algeria to create a modern, egalitarian democratic state and demonstrate how inhospitable the parents' homeland is for the westernised *beurs*.

L'Autre Monde centres on Yasmine (Marie Brahimi), a student from Créteil, who has decided to go to Algeria to search for her *beur* fiancé, Rachid (Nazim Boudjenah), who has joined the Algerian army. Set initially in Paris in the weeks before Christmas, with opera playing on the soundtrack, the film documents the desires and fears of the apparently integrated young *beur* woman as she purchases a burka in Belleville prior to her flight to Algiers. It then follows her trajectory across Algeria, from cosmopolitan Algiers via a countryside traversed by terror to the desert landscapes of the south where she and her fiancé meet their deaths. Combining features of melodrama, the road movie and the political thriller, the narrative is propelled by Yasmine's quest for her fiancé and determination to overcome the obstacles which stand in her path. On the one hand she has to persuade the army officer (played by filmmaker Bahloul) to give her information about the possible whereabouts of Rachid and his fellow deserter, Abdullah, the only survivors of a terrorist massacre. On the other she has to avoid the pitfalls awaiting the unwary, 'foreign' woman traveller. She witnesses the police and army effecting various searches and controls, she narrowly escapes being raped and killed when the bus she is travelling in is attacked by terrorists, she saves Hakim (Karim Bouaiche) – the terrorist who has helped her get away – from a police check, but she is the victim of his deathly violence when he sees her making love to the man he thought was her brother. An insert sequence shows the army officer being ambushed and shot dead by the remains of the terrorist group.

Yasmine's lack of awareness makes her a key, if unwitting, player in the narrative, rather than just a witness to events, as suggested by her diary. Wherever she goes, people die because of her journey – her fellow travellers in the ambushed bus, the peasant family which feeds her, the army officer who helps her, and, in the end, Rachid and the people he lives with who give her hospitality. Yet, thanks to a weak script and poor acting, she seems to remain detached from events, unmoved by the horror around her, unaware of the effect her presence has on Hakim (who speaks French and is familiar with French television), and imposing her own agenda (sexual pleasure) on her traumatised fiancé. The long final section of the film seems literally to take place in 'another world', an isolated labyrinthine fort in the desert inhabited by a curious group of misfits (prostitutes and deserters). Allouache draws the film to a climax by focusing on sexual relationships, particularly that of the *beur* couple, to make the link between sexual repression and terrorism, embodied in the disturbing figure of the unseen, watching terrorist youth who is ultimately the only survivor. The final shot of Hakim reading Yasmine's diary and shaking his head is followed by a slow-motion close-up flashback shot of Yasmine clothed in her burka running in the desert. However, the plot is unconvincing because of the simplistic one-dimensional characterisation of both Yasmine and Hakim (who bears an uncanny physical resemblance to Rachid).

If the plot is schematic and unconvincing, the film's cinematography (shot by Hélène Louvart in semi-clandestine conditions) creates a loving and convincing evocation of the land and landscape of Algeria. As Yasmine makes her way from the centre and outskirts of Algiers via a mountain town, lush woods and valleys, to a desert town and the desert itself, the imagery moves progressively southwards, further and further away from France and French influences (though it is still possible to capture French radio). There is undoubtedly an element of nostalgia in this capturing of the landscape, particularly through the unmotivated, fetishised shots of the desert which, for Allouache, represent 'a different life, a different tempo, a different relationship with the land' (Alion 2001: 140). But ultimately even the desert, the source of Algerian identity, is shown to be traversed by terror.

The young Swiss *beur* heroine of *La Fille de Keltoum* is given a more credible motive for travelling to Algeria, namely the desire to track down her birth mother and understand why she let her be adopted. The film, shot in CinemaScope, begins with shots of Rallia (Cylia Malki) travelling on a yellow bus amid spectacular, arid mountain scenery, and ends with her catching the bus in the opposite direction to return to Switzerland. In the course of her sojourn in Algeria, she not only discovers the true identity of her mother and the nature of the harrowing circumstances which led to her being sold for adoption as a baby, but also experiences for herself the harsh treatment of women in Algeria and the everyday presence of violence and terrorism.

In the first part of the film, Rallia experiences life in a remote mountain village, where she discovers her grandfather and mentally disturbed aunt Nedjma (Baya Belal) living a scratch existence, her aunt making a living by transporting water by donkey. Her mother, Keltoum,[20] works in a distant seaside resort, and Rallia eventually decides to go and find her. Accompanied by her crazy aunt, who wants to protect her (like Yasmine, Rallia is completely unaware of the dangers she faces), Rallia takes to the road and learns more of the horrors of life in contemporary Algeria. At the first stop, when the men who have given them a lift go to eat, she discovers that women are not allowed into the café, even for a drink of water. Outside, a man drags his wife along on the end of a rope before repudiating and abandoning her. Overnight, terrorists kill the woman who has taken shelter with Rallia and her aunt, because she has recognised one of them. During their next lift, the lorry they are travelling in is ambushed by mountain villagers who want the sacks of grain it is transporting; later the lorry driver tries to rape them for joining in with the villagers. At another stop, a Belgian tourist wearing Western attire is physically attacked by an Islamic fundamentalist who accuses her just of looking at him. Rallia becomes more and more alienated from her surroundings, and tries to separate herself from her aunt. She also says she wants to kill Keltoum for abandoning her. However, when she eventually tracks her down at the resort (where Nedjma sees the sea for the first time in her life), Keltoum proves to be distant and unsympathetic. It transpires that Rallia is actually Nedjma's daughter, born after she was raped by a soldier and went out of her mind, and sold so as to pay for the family to have access to water.

The narrative is thus critical of the way the newly independent Algeria of the 1960s and 1970s failed to provide for those in need and implicitly sanctioned rape and the trade in babies (Keltoum had earlier sold her own baby). It also condemns the continuing effects of the misogynistic Islamic patriarchal system. Thus, although the final revelation leads to a moment of delight in Rallia's new relationship with Nedjma, the moment does not last, Rallia (a fashion model) is unable to adapt to life in Algeria, and she leaves abruptly, her mother running alongside the bus. Despite all she has gone through, Rallia's experiences appear to leave her with little feeling for the country, and no political awareness. Like *L'Autre Monde*, the film's political impact is undermined by the (presumably unintended) vacuous nature of its female protagonist and by its use of visual spectacle to construct a 'symbolic' Algeria, rooted in the timeless beauty of rugged mountain landscapes and peasant traditions. As suggested by its soundtrack of nostalgic music (by Sandoval) rather than authentic Arab music, the film is overtly geared to Western audiences.

Le Harem de Mme Osmane/*The Harem of Madame Osmane* (2000) and *Le Soleil assassiné*/*The Assassinated Sun* (2003)

Le Harem de Mme Osmane and *Le Soleil assassiné* are both more obviously exilic films in their constructions of past moments in recent Algerian history. On the one hand, they elucidate the ways in which independent Algeria fell short of the ideals of the Algerian revolution; on the other, they express the anxieties and longings of those who suffered as a result.

Le Harem de Mme Osmane, a first feature by Nadir Moknèche[21], is set in Algeria in the early 1990s at the beginning of the civil war (though actually

shot in Morocco) and constitutes a tribute to women of his mother's generation. Displaying a camp style reminiscent of films by Pedro Almodóvar, it
features a household of outrageous women, headed by the tyrannical Mme
Osmane (Carmen Maura), a former militant whose husband has left her to go
to France. Mme Osmane's problems with the régime, and with her daughter's
desire to marry a teacher with traditional Islamic values, lead tragically to the
daughter's death (shot by the army for driving during curfew). The visual,
verbal and behavioural flamboyance of Mme Osmane and her harem (particularly Biyouna's role as Meriem) functions both as resistance to and critique of
the ways in which their activities have become restricted and policed. The film
thus harks back nostalgically to a time when women were able to lead more
active, independent lives.

Bahloul's most recent film, *Le Soleil assassiné*, shown at the London Film
Festival in October 2003, also reconstructs a particular period in post-independence Algeria, namely the last few years of the life of *pied noir* poet Jean
Sénac. Algerian-identified Sénac was a French-speaking Catholic homosexual
who had refused to leave Algeria with other *pieds noirs* in 1962, and whose
weekly radio broadcasts of poetry in French had a great influence on young
Algerian writers (including Bahloul himself). Focusing on two young men
befriended by Sénac after they have been disqualified for writing and performing a play in French instead of Arabic, the film traces the gradual harden-
ing of the régime towards the poet and the growing disillusion of the young
intellectuals as they realise that the ideal of an all-inclusive Algerian society
which he embodies is being wilfully destroyed. The film ends after Sénac's
murder, as one of the two young men sets off on the ferry for France, vowing
never to set foot in his country again. It thus dramatises the growing illiberal-
ism of the Algerian state, makes claims for an identity which transcends the
narrowly nationalistic, and accounts for the choice made by many Algerian
intellectuals to live in exile in France.

Conclusion

This survey of émigré Algerian films made since the 1980s indicates a shift in
perspective from films (still being made) about the transient immigrant/
visitor in Paris to films about more settled immigrant communities in, or on
the outskirts of, Paris, to films which set about rediscovering Algeria. Clearly
there are elements of overlap with *beur*-authored films in their desire to
address the 'here and now' of minority identities and the problems of 'belonging' in contemporary France. But their films also tackle topics which are rarely
addressed in *beur* cinema (notably the role of Islam) and do so in ways which
more obviously draw on conventional film genres. More significantly, their
concerted double focus on both France and contemporary Algeria, and their

foregrounding of the points of view of first-generation (im)migrants as well as (or instead of) the *beurs,* demonstrate a more transnational, exilic concern with the 'here and there, now' as well as, in the last films mentioned, the 'there and then'. The particular inscriptions of exile and belonging in these films point both to the heterogeneity of 'accented cinema' and to the importance of the directors' individual experiences of deterritorialisation.

Notes

1 Part of this chapter was presented at the ASCA conference on 'Accented Cultures: Deterritorialization and Transnationality in the Arts and Media', held at the University of Amsterdam in June 2003.

2 A discussion of the corpus of films by *pied noir* filmmakers (former French colonialists who left Algeria after the War of Independence) is beyond the scope of this study. However, *L'Autre Côté de la mer* (1997) by Dominique Cabrera stands out as a significant attempt to understand contemporary tensions informing multi-ethnic, multicultural France and Franco-Algerian relationships. The film constructs a dialogue between a French settler in Algeria who needs an eye operation in France and a young, apparently integrated *beur* eye surgeon who has denied his roots (see Tarr with Rollet 2001: 153–5).

3 Screenings during the Year of Algeria in France have included a number of Algerian films made with French funding, including *Rachida* (Yamina Bachir-Chouikh, 2002).

4 Of these, only Allouache is not listed in Stéphane Roux's otherwise very comprehensive dictionary of French (*sic*) directors (Roux 2002). Mention should also be made of female director Amal Bedjaoui (born in Algiers, but trained in New York and Paris), whose first medium length film, *Un fils* (2003), has been very successful on the festival circuit. *Un fils* sensitively addresses the problems of a young man of Maghrebi origin, a transvestite and prostitute, and his relationship with his father.

5 Mostéfa Djadjam, an Algerian actor who first appeared as a child in Allouache's *Les Aventures d'un héros* (1978) and now works in France, has made a fascinating first film, *Frontières* (2002), co-written with Agnès de Sacy, which addresses the case not of Maghrebi immigrants, but of a mixed group of mostly francophone sub-Saharan African migrants seeking exile in France. The film traces the ups and downs of their clandestine border crossings from Senegal to Tangiers, ending in failure and tragedy for the few left to attempt to cross the straits of Gibraltar. It appeared at the same time as Michael Winterbottom's *In This World* (2002) but has not been given the same sort of distribution.

6 A desired 'return' to Algeria figures only in Ghorab-Volta's *Souviens-toi de moi* (see chapter 5), and only on the occasion of a family holiday.

7 Kechiche, who was born in Tunis in 1960, came to France at the age of five, and has forged a career as an actor on both sides of the Mediterranean.

8 The latest in this series of films is Allouache's camp hit comedy *Chouchou* (2003), co-written with Gad Elmaleh and based on his stage show, which stars Elmaleh as

the eponymous Chouchou, a lovable gay transvestite Algerian *sans-papiers* in Paris. Significantly, the Maghrebi immigrant falls in love (with gay, white Stanislas de Latour-Maubourg, played by Alain Chabat), gets 'married', to everyone's approval, and is allowed to stay in France. But as one reviewer said, 'the testosterone of the heterosexual Maghrebi is threatening!' ('la testostérone du Maghrébin hétéro fait peur!'). While the film may celebrate the fluidity of gender, sexuality and identity, its acceptance of Algerian others is limited to those whose sexuality poses no threat.

9 See Smith (1995) for a discussion of immigrant films of the 1970s.

10 Numerous *beur* films feature central characters who dream of crossing borders (for example to Denmark in *La Vago*, Canada in *Malik le maudit*, Spain in *Bye-Bye*, Goa in *L'Honneur de ma famille*, Switzerland in *Origine contrôlée*) but are never shown arriving.

11 Allouache subsequently travelled to Lebanon to film *Alger-Beyrouth: pour mémoire* (1998), another study of exile and displacement.

12 See Rosello (2001: 85–118) for a compelling analysis of *Salut cousin!*

13 *La Faute à Voltaire* is the only film discussed in this section to have been made after the mass protests at the treatment of the *sans-papiers* in France but, like *Chouchou*, it does not link its protagonist with the *sans-papiers* or with political protest. Pleas in favour of the *sans-papiers* movement have since been incorporated into fiction films such as Cheik Dutouré's *Paris selon Moussa* (2003) and Nadia El Fani's futuristic transnational comedy *Bedwin Hacker* (2003). A low-budget Tunisian film, *Bedwin Hacker* pits a Tunisian woman hacker against a Parisian woman security officer and constitutes a protest against all borders and labels.

14 It took Kechiche five years to find funding for the film, and he was obliged to cut out scenes set in Tunisia.

15 See also *Paria* (Nicolas Klotz, 2002) for a study of homelessness.

16 In 1997, *raï* star Cheb Hasni was assassinated under the order of religious extremists and many leading *raï* musicians live in exile for fear of persecution.

17 Bahloul's earlier films are inflected by the presence of strong, poetically charged figures of Maghrebi origin who remind the central protagonists of their origins, be it the mother in *Le Thé à la menthe*, the vampire in *Un vampire au paradis*, or the wise man in *Les Soeurs Hamlet*.

18 Marie-Josée Nat played the lead role in Michel Drach's *Elise ou la vraie vie* (1970), based on the novel by Claire Etcherelli, one of the first films to address the plight of first-generation Maghrebi immigrants in France.

19 Gaël Morel's *Le Chemin de l'oued* (2003) features the adventures of mixed-race Samy (played by Nicolas Cazalé, himself an actor of mixed-race origins) in Kabylia, Algeria, after he has been dispatched by his Algerian mother to stay with his dying grandfather in order to avoid being arrested on a manslaughter charge. Samy finds himself out of his depth when it comes to Algerian customs and politics, and he and his cousin end up getting ambushed and executed by terrorists as he is about to leave for 'home' (France). The film is acutely sensitive to the beauties and physicality of the male body (as in *A toute vitesse*).

20 The name could be an ironic reference to the role of the idealised, devoted mother played by actress Keltoum in Mohamed Lakhdar-Hamina's *Le Vent des Aurès* (1966).

21 Moknèche has since made a second feature, *Viva l'Aldjérie* (2004), which also focuses on the trials and tribulations of a community of women, this time set in present-day Algiers.

Conclusion

The body of films discussed in this book, the products of *beur*, *banlieue* and Algerian filmmaking in France, constitute a challenging intervention to narratives of nation in contemporary French cinema. Pursuing a specifically French problematic, the place within French society of France's postcolonial ethnic others, they construct very different images of France from those which have conventionally dominated France's cinema exports. Thanks in no small measure to the influence of the filmmakers discussed here, images of a plural multi-ethnic France are no longer relegated to the margins of French cinema, but are now regularly visible in the mainstream. Across a range of comedies and dramas, action films and *auteur* films, *beur* and black actors are able to embody characters who are not exoticised or demonised (though this phenomenon has not completely disappeared) but whose interactions with France's white citizens are increasingly normalised.

The argument of this book is that the reframing of difference is particularly significant in the work of filmmakers of Maghrebi descent, because their relationship to Frenchness is different from that of both majority white and émigré Algerian filmmakers (whose position as outsiders is arguably less pressured). For filmmakers of Maghrebi descent, filmmaking is more than just a question of representation, it is also a way of negotiating their own position within French society. It was argued in the introduction that the majority of French citizens of Maghrebi descent seek to negotiate identities which confirm their Frenchness whilst retaining elements of difference. *Beur*-authored films employ strategies which confirm this desire, seeking both to demonstrate that the *beurs* are French citizens like any others, and, nevertheless, that they have their own specific history and culture. In so doing, they mark their own difference from the majority of white-authored films.

The reframing of difference in *beur* filmmaking has been dominated by the need to counter the stigmatisation of the *beurs*, and the *banlieues*, in dominant media discourses, including the cinema. *Beur*-authored films are therefore informed by the need to reassure majority audiences that fears about 'other-ness' are unfounded. Thus, they draw on realist modes of filmmaking to demonstrate the basic humanity of the *beurs*, placing them at the centre of the diegesis, privileging points of view which make them the subjects rather than the objects of the gaze, and constructing them as complex individuals whose feelings and emotions are likely to elicit sympathy. The repeated trope of peer group friendships across ethnic difference, from the unemployed school-leavers of *Le Thé au harem d'Archimède* to the unemployed thirty-year-olds of *La Maîtresse en maillot de bain*, underlines the fact that the *beurs* share certain modern attitudes and aspirations with their peers, as well as highlighting shared economic disadvantages.

By establishing commonalities between *beurs* and others, these films clearly demonstrate the unacceptability of racist attitudes and behaviour. Rather than addressing the issue in a didactic way, however, they tend to treat it with humour and wit, as in *Douce France* or *Le Ciel, les oiseaux . . . et ta mère*. They denounce demonstrably unjust differences of treatment based on ethnic ori-gins, such as the *double peine*, and also quietly draw attention to other forms of injustices and inequalities, such as unemployment, poverty, poor housing and the fate of immigrants. *Wesh wesh*'s heartfelt indictment of the police and the state is unusual, and it is generally left to white filmmakers to express anger and rage, as in *La Haine*, *Raï* and *Ma 6-T va crack-er*.

At the same time, however, unlike most white-authored films, *beur*-authored films also tend to incorporate representations of the Maghrebi family (though not, significantly, in the hit comedies by Smaïn and Bensalah). The presence of the family is an important indicator of the *beurs*' culture of origin, whether as a way of paying tribute to the languages and lifestyles of first-generation immi-grants, as the site of conflict between the generations, or – in those films shot in the past – as a way of reconfiguring dominant histories of immigration. In each case, differences between the parents' customs and values and the aspects of Western lifestyles to which their children aspire (along with their non-*beur* peers) highlight the specificity of the *beurs*' attempts to negotiate their plural/hybrid identity in France. In contrast, white-authored films usually represent the *beurs* in isolation from their families, making their distance from their cul-ture of origin a sign of their integration.

Nevertheless, there are a number of absences in the representation of the *beurs*' culture of origin, which may reflect the need not to alienate a major-ity audience. First, even though adherence to Islam (however token) is per-ceived as a key component of the *beurs*' identity (and Islam is a key factor underlying Arabophobia in France), *beur* filmmakers have represented Islam through little more than picturesque references to the celebration of Eid or Ramadan. There is no study of practising Muslims, nor of the circumstances which might encourage young people from the *banlieue* to turn to Islam (except in *Douce France*'s rather superficial treatment of the wearing of the veil). The topic is foregrounded only in *La Nuit du destin* by Algerian émigré filmmaker Bahloul. Similarly, there is only a limited critique of the effects on the second and third generations of the Arabo-Berber-Islamic sex/gender system. Arranged marriages are condemned in *Cheb* and *Douce France*, but otherwise the male-authored *beur* films do not address the question of patriarchal violence against women.

This is in part because the construction of masculinity in these films is geared towards challenging negative associations of *beur* youths with sexuality, violence and criminality. *Beur* films, with their emphasis on the experiences of everyday life, generally lack goal-directed narratives and represent their protagonists, however sympathetic, as lacking in agency, their minor acts of delinquency the inevitable consequence of an impossible socio-economic situation. Even more troubling, they seem unable to represent the *beurs* as able to assume a mature masculine identity by growing up and settling down. There are few *beur*-authored narratives structured around a romance, and no happy endings in which a *beur* settles down with a job and a family. The trope of inter-racial romance, potentially a sign of successful integration, is also a significant absence. In 1996, Dina Sherzer's analysis of French colonial and postcolonial films led her to conclude that, at least in realist films, 'inter-racial relationships lead to tragedy' (Sherzer 1996: 243). In 2003, inter-racial relationships can be found in films by white and Maghrebi filmmakers, and in the occasional *beur* film (*Hexagone*, *Souviens-toi de moi* and *La Faute à Voltaire*), but they rarely lead to the establishment of a mixed-race couple. Even Bensalah's comedies end with only a hint of the possibility of a mixed-race romance. In general, then, it would seem that filmmakers of Maghrebi descent fear playing into the majority population's fantasies of the potency of the heterosexual *beur* male, preferring to maintain an image of the *beur* as a lovable loser. They are also unwilling to address other issues related to sexuality. With the important exceptions of *Miss Mona* and *Origine contrôlée* (which each set up a mixed-race white/Algerian same-sex male couple), gays, transvestites and prostitutes of Maghrebi origin are to be found only in films by white and Algerian filmmakers.

This cautious approach to the representation of difference is mirrored in the ways in which *beur* filmmakers construct space. First, it is clear that *beur*-authored *banlieue* films set out to provide a different construction of the *banlieue* from white-authored films, placing less emphasis on drugs and violence, more on the *banlieue* as a multi-layered site of social relations. However, from *Le Thé au harem* to *Wesh wesh*, it is also evident that their films have difficulty in finding a place for their *beur* (and other *banlieue*) protagonists to settle. Though there may be opportunities for 'poaching' activities in the interstices of regulated spaces, they have no space to call their own. If there are exceptions, they are to be found in the films directed by *beur* women. Indeed, women filmmakers are now playing an important role in challenging dominant representations of Maghrebi women and renegotiating their identities in French cinema. Mimouna in *Souviens-toi de moi*, Aya in *Sous les pieds des femmes* and Zouina in *Inch'Allah dimanche* are all strong, active female subjects who manage to negotiate spaces which, provisionally, allow them to reconcile different aspects of their plural identities. But the best that can be hoped for in the male *beur*-authored films is the retention of peer group friendships or family bonds and the hope (but rarely the actualisation) of a new start. Whereas *Le Thé au harem* ends with Madjid being taken into police custody and *Wesh wesh* ends with Kamel being killed by the police, *La Maîtresse en maillot de bain* ends with Karim back in the classroom. It is a matter of concern that *beur* filmmakers are as yet not able to construct narratives of empowerment which allow their *beur* protagonists to resolve their lack of place in France.

In 1993, Susan Hayward wondered if *beur* cinema would get recuperated, be returned to the outer margins or sustain its visibility on the periphery (Hayward 1993: 288). Ten years later, the diversity of *beur* filmmaking testifies to each of these possibilities. Bensalah's *Le Raïd* demonstrates how the themes of *beur* filmmaking can be recuperated by *beur* filmmakers as well as by white filmmakers (as in the *Taxi* trilogy), while Ameur-Zaïmèche's difficulties in making *Wesh wesh* illustrate how *beur* filmmaking may still take place in the interstices of the French film industry. However, the regular if limited appearance of more and more films by filmmakers of Maghrebi descent suggests that *beur* filmmaking is now an established part of the French cinema landscape (even if the label itself is not). These films overturn cinematic expectations as to where the cultural life of the nation is taking place and challenge the history of France and the nature of Frenchness through their stories of French people of Maghrebi descent.

Most *beur*-authored films achieve limited audiences and, despite their potential transnational appeal, do not get distributed abroad. As low-budget personal films, they differ from mainstream, star-studded French film productions anxious to compete with American imports. However, their narratives of place and identity in postcolonial France are identifiably French stories. *Beur* filmmaking, then, can be seen as by, for and about the French, understood as a plural, multi-ethnic society; and, paradoxically, filmmakers of Maghrebi descent can themselves be seen as positive models of integration in France, entering but also reframing the symbolic spaces of French culture.

Filmography

Note: Films are listed according to their year of release and not their year of production (dates given refer to their theatrical release in Paris). Viewing figures have been compiled from *Les Fiches du cinéma* (available on the Bibliothèque du Film database) and with the help of the Centre Nationale de la Cinématographie (February 2004). Most have not been distributed in Britain, but many are available on videotape or DVD in France or, if set in Paris, can be viewed at the Forum des Images, Paris. The running time of short or medium-length films is given in brackets.
* Indicates a film by a director of Maghrebi descent.
+ Indicates a film by a Maghrebi director working in France.
(P) Indicates that viewing figures are only available for Paris.

	Film	Director(s)	Release date	Viewership
	1981			
*	*C'est Madame la France que tu préfères?* (20 mins)	Farida Belghoul	–	–
	1982			
	Balance, La	Bob Swaim	10 November	1,068,714
	Grand frère	Francis Girod	11September	1,120,418
+	*Sacrifiés, Les*	Okacha Touita	–	16,302
	1983			
*	*Départ du père, Le* (20 mins)	Farida Belghoul	–	–
	Tchao Pantin	Claude Berri	21 December	3,829,139
*	*Vago, La* (32 mins)	Aïssa Djabri	–	–
	1984			
	Laisse béton	Serge Le Péron	14 March	94,655
	1985			
*	*Baton Rouge*	Rachid Bouchareb	11 December	72,222
*	*Enfant des étoiles, L'*	Mohamed Benayat	–	–
	Police	Maurice Pialat	04 September	1,830,970

+	*Thé à la menthe, Le*	Abdelkrim Balhoul	06 March	36,603
*	*Thé au harem d'Archimède, Le*	Mehdi Charef	01 May	171,221
	Train d'enfer	Roger Hanin	09 January	220,056
	1986	–	–	–
	1987			
	Innocents, Les	André Téchiné	23 December	189,354
*	*Miss Mona*	Mehdi Charef	28 January	108,863
	Oeil au beurre noir, L'	Serge Meynard	04 November	235,314
	Pierre et Djemila	Gérard Blain	27 May	32,944
	1988			
*	*Camomille*	Mehdi Charef	04 May	34,488
	De bruit et de fureur	Jean-Claude Brisseau	03 June	129,372
+	*Un amour à Paris* (1986)	Merzak Allouache	03 February	5,137
	1989			
+	*Nuit du doute, La* (25 mins)	Cheikh Djemaï	–	–
	1990	–	–	–
	1991			
*	*Cheb*	Rachid Bouchareb	05 June	62,096
	Mohamed Bertrand-Duval	Alex Métayer	09 October	12,710
	Thune, La	Philippe Galland	20 November	39,582
	1992			
*	*Années déchirées, Les* (TV)	Rachid Bouchareb	–	–
*	*Au pays des Juliets*	Mehdi Charef	11 May	8,120
	L627	Bertrand Tavernier	09 September	715,297
	Sale temps pour un voyou	Amor Hakkar	–	>5,000
+	*Un vampire au paradis*	Abdelkrim Balhoul	26 August	44,082
	1993			
	Histoires d'amour finissent mal en général, Les	Anne Fontaine	02 June	19,300
	Métisse	Mathieu Kassovitz	18 August	72,038
	1994			
	Frères: la roulette rouge (TV)	Olivier Dahan	–	–
*	*Hexagone*	Malik Chibane	03 February	40,404
*	*Poussières de vie*	Rachid Bouchareb	18 January	16,000
	1995			
*	*Bye-Bye*	Karim Dridi	30 August	121,309
*	*Douce France*	Malik Chibane	22 November	18,273

Etat des lieux	Jean-François Richet	14 June	45,979
Haine, La	Mathieu Kassovitz	31 May	1,978,328
* *Krim*	Ahmed Bouchaala	31 May	>5,000
* *Pigalle*	Karim Dridi	01 February	47,212
Raï	Thomas Gilou	26 June	126,419
Sa vie à elle (TV)	Romain Goupil	–	–

1996

A toute vitesse	Gaël Morel	25 September	77,013
Cri de Tarzan, Le	Thomas Bardinet	13 March	>5,000
* *Deux Papas et la maman, Les*	Smaïn et Longwal	24 April	1,080,519
N'oublie pas que tu vas mourir	Xavier Beauvois	03 January	119,290
Plus Beau Métier du monde, Le	Gérard Lauzier	11 December	1,235,819
+ *Salut cousin!*	Merzak Allouache	20 November	47,503
* *Souviens-toi de moi* (59 mins)	Zaïda Ghorab-Volta	24 January	6,623
Zone franche	Paul Vecchiali	18 December	>5,000

1997

+ *100% Arabica*	Mahmoud Zemmouri	05 November	154,323
Assassin(s)	Mathieu Kassovitz	21 May	446,548
Autre Côté de la mer, L'	Dominique Cabrera	21 May	169,520
Clubbed to Death	Yolande Zauberman	25 June	12,600
De l'autre côté du périph' (doc)	Bertrand et Nils Tavernier	–	–
* *Honneur de ma famille, L'* (TV)	Rachid Bouchareb	–	–
Ma 6-T va crack-er	Jean-François Richet	18 May	69,534
* *Malik le maudit* (60 mins)	Youcef Hamidi	03 September	>5,000
* *Nés quelque part* (TV)	Malik Chibane	–	–
* *Sous les pieds des femmes*	Rachida Krim	26 November	24,200
Vie de Jésus, La	Bruno Dumont	04 June	150,000
Vive la République!	Eric Rochant	05 November	145,607

1998

+ *Alger-Beyrouth: pour mémoire* (TV)	Merzak Allouache	–	–
D'une brousse à l'autre (doc)	Jacques Kebadian	2 September	7,532
Gone du Chaâba, Le	Christophe Ruggia	15 January	396,290
Hors jeu	Karim Dridi	25 November	18,652
* *Laisse un peu d'amour* (TV)	Zaïda Ghorab-Volta	–	–
* *Mémoires d'immigrés* (doc)	Yamina Benguigui	04 February	82,200

+	*Soeurs Hamlet, Les* (1996)	Abdelkrim Balhoul	18 February	>5,000
	Taxi	Gérard Pirès	08 April	6,294,033
	Zonzon	Laurent Bouhnik	26 August	206,778

1999

	Ça commence aujourd'hui	Bertrand Tavernier	12 March	860,736
	Calino Maneige	Jean-Patrick Lebel	23 June	>5,000
*	*Ciel, les oiseaux … et ta mère, Le*	Djamel Bensalah	20 January	1,206,753
*	*Cour interdite*	Djamel Ouahab	21 April	>5,000
	Etrangers, Les (TV)	Philippe Faucon	–	–
	Karnaval	Thomas Vincent	03 March	171,517
	Nos vies heureuses	Jacques Maillot	1 December	40,016
+	*Nuit du destin, La*	Abdelkrim Balhoul	05 May	>5,000
	Petits frères	Jacques Doillon	07 April	176,880
*	*Vivre au paradis*	Bourlem Guerdjou	17 March	80,534

2000

*	*Comme un aimant*	Kamel Saleh, Akhenaton	31 May	251,598
	Drôle de Félix	Olivier Ducastel, Jacques Martineau	19 April	82,632
+	*Harem de Mme Osmane, Le*	Nadir Moknèche	12 July	64,837
*	*Marie-Line*	Mehdi Charef	20 December	217,000
*	*Old School*	Kader Ayd, Karim Abbou	05 July	35,346
	Ressources humaines	Laurent Cantet	15 January	130,692
	Rivières pourpres	Mathieu Kassovitz	27 September	640,271
	Sauve-moi	Christian Vincent	06 September	25,772
	Squale, La	Fabrice Génestal	29 November	58,000
•	*Total Western*	Eric Rochant	05 July	80,753

2001

*	*17 rue Bleue*	Chad Chenouga	21 November	>5,000
+	*Autre Monde, L'*	Merzak Allouache	07 November	11,453
	Change-moi ma vie	Liria Bégéja	28 November	44,610
	Chaos	Coline Serreau	03 October	1,160,913
	Cités de la plaine	Robert Kramer	10 January	>5,000
	De l'amour	Jean-François Richet	11 April	199,910
	Histoires de vies brisées (doc)	Bertrand Tavernier		8,030
*	*Faute à Voltaire, La*	Abdel Kechiche	21 February	81,172
	Gamer	Zak Fishman	21 March	87,387
*	*Inch'Allah dimanche*	Yamina Benguigui	05 December	126,593
	Ligne 208	Bernard Dumont	31 January	>5,000
*	*Little Senegal*	Rachid Bouchareb	18 April	269,187
	Loin	André Téchiné	29 August	158,346
*	*Origine contrôlée*	Ahmed and Zakia Bouchaala	24 January	69,126

	Pas d'histoire! Douze films sur le racisme au quotidien	Vincent Lindon et al.	17 January	115,881
	Samia	Philippe Faucon	03 January	180,851

2002

	L'Afrance	Alan Gomis	30 January	–
	Bruit, l'odeur et quelques étoiles, Le	Eric Pittard	19 November	16,000
	Féroce	Gilles de Maistre	17 April	107,892
*	*Fille de Keltoum, La*	Mehdi Charef	10 April	10,214
+	*Frontières*	Mostéfa Djadjam	13 March	>5,000
*	*Jeunesse dorée*	Zaïda Ghorab-Volta	27 March	5,176
*	*Maîtresse en maillot de bain, La*	Lyèce Boukhitine	02 January	20,734
	Mentale, La	Manuel Boursinhac	23 October	359,866
	Paria	Nicolas Klotz	05 November	6,222
*	*Raïd, Le*	Djamel Bensalah	27 March	1,453,610
	Taxi 2	Gérard Krawczyk	29 March	10,345,901
*	*Wesh wesh, qu'est-ce qui se passe?*	Rabah Ameur-Zaïmèche	30 April	63,997

2003

	Bedwin Hacker	Nadia El Fani	16 July	>5,000
	Chemin de l'oued, Le	Gaël Morel	16 April	6,986
+	*Chouchou*	Merzak Allouache	19 March	3,876,572
*	*Fureur*	Karim Dridi	16 April	16,865 (P)
	On n'est pas des marques de vélo (doc)	Jean-Pierre Thorn	24 September	>5,000 (P)
	Paris selon Moussa	Cheik Dutouré	11 June	5,078
	Rêves de France à Marseille (doc)	Jean-Louis Comolli, Michel Samson	26 November	>5,000
	Taxi 3	Gérard Krawczyk	29 January	6,150,841
	Travail d'arabe	Christian Philibert	09 July	48,240
	Un fils (58 mins)	Amal Bedjaoui	–	–
	Vivre me tue	Jean-Pierre Sinapi	25 June	17,071 (P)

Bibliography

Agard, S. (2004), 'Les Cinéastes et les "*sans-papiers*": contester ou filmer?', in G. Hayes and M. O'Shaughnessy (eds), *Cinéma et engagement*, Paris: L'Harmattan, 241–53.

Alion, Y. (2001), 'L'Autre Monde: entretien avec Merzak Allouache', *Avant-scène du cinéma*, 506, 139–42.

Amara, F. (2003), *Ni Putes Ni Soumises*, Paris: Editions la Découverte.

Amiel, V. (2000), '*Gauche/Droite*, une série', *Positif*, 472 (June), 20–3.

Amrane-Minne, D. D. (1994), *Des femmes dans la guerre d'Algérie*, Paris: Karthala.

Anderson, B. (1983), *Imagined Communities: Reflections on the Origin and Spread of Nationalism*, London: Verso.

Armes, R. (1996), *Dictionnaire des cinéastes du Maghreb/Dictionary of North African Film Makers*, Paris: Editions ATM.

Ashcroft, B., Griffiths, G. and Tiffin, H. (1989), *The Empire Writes Back: Theory and Practice in Post-colonial Literatures*, London and New York: Routledge.

Bachmann, C. (1994) 'Jeunes et banlieues', in G. Ferréol (ed.), *Intégration & exclusion dans la société française contemporaine*, Lille: Presses Universitaires de Lille, 129–51.

Baldizzone, J. (1994), 'Villes et banlieues dans le cinéma français', *Cahiers de la Cinémathèque*, 59/60 (February), 75–80.

Bazin, H. (1995), *La Culture hip hop*, Paris: Desclée de Brouwer.

Begag, A. (1986), *Le Gone du chaâba*, Paris: Seuil.

Begag, A. (2003), *L'Intégration*, Paris: Le Cavalier Bleu.

Begag, A. and Chaouite, A. (1990), *Ecarts d'identité*, Paris: Seuil.

Belghoul, F. (1985), '*Le Thé au harem d'Archimède* de Mehdi Charef', *Cinématographe*, 110, 32–3.

Bellil, S. (2002), *Dans l'enfer des tournantes*, Paris: Denoël.

Benaïcha, B. (1992), *Vivre au paradis: D'une oasis à un bidonville*, Paris: Desclée de Brouwer.

Ben Jalloun, T. (1997), *Hospitalité française: racisme et immigration maghrébine*, Paris: Seuil. [First published 1984.]

Berardinelli, J. (2000), '*100% Arabica*', http://movie-reviews.colossus.net/movies/o /100arabica.html.

Beugnet, M. (2000a), 'Le Souci de l'autre: réalisme poétique et critique sociale dans le cinéma français contemporain', *Iris*, 29, 53–66.

Beugnet, M. (2000b), *Marginalité, sexualité, contrôle dans le cinéma français contemporain*, Paris: L'Harmattan.

Bhabha, H. K. (1994), *The Location of Culture*, London and New York: Routledge.

Biskend, P. (1991), 'The Colour of Money', *Sight and Sound* (August), 6.

Bosséno, C. (1983), '"Le Garage", "Zone immigrée", "La mort de Kader": Des films provocateurs', *Cinémas de l'émigration 3*, *CinémAction*, 24, 128–31.

Bosséno, C. (1992), 'Immigrant Cinema: National Cinema – The Case of Beur film', in R. Dyer and G. Vincendeau (eds), *Popular European Cinema*, London and New York: Routledge, 47–57.

Bouamama, S. (1994), *Dix ans de marche des Beurs: chronique d'un mouvement avorté*, Paris: Declée de Brouwer.

Cadé, M. (1994), 'Des immigrés dans les banlieues', *Cahiers de la Cinémathèque*, 59/60 (February), 125–7.

Cadé, M. (1999), 'Du côté des banlieues, les marques d'un territoire', *La Marginalité à l'écran*, *CinémAction* 91, 172–80.

Cadé, M. (2000), 'A la poursuite du bonheur: les ouvriers dans le cinéma français des années 1990', *Cahiers de la Cinémathèque*, 71 (December), 59–72.

Cahiers de la Cinémathèque (1994), 59/60 (February).

Camhi, L. (1997), *Village Voice*, 25 February.

Cesari, J. (1999), 'De l'islam en France à l'islam de France', in P. Dewitte (ed.), *Immigration et intégration: l'état des savoirs*, Paris: La Découverte, 222–31.

Charef, M. (1983), *Le Thé au harem d'Archi Ahmed*, Paris: Mercure de France.

Charef, M. (1989), *Le Harki de Meriem*, Paris: Mercure de France.

Charity, T. (1995), 'The Riot Act', *Time Out*, 15–22 November, 26–7.

Chauville, C. (ed.) (1998), *Dictionnaire du jeune cinéma français*. Paris: Editions Scope.

Chibane, M. (1994), Pressbook for *Hexagone*, Paris.

CinémAction/Tumulte (1981), 'Cinéma contre racisme: visages des communautés immigrées', Special Issue.

CinémAction (1983), 'Cinémas de l'émigration 3', 24.

CinémAction/Hommes et Migrations (1990), 'Cinémas métis – de Hollywood aux films beurs', 56 (July).

Cinématographe (1985), 'Dossier: Cinéma Beur', 112, 1–27.

Clarke, D. B. (ed.) (1997), *The Cinematic City*, London and New York: Routledge.

Copferman, A. (2002), 'Opéra sur une bavure', *Les Echos*, 21 November.

Dayan-Herzbrun, S. (2000), 'The Issue of the Islamic Headscarf' in J. Freedman and C. Tarr (eds), *Women, Immigration and Identities in France*, Oxford: Berg, 69–82.

de Certeau, M. (1984), *The Practice of Everyday Life*, trans. S. F. Rendall, Berkeley: University of California Press. [(1980), *L'invention du quotidien*, 1, *Arts de faire*, Paris: Gallimard.]

de Plunkett, P. (1995), '*La Haine*, la France et les Municipales', *Le Figaro Magazine*, 10 June.

Delesalle, N. (1999), 'En France l'égalité se fait attendre', *Télérama*, 2597, 20 October.

Deleuze, G. and Guattari, F. (1987) *Capitalism and Schizophrenia*, vol. 2, *A Thousand Plateaus*, trans. B. Massumi, Minneapolis: University of Minnesota Press, 464–70. [(1980), *Capitalisme et schizophrenie*, vol. 2, Mille plateaux, Paris: Minuit].

Deliba, F. (2003), Interview in *Où va le cinéma algérien?*, *Cahiers du Cinéma*, Special Issue (February–March).

Dewitte, P. (ed.) (1999), *Immigration et intégration: l'état des savoirs*, Paris: La Découverte.

Dhoukar, H. (1990), 'Les thèmes du cinéma beur', *CinémAction* 56, 152–60.

Djura, (1993) *La Saison des narcisses*, Paris: Michel Lafon and Livre de poche.

Durmelat, S. (1998), 'Petite histoire du mot *beur*', *French Cultural Studies*, 9, 2, 191–207.

Durmelat, S. (2000), 'Transmission and Mourning in *Mémoires d'immigrés: l'heritage maghrébin*: Yamina Benguigui as "Memory Entrepreneuse"', in J. Freedman and C. Tarr (eds), *Women, Immigration and Identities in France*, Oxford: Berg, 171–88.

Durmelat, S. (2001), 'On Natives and Narratives from the *Banlieues*', in S. Ireland and P. J. Proulx (eds), *Immigrant Narratives in Contemporary France*, Westport and London; Greenwood Press, 117–25.

Fahdel, A. (1990), 'Une esthétique beur?', *CinémAction*, 56, 147–8.

Faroult, D. (2004), 'Jean-François Richet, un cinéaste "militant"?' *CinémAction: le cinéma militant reprend le travail*, 110, 197–200.

Faucon, P. (2001), Interview in *L'Humanité*, 03 January.

Fielder, A. (2001), 'Poaching on Public Space: Urban Autonomous Zones in French *Banlieue* Films', in M. Shiel and T. Fitzmaurice (eds), *Film and Urban Societies in a Global Context*, Oxford: Blackwell, 270–81.

Flanquart, H. (2003), *Croyances et valeurs chez les jeunes Maghrébins*, Brussels: Editions Complexe.

Forbes, J. (2000), '*La Haine*', in J. Forbes and S. Street (eds), *European Cinema: An Introduction*, Basingstoke and New York: Palgrave, 171–80.

Foucault, M. (1977), *Discipline and Punish*, trans. A. Sheridan, New York: Pantheon. [First published 1975.]

Freedman, J. (2000), 'Women and Immigration: Nationality and Citizenship', in J. Freedman and C. Tarr (eds), *Women, Immigration and Identities in France*, Oxford: Berg, 13–28.

Gaillac-Morgue (1995), 'La Grande Peur du prolétariat qui a hanté les fantasmes bourgeois tourne aujourd'hui à la grande peur des cités', *Match de Paris* (May).

Ghorab-Volta, Z. (2002), 'Je hais les ghettos', *Libération*, 27 March 2002.

Gillespie, M. (1995), *Television, Ethnicity and Cultural Change*, London and New York: Routledge.

Göktürk, D. (2000), 'Turkish Women on German Streets: Closure and Exposure in Transnational Cinema', in M. Konstantarakos (ed.), *Spaces in European Cinema*, Exeter and Portland: Intellect, 64–76.

Grand Maghreb, Image(s) du maghrébin dans le cinéma français, 57, 19 April 1989.

Grosz, E. (1995), 'Woman, Chora, Dwelling', in S. Watson and K. Gibson (eds), *Postmodern Cities and Spaces*, Oxford: Blackwell, 47–58.

Guénif Souilamas, N. (2000), *Des 'beurettes' aux descendantes d'immigrants nord-africains*, Paris: Bernard Grasset.

Hall. S. (1992a), 'New Ethnicities', in J. Donald and A. Ranansi (eds), *'Race', Culture and Difference*, Milton Keynes: Open University, 252–9.

Hall. S. (1992b), 'European Cinema on the Verge of a Nervous Breakdown', in D. Petrie (ed.), *Screening Europe: Image and Identity in Contemporary European Cinema*, London: British Film Institute Working Papers, 45–53.

Hargreaves, A. G. (1991), *Voices from the North African Immigrant Community in France: Immigration and Identity in Beur Fiction*, Oxford and New York: Berg.

Hargreaves, A. G. (1995), *Immigration, 'Race' and Ethnicity in Contemporary France*, London and New York: Routledge.

Hargreaves, A. G. (1999), 'No Escape? From "cinéma beur" to the "cinéma de la banlieue"', in E. Ruhe (ed.), *Die Kinder der Immigration/Les Enfants de l'immigration*, Würzburg: Konigshausen & Neumann, 115–28.

Hargreaves, A. (2000), 'Resuscitating the Father: New Cinematic Representations of the Maghrebi Minority in France', *Sites: The Journal of 20th Century/Contemporary French Studies*, 4, 2, 343–51.

Hargreaves, A. G. (2003), 'La Représentation cinématographique de l'ethnicité en France: entre stigmatisation, reconnaissance et banalisation', *Questions de communication*, 4 (October).

Hayward, S. (1993), *French National Cinema*, London and New York: Routledge.

Higbee, W. (2001a), 'Hybridity, Space and the Right to Belonging: Maghrebi-French Identity at the Crossroads in Karim Dridi's *Bye-Bye*', in L. Mazdon (ed.), *France on Film: Reflections on Popular French Cinema*, London: Wallflower Press, 51–64.

Higbee, W. (2001b), 'Screening the "Other" Paris: Cinematic Representations of the French Urban Periphery in *La Haine* and *Ma 6-T va crack-er*', *Modern & Contemporary France*, 9, 2, 197–208.

Highmore, B. (2002), *Everyday Life and Cultural Theory: An Introduction*, London and New York: Routledge.

Higson, A. (1989), 'The Concept of National Cinema', *Screen*, 30, 4, 36–47.

Hirschauer, E. (1999), '*Vivre au paradis*', *Le Progrès de Lyon*, 17 March.

hooks, b. (1989), *Black Looks: Race and Representation*, London: Turnaround.

Ireland, S. (1997) 'Displacement and Identity in the *Beur* Novel', http://tell.fll.purdue.edu/RLA-archive/1997/French-html/Ireland,Susan.htm..

Ireland, S. (2001), 'Mounsi's *Territoire d'outre-ville*', in S. Ireland and P. J. Proulx (eds), *Immigrant Narratives in Contemporary France*, Westport, Connecticut and London: Greenwood Press, 69–81.

Jameson, F. (1986), 'Third World Literature in the Era of Multinational Capitalism', *Social Text*, 15 (Fall).

Jeancolas, J.-P. (1997), 'Une bobine d'avance: du cinéma et de la politique en février 1997', *Positif*, 434, 56–8.

Jousse, T. (1995a), 'Prose combat', *Cahiers du cinéma*, 492, 32–5.

Jousse, T. (1995b), 'Le banlieue-film existe-t-il?', *Cahiers du cinema*, 492, 37–9.

Kassovitz, M. (1995), Interview in *L'Express*, 11 May.

Kechiche, A. (2000), 'Director's Note', *Venice Film Festival Catalogue*, 132.

Kédadouche, Z. (2002), *La France et les beurs*, Paris: La Table Ronde.

Konstantarakos, M. (1998), 'Le Renouveau du cinéma français dans les années 90: s'agit-il d'une nouvelle nouvelle vague?', in F. Wilde (ed.) *Film in the 1990s, Contemporary French Civilization*, 22, 2, 140–71.

Konstantarakos, M. (1999), '*La Haine* and the *cinéma de banlieue*', in P. Powrie (ed.), *Contemporary French Cinema: Continuity and Difference*, Oxford: Oxford University Press, 160–71.

Konstantarakos, M. (2000), *Spaces in European Cinema*, Exeter and Portland: Intellect.

Lançon, P. (2001), 'Coline s'en va-t-en guerre', *Libération* 16 November.

Lallouette, F. (1993), 'Lola l'Antillaise et l'amour', *Journal du dimanche*, 15 August.

Larcher, J. (2000), '*Marie-Line* de Mehdi Charef', *Cahiers du Cinéma*, 552, 87–8.

Lepage, E. (2000), 'Les Enfants terribles', *Le Nouvel Observateur*, 23 November.

Lochak, D. (1997), 'Les Politiques de l'immigration au prisme de la législation sur les étrangers', in D. Fassin *et al.* (eds), *Les Lois de l'inhospitalité: les politiques de l'immigration à l'épreuve des sans-papiers*, Paris: La Découverte.

Mahoney, E. (1997), '"The People in Parentheses": Space under Pressure in the Postmodern City', in D. B. Clarke (ed.), *The Cinematic City*, London and New York: Routledge, 168–85.

Marie, M. (ed.) (1998), *Le Jeune Cinéma français*, Paris: Nathan.

Maspero, F. and Frantz, A. (1990), *Les Passagers du Roissy-Express*, Paris: Editions du Seuil.

Masson, C. (1998), 'Entretien avec Jean-François Richet, réalisateur', in M. Marie, (ed.), *Le Jeune Cinéma français*, Paris: Nathan, 112–15.

McKinney, M. (2000), 'Ethnic Minority Women in Comic Books', in J. Freedman and C. Tarr (eds), *Women, Immigration and Identities in France*, Oxford and New York: Berg, 85–102.

Médioni, G. (1999), 'Sous la cité, la plage', *L'Express*, 21 January.

Mélinard, M. (2001), 'A la recherché des cites des champs', *L'Humanité*, 11 May.

Mercer, K. and Julien, I. (eds) (1986), *Black Film, British Cinema*, London: ICA Documents 7.

Minces, J. (1989), 'Sont-ils tous des délinquants?', in *Grand Maghreb, Image(s) du maghrébin dans le cinéma français*, 57, 26–31.

Mohamed (1981), 'Un outil d'enquête', *CinémAction/Tumulte*, Special Issue, 86–8.

Moinereau, L. (1994), 'Paysages de cinéma: les figures emblématiques d'une banlieue imaginaire', *Cahiers de la Cinémathèque*, 59/60, 35–46.

Morley, D. (ed.) (2001), *Home Territories, Media, Mobility and Identity*, London and New York: Routledge.

Mullier, N. (2004), 'Fiche d'activités ECJS; lutter contre le racisme au lycée', *Le Café pédagogique*. Available online at www.cafepedagogique.net/dossiers/racisme04/index.php?p=fiche_ecjs

Naficy, H. (2001), *An Accented Cinema: Exilic and Diasporic Filmmaking*. Princeton and Oxford: Princeton University Press.

Nordmann, C. (ed.) (2004), *Le Foulard islamique en questions*, Paris: Editions Amsterdam.

O'Shaughnessy, M. (2003), 'Post-1995 French Cinema: Return of the Social, Return of the Political?', *Modern & Contemporary France*, 11, 2, 189–203.

Petrie, D. (1992), 'Introduction: Change and Cinematic Representation in Modern Europe', in D. Petrie, (ed.), *Screening Europe: Image and Identity in Contemporary European Cinema*, London: British Film Institute Working Papers, 1–8.

Powrie, P. (1997), *French Cinema in the 1980s: Nostalgia and the Crisis of Masculinity*, Oxford: Clarendon Press.

Powrie, P. (ed.) (1999), *French Cinema in the 1990s: Continuity and Difference*, Oxford: Oxford University Press.

Prédal, R. (2002), *Le Jeune Cinéma français*, Paris: Nathan.

Reader, K. (1995), 'After the Riot', *Sight and Sound*, 5, 11, 12–14.

Reynaud, B. (1996), 'Le 'hood: *Hate* and Its Neighbours', *Film Comment*, 32, 2, 54–8.

Rosello, M. (1998), *Declining the Stereotype, Ethnicity and Representation in French Cultures*, Hanover and London: Dartmouth College, University Press of New England.

Rosello, M. (2001), *Postcolonial Hospitality: The Immigrant as Guest*, Stanford: Stanford University Press.

Rosello, M. (2003), 'Tactical Universalism and New Multiculturalist Claims', in C. Forsdick and D. Murphy (eds), *Francophone Postcolonial Studies: A Critical Introduction*, London: Arnold, 135–44.

Roux, S. (2002), *Dictionnaire des réalisateurs français*, Paris: Dualpha.

Roze, A. (1995), *La France Arc-en-ciel*, Paris: Editions Julliard.

Sassen, S. (1991), *The Global City*, Princeton and Oxford: Princeton University Press.

Saussier, G. (2001), 'Situations du reportage, actualité d'une alternative documentaire', *Communications, le parti pris du document*, 71 (October), 307–31.

Sherzer, D. (1996), 'Race Matters and Matters of Race: Interracial Relationships in Colonial and Postcolonial Films', in D. Sherzer (ed.) *Cinema, Colonialism, Postcolonialism: Perspectives from the French and Francophone Worlds*, Austin: University of Texas Press, 229–48.

Sherzer, D. (1999) 'Comedy and Interracial Relationships: *Romuald et Juliette* (Serreau, 1987) and *Métisse* (Kassovitz, 1993)', in P. Powrie (ed.) *Contemporary French Cinema: Continuity and Difference*, Oxford: Oxford University Press, 149–59.

Shohat, E. and Stam, R. (1994), *Unthinking Eurocentrism*, London and New York: Routledge.

Silverman, M. (1992), *Deconstructing the Nation: Immigration, Racism and Citizenship in Modern France*, London and New York: Routledge.

Smith, A. (1995), 'The Problems of Immigration as Shown in French Cinema of the 1970s', *Modern & Contemporary France*, NS3, 1, 41–50.

Stora, B. (1992), *Ils venaient d'Algérie: l'immigration algérienne en France 1912–1992*, Paris: Fayard.

Tarr, C. (1997), 'French Cinema and Post-colonial Minorities', in A. G. Hargreaves and M. McKinney (eds), *Postcolonial Cultures in France*, London and New York: Routledge, 59–83.

Tarr, C. (1999), 'Gender and Sexuality in *Les Nuits fauves*', in P. Powrie (ed.), *French Cinema in the 1990s: Continuity and Difference*, Oxford: Oxford University Press, 117–26.

Tarr, C. (2000), 'Where Women Tread: Daughters and Mothers in *Souviens-toi de moi* and *Sous les pieds des femmes*', in J. Freedman and C. Tarr (eds), *Women, Immigration and Identitites in France*, Oxford and New York: Berg, 153–69.

Tarr, C. with Rollet, B. (2001), *Cinema and the Second Sex, Women's Filmmaking in France in the 1980s and 1990s*, New York and London: Continuum.

Tobin, Y. (1995), 'Etat des (ban)lieues', *Positif* (September), 28–30.

Trémois, C.-M. (1997), *Les Enfants de la liberté, le jeune cinéma français des années 90*, Paris: Editions du Seuil.

Tribalat, M. (ed.) (1991), *Cent ans d'immigration: étrangers d'hier, Français d'aujourd'hui*, Paris: Presses Universitaires de France/INED.

Tribalat, M. (1995), *Faire France*, Paris: La Découverte.

Tribalat, M. (2003), 'On a sorti d'un chapeau 5 millions de musulmans', *L'Express*, 4 December 2003. Available online at www.lexpress.fr/info/societe/dossier/mosquees /dossier.asp?ida=415635.

Vanoye, F. (1998), 'Le Cinéma français contemporain: sous le signe du lien', in M. Marie (ed.), *Le Jeune Cinéma français*, Paris: Nathan, 56–63.

Videau, A. (1995), 'Cinéma: les banlieues sont de sortie', *Hommes et migrations* 1192, 60–4.

Vincendeau, G. (1987), 'Women's Cinema, Film Theory and Feminism in France', *Screen*, 28, 4, 4–18.

Vincendeau, G. (1992), 'Family Plots: The Father and Daughters of French Cinema', *Sight & Sound*, NS 1, 1, 14–17.

Vincendeau, G. (2000), 'Designs on the *Banlieue*: Mathieu Kassovitz's *La Haine*', in S. Hayward and G. Vincendeau (eds), *French Film: Texts and Contexts*, London and New York: Routledge, 310–27.

Vincent, C. (2003), '*Sauve-moi*: Anecdotes', www.allocine.fr/film/anecdote_gen_cfilm.

Wallet, J.-W., Nehas A. and Sghiri, M. (1996) *Les Perspectives des jeunes issus de l'immigration maghrébine*, Amiens, Licorne and Paris: L'Harmattan.

Wayne, M. (2002), *The Politics of Contemporary European Cinema: Histories, Borders, Diasporas*, Bristol: Intellect Books.

Wihtol de Wenden, C. (1999), 'Les "jeunes issus de l'immigration", entre intégration culturelle et exclusion sociale', in P. Dewitte (ed.), *Immigration et intégration: l'état des savoirs*, Paris: La Découverte, 232–7.

Willeman, P. (1989), *Questions of Third Cinema*, London: British Film Institute.

Wood, N. (1999), *Vectors of Memory: Legacies of Trauma in Postwar Europe*, Oxford: Berg.

Woodward, K. (ed.) (1997), *Identity and Difference*, London, Thousand Oaks and New Delhi: Sage Publications, in association with The Open University.

Zem, R. (1998), Interview with Eugénie Bourdeau, in M. Marie (ed.), *Le Jeune Cinéma français*, Paris: Nathan, 108–11.

Index

Notes: page numbers in **bold** refer to main entries, page numbers in *italic* refer to illustrations; 'n.' after a page reference indicates the number of a note on that page.